The Greenwood Encyclopedia of Homes through World History

The Greenwood Encyclopedia of Homes through World History

Volume 1

From Ancient Times to the Late Middle Ages, 6000 BCE–1200

James Steele

With research by Olivia Graf

Greenwood Press
Westport, Connecticut · London

Library of Congress Cataloging-in-Publication Data

Steele, James, 1943–
    The Greenwood encyclopedia of homes through world history / James Steele ;
    with research by Olivia Graf.
       p. cm.
    Includes bibliographical references and index.
    ISBN 978–0–313–33788–8 (set : alk. paper) — ISBN 978–0–313–33789–5 (vol. 1 : alk.
    paper) — ISBN 978–0–313–33790–1 (vol. 2 : alk. paper) — ISBN 978–0–313–33791–8
    (vol. 3 : alk. paper)
1. Architecture, Domestic—History—Encyclopedias. 2. Dwellings—History—
Encyclopedias. I. Greenwood Press (Westport, Conn.) II. Title. III. Title: Encyclopedia of
homes through world history.
NA7105.S74   2009
728—dc22   2008018310

British Library Cataloguing in Publication Data is available.

Library of Congress Catalog Card Number: 2008018310
ISBN: 978–0–313–33788–8 (set)
        978–0–313–33789–5 (vol. 1)
        978–0–313–33790–1 (vol. 2)
        978–0–313–33791–8 (vol. 3)

First published in 2009

Greenwood Press, 88 Post Road West, Westport, CT 06881
An imprint of Greenwood Publishing Group, Inc.
www.greenwood.com

Printed in the United States of America

The paper used in this book complies with the
Permanent Paper Standard issued by the National
Information Standards Organization (Z39.48–1984).

10 9 8 7 6 5 4 3 2 1

Contents

Contents

Acknowledgments

The author would like to thank Olivia Graf and Hannah Choi for their assistance in researching and processing this volume. I would also like to recognize the assistance of Ken Breish, Hugo Carvallo, Christopher Steele, Rasem Badran, Ismail Serageldin, the Age Khan Trust for Culture, the Archivists at the World Bank in Washington, D.C., Syed Iskandar, Ezrin Arbi, Rami Dahan, Abdul Halim Ibrahim, Stefanos Polyzoides, Dimitri Porphyrios, Midori Mazuzawa, Luo Di, Qao Qin, Viniak Bharne, and Abdel Wahed El Wakil.

Introduction

THE HOUSE AS THE TANGIBLE RECORD OF SOCIOLOGICAL INTERACTION AND ENVIRONMENTAL ADAPTATION

Histories of architecture in both the near and distant past have concentrated exclusively on the Western tradition or on cultures that could convincingly be rationalized as contributing to that tradition. It is only recently that non-Western societies have begun to be represented in their own right, and this series is part of that movement toward the recognition and celebration of diversity in the world and its expression in the art and craft of architecture. It focuses on the house, which is the most personal and descriptive of social artifacts, revealing cultural mores and values in a way that other methods of collective expression cannot. The series does not aim to be encyclopedic, but rather to present enough of a representative sampling of examples from around the world to be able to highlight some important recurring themes and some critical comparisons.

Chapter headings have been selected to allow that sampling to be as global as possible, and every effort has been made to ensure that the sections within each chapter, which are the individual examples, are well balanced, qualified only by the amount of information available at the time of writing, in what is still largely unexplored territory. The chapters are the following: The Americas, Africa, Asia and Australasia, Europe and the Western Mediterranean, and East and Southeast Asia. The titles reflect recently expressed regional preferences, and groupings, with "Australasia," which has the same politically freighted content as the recent use of the term "West Asia," instead of the "Middle East," indicating a new point of reference in those areas of the world.

PRECEDENTS

Henri Lefebvre, in his landmark work *The Production of Space*, which first appeared in French in 1974 and then in English in 1991, epitomizes the substantially different kind of examination of domestic architectural artifacts now being undertaken by spatial geographers. Lefebvre was one of the first to theorize extensively about the spatial implications of the various categories of social difference. His book superseded Michel Foucault's theory about the contextualization of power and expanded it to an international scale in parallel with the growing phenomenon of globalization. Lefebvre admittedly had an agenda of advancing what he described as "the meta-Marxist critique of the representations of power" to include the spaces used in everyday life as the new arena where the struggle for control is acted out. This made the house, to him, just as important as the workplace, or other obvious places where surveillance is carried out by the state, such as a prison, as a subject for consideration in this argument, which has been given far more visibility by Foucault. Lefebvre, however, has convincingly proposed that the global geography of capitalism has substantially changed, and his hypothesis about space includes developing and developed nations alike. This is in direct contradiction to common assumptions about the homogenizing effects of globalization. His work has had the direct effect of heightening the importance of theoretical and practical questions related to the investigation of architectural space in general and houses in particular.[1]

At the same time that *The Production of Space* first appeared, Pierre Bourdieu published his masterpiece, "The Berber House," which has now become a paradigm of a description of the interaction between human values and behavior and the domestic setting that those values formulate and then modify, in return. His methodology in that study is to constantly juxtapose his description of a part of the house with the deeper cultural significance it has for the family, so that various layers of meaning related to it are eventually revealed. He says that

> The low and dark part of the house, [for example,] is opposed to the high part as the feminine is to the masculine; besides the fact the division of work between the sexes, which is based upon the same principle of division as the organization of space, entrusts to the woman the responsibility of most objects which belong to the dark part of the house.[2]

The distinctions between Western and non-Western culture, which play such a critical role for Lefebvre and others in discussions about the history of architecture today, are of little or no consequence during the period covered by this first volume in this series, but do in the other two, given the extent of the cross-fertilization that has resulted from globalization. While the civilizations that are generally considered to have had a function in the development of Western culture are represented here, the part that they played in doing so is a post-materialistic construct and is hardly objective.

A WELLSPRING OF RECOGNITION

The theoretical revolution instigated by Lefebvre and Bourdieu, of reaching a broader cultural understanding of diverse societies through the analysis of housing types, has not been confined to architectural historians, but has also engaged archaeologists, anthropologists, social scientists, semioticians, human geographers, ethnographers, and environmental psychologists as well. Although the methods that have been used in each case have been specific to each discipline, the basic multivalent premise is the same. It is that the historical monuments that have survived have done so because they are built of durable materials that could only be afforded and built by the more economically advantaged segment of society, but that these are not fully representative of it. The remnants of the houses of all classes must be considered to present a more balanced view. That view seeks to understand individual behavior as a barometer of the cultural values of a given society at a specific time, and to extrapolate these from the built remainder rather than focusing on stylistic issues alone.

There have been several pioneers in each of the fields mentioned as well, who have been engaged in what has been referred to as "ethnoarchaeological" research, some since the early 1960s.[3] But one concentration, which is relatively recent and common to all these fields, is the interactive, or sociological-ecological model. It has been described as proposing that

> the relationship between the environment and behavior [is] interdependent and mutually determinative. This model stresses the dynamic interaction within a people-built environmental system, involving both change and adaptation. Human behavior influences the organization of the built environment, and the built environment influences behavior; each can be modified by the other.[4]

Within this model, seven factors have been identified as the determinants of house form, regardless of social, cultural, or geographic identity. These are the following: climate, topography, available materials, level of technology, economic resources, function, and cultural convention.[5] These have informed the discussion that follows.

COMMON THEME

In addition to these seven factors, there are several common themes that begin to emerge related to the housing types discussed in this first volume, prior to the standardizing mechanisms introduced during the Industrial Revolution. The first of these, in no particular order of appearance, is that of sophistication. The Prehistoric Period of human development worldwide was far more complex and advanced than is commonly thought. New archaeological discoveries have now forced us to reevaluate our opinion of human culture, including our ability to produce art, think symbolically, engage in ritual, and understand mathematics and astronomy, as well as the deep human need to make sense of the cosmos through formalized religion.

The Lascaux caves, for example, provide a perfect case and point. They were sealed shortly after they were painted and were like new when they were discovered, even though the carbon dioxide produced by hundreds of thousands of tourists that have visited since then have caused irreparable harm to the paintings on the walls there. A nearly 50 feet long subterranean hall along with its subsidiary chambers contains a breathtakingly realistic frieze of animals, which has been foreshortened to make the best use of the space, and is dominated by a line of six large bulls, painted in black outline, that is nearly 18 feet long. Another frieze of deer seems to overlap them, balancing the composition.

These friezes in the Lascaux caves are an astonishing display of human perception and sensitivity painted by different artists from the same time to a unified, prearranged plan, sometime between 15,000 and 10,000 B.C. Archaeologists feel that they were painted by hunters of the Magdalenian culture as a gesture of sympathetic magic, in which the hunters felt that by representing these animals, they would ensure themselves and their dependants a constant supply of food. One problem with this theory, however, which hints at an even more mystical purpose for the paintings, is that reindeer, which are known to have been a favorite food source during the Paleolithic Period, are not included here.

The caves were closed in 1963 because of a fungus that started to form on the paintings and on the cave walls and floor because of the large number of visitors that trooped through them. Before that happened, however, Pablo Picasso was able to see them and said, after he did so, that "we are incapable of producing anything as beautiful and have learned nothing since."

ÇATAL HÜYÜK

If sympathetic magic was the motive behind this Prehistoric equivalent of the Sistine Chapel, it appears again in an equally impressive way about 4500 B.C. near Konya in Turkish Anatolia in a Neolithic settlement called Çatal Hüyük. This Prehistoric town, which covers about 26 acres, was uncovered by archaeologist James Mellaart in 1967 and continues to surprise those who have come after him because of its sophistication and complexity.

The houses were all made of sun-dried brick and were arranged in a honeycomb pattern, with entrances on flat roofs, on the south side, to keep away from the cold, prevailing wind. Several houses usually shared a communal court, with one unit, which seemed to serve as a shrine that was decorated with the heads and horns of cattle, either real or plaster. Painted murals covered plastered walls. The houses had raised platforms for inhumation burials; that is, the bones were stripped of flesh first, and then wrapped. The skulls were colored with red pigment. This settlement marks an important transition point between the hunters of Lascaux in Paleolithic times and a people adapting themselves to life in a community. There is a bit of uncertainty that can be seen in their testing of nearly 14 different food plants, which they tried to cultivate. The murals, tools, pottery, and weapons show artistic craftsmanship of a very high level.

Çatal Hüyük has been only partially excavated, and it is much larger than originally thought. It is known to have carried out trade with villages nearly 100 miles away. It is also the largest site in the Near East and Asia Minor, with the first evidence of domesticated cattle. There were probably 1,000 houses there, with an overall population of 5,000 to 6,000 people. The high level of standardization and deliberate planning seen in the architecture and furnishings of the houses show a high level of cohesion and cooperation within the community, and suggest an organizing authority, which extended to ritual activity, and the specialization of labor.

A similar discovery in Jericho, Israel, which dates from the eighth century B.C. shows that Çatal Hüyük was not an isolated phenomenon. Flat-roofed dwellings of a similar kind can also be found much later, in Mesa Verde, Colorado, and Chaco Canyon, New Mexico, which were both built about 350 A.D., and continuously inhabited for over 800 years. These had sacred, subterranean rooms called *kivas*, where religious and magical rites were performed. These early achievements, and others that now seem to be continuously coming to light, reinforce the tide of changing opinion about the level of sophistication of our prehistoric ancestors, and this is underscored in the presentation of the houses of that period from different parts of the world that are discussed here.

THE RELATIVITY OF THE AGRICULTURAL REVOLUTION

A second theme, conveyed more extensively elsewhere by such notable historians of domestic architecture as Norbert Schoenauer, is that the "Neolithic revolution" in which nomadic hunter-gatherer societies supposedly adopted agriculture and became more sedentary in urban environments did not happen all at once, but in stages that occurred at different times in different ways throughout the world. This layering of settlement patterns had direct implications on housing typologies.

As indicated in the development of Çatal Hüyük, the transfer from a hunting and gathering culture to agricultural communities is one of the most momentous events in human development. This was brought on by climatic changes that took place after the Ice Age, which reached its peak about 18,000 B.C. Over the next 10,000 years there was a progressive rise in temperature, which encouraged agriculture in the Near East, and cities were the result. Agriculture demands a stationary, rather than nomadic, lifestyle, good organization, planning, astronomy, and mathematics for record keeping, which also give rise to architecture. These sprang up almost at the same time in both Egypt and Mesopotamia, which had an important influence on both the East and the West. Archaeologists usually use the two criteria of writing and the creation of cities as the basis for civilization, but urban settlements existed in the Protoliterate Period, that is, before written history in the Fertile Crescent as well. Pictographic writing came first, then cuneiform by 3000 B.C.

The crops and animals that were the basis of the first agricultural economies were two types of wild wheat, mild barley, legumes and lentils, domesticated cattle, sheep, goats, and pigs. As people began to rely on agriculture, social behavior began to change. A year's supply of grain for a family of four, which is about one metric ton, can only be harvested during a brief period in the spring when the crop ripens, and it cannot be carried around. So then need for stability is key, and permanent settlements are the result.

The first literate, urban society was during the "Uruk" period in Mesopotamia, and by 4000 B.C., there were a number of cities in Sumeria that each had a high degree of economic independence. Warka, which is 150 miles southeast of Baghdad, and 12 miles from the Euphrates, is one of the largest cities in this period, covering 3.5 square miles

SOCIAL STRATIFICATION

A third theme that transcends cultural difference is the variation of housing types found in each region related to class distinctions. Select egalitarian exceptions aside, settlement prompted, or even necessitated, social stratification, and the archaeological evidence behind each of the examples presented here point to a wide range of habitation used by several social levels. Because those of higher economic means could afford better, and more durable, building materials, their houses have tended to last longer than those of the less fortunate, which were more perishable. With better technology available to them and more sophisticated techniques now being used, archaeologists have been more confidently able to determine what those more ephemeral dwellings looked like, but large gaps in our knowledge of them still exist.

TRADITIONAL WISDOM ABOUT THE ENVIRONMENT

What is becoming increasingly clear, and is a fourth theme here, is that in many cases the way that the common people have lived has remained unchanged for millennia in many parts of the world. The remains of houses that have been uncovered in the Mayan Kingdom of Mesoamerica seem to be identical to those of the *milpas* that can be seen in Yucatan today. The mud brick houses of Ur in Mesopotamia in 2000 B.C. are very similar to village dwellings in parts of Iraq right now. Carvings on the walls of Angkor Wat and the Bayon in Cambodia also show that the basic house form of the Khmers, who provided the sustenance for that culture and helped to build those extraordinary monuments, was remarkably similar to the houses that can be seen in the agricultural villages spread throughout the country today. The ancient houses of the common people have perished, but the type has survived. Why? These similarities lend credibility to the view that once a successful residential prototype, such as the igloo or the Bedouin tent of the yurt, evolved in response to singular environmental and cultural imperatives and represent a precious reposition of hard-won collective wisdom. New kinds of socioeconomic pressure have forced and tempted people in various cultures to change. Air-conditioned, bunker-like concrete block cells are quickly replacing the traditional wooden *rumah ibu* throughout Malaysia, in spite of the fact that it is a masterpiece of environmental responsiveness and such an indelible part of Malaysian identity. The desire to conform to developed world standards and models is a powerful force for change in spite of the efficacy and longevity of proven vernacular convention. This pattern prevails throughout the developing world, from Alaska to Zimbabwe, but there are some holdouts still surviving that give us the chance to see building traditions that have remained the same for centuries because they have proven socially, economically, and environmentally effective.

The issue of environmental appropriateness and sensitivity is an important determinant in both the form, layout, and materials used in houses in each of the regions presented here. A growing awareness of this relationship has led architects and planners to revise their attitude about vernacular houses, from that of regarding them as a quaint curiosity to a new appreciation of the accumulated human wisdom that they embody and the lessons they collectively have to teach us now. The smugness and sense of superiority that seemed to typify the manifesto issued by those in the Modern Movement, who regarded tradition as irrelevant and looked to technology to solve every problem, are slowly being replaced by a respect for historical solutions to environmental conditions and differences. This shift is due, in no small part, to the recent validation of scientific studies of global warming and climate change, showing that technology presents as many problems as it does solutions.

CULTURAL PRIORITIES

A sixth theme related to that of the fragility and impermanence of the houses of people at the lower end of the social ladder, irregardless of which region they lived in, is the issue of the relative importance of public spaces over private life, or a preference for the *res publica* over domestic comfort. Time and again, in the Pharonic, Khmer, Mayan, Megalithic, and Greek cultures perhaps more obviously than others, the emphasis was on the collective rather than the individual. The result was that the focus of energy and resources was on the building of monuments and ceremonial centers, with less emphasis given to houses, especially that of those with fewer advantages.

THE APPRECIATION OF AUTHENTICITY

A seventh and final theme that is prevalent throughout this volume is the tendency of a younger culture to borrow from an older more established one. This involves a pattern of conscientious syncretism, which runs the gamut from the deliberate borrowing of easily recognizable symbols to the total assimilation of architectural forms. There are many examples of this tendency here, from the Incan adaptation of Chimu culture, to the extensive borrowing that characterized the Romans' relationship with the Etruscans, who were their predecessors in Latium, or the Byzantine influence on the Ottoman Turks, although the list is far more extensive. Within this syncretism, however, in each case, individual residential proclivities eventually emerge, as collective identity begins to solidify and become more confident, reinforcing the strong connection between cultural patterns and domestic form.

1

The Americas

HOUSES OF THE ADENA TRIBE IN THE OHIO VALLEY

Hundreds of mounds, which have been attributed to the Adena tribe and which dot the landscape throughout the northeastern United States, have occupied archaeologists since the beginning of the nineteenth century. But as with other ancient monument-building civilizations, little attention has been focused on how the Adenas lived their daily lives. The mounds they built, which mysteriously have forms that are best appreciated from the air, occur in several sizes and shapes. These can be categorized as either geometric or representational, depicting animals or reptiles that the Adenas held sacred. Thomas Jefferson advocated documentation of the different tribes and their monuments. Explorers such as Meriwether Lewis and George Rogers Clark helped in this process with their famous eponymous expedition and uncovered and documented several of the many different mounds in the Ohio area. Albert Gallatin, Secretary of the Treasury during Jefferson's presidency, supported Ephraim George Squier and Edwin H. Davis in their writing of *Ancient Monuments of the Mississippi Valley*, as well as documenting many tribal rituals. These visionaries have helped to raise awareness about monuments that would otherwise have been destroyed. Early archaeologists, as a product of the rationalist Enlightenment tradition, categorized them as having either a functional purpose or merely an aesthetic one. They further classified them, if functional, into material used (earth or stone) and possible purpose (enclosure or ceremonial). If they considered the mound to have not had a functional purpose, it was classified as being either "ornamental" or "sculptural."[1]

Centered in the Northeastern United States

The Adena culture was centered around what is now Chillicothe, Ohio, with evidence that its influence spread as far east as the Chesapeake Bay. The earliest artifacts that have been found date from about 300 B.C., but it is believed that the Adena occupied this region from a much earlier date. The Hopewell tribe, which represents a parallel culture, also built large earth and stone landforms and had a territory that overlapped that of the Adena. The societies have so many similarities that archaeologists originally believed that they coexisted. The Hopewell tribe, however, favored octagonal forms while the Adena mounds in the geometric category were far less complex. The most obvious and famous example of this may be the two attached Adena fortifications that were the basis for what is now Circleville, Ohio, surveyed by Caleb Atwater in 1820. He described it as being

> two forts, one being an exact circle and the other being an exact square, the former is surrounded by two walls, with a deep ditch between them. The latter is encompassed by one wall, without any ditch. The former was 69 rods in diameter ... the latter is 55 rods square ... the walls are at least 20 feet in height ....[2]

The pristine geometric beauty of this extremely important historical site did not survive for long, however, after the town of Circleville was built on top of it.

The Use of the Mounds

The Adena used the mounds for temples and tombs, based on the artifacts that have been found in them. Although many of them have been looted, pottery and jewelry associated with burials have been found inside. These burials indicate that this culture was deeply attuned to rituals related to the cycle of life and the seasons, as well as to agriculture and the passage of time. The tombs were raised well above the flood plain, and some of them contain several generations of individuals who were buried in successive layers in the same crypt. There is evidence that these burial mounds grew as the population increased, and in one case, in Portsmouth, Ohio, several large circular burial mounds have smaller mounds surrounding them.[3]

In other instances, excavation of mounds have indicated that some of them formed sacred areas used as temples, which were burned before the mounds were built on top of them.[4] Based on the artifacts that have been found, these temples had a wood frame and mud walls, and were about 12 feet high inside. Whether the temples were burned deliberately or were destroyed as part of a conflagration resulting from an invasion from another tribe is not clear, although destruction by others and the subsequent commemoration of the sacred site by covering it with a mound seems more likely. This is because, unlike other regions in the Americas, such as the central valley of Mexico, this area was very porous and vulnerable to attack, which may explain why it never became the source of highly developed civilizations, such as those in Mesoamerica.[5] At its western extent, near the Mississippi, the Adena culture was subject to annual flooding, which was also the case near the Ohio River. These rivers also made it easy for enemies to attack them. The mounds, then, were obviously a way of making their territory more secure, giving it a sense of protection and enclosure.

This openness also encouraged interaction between the Adena and the other tribes near them, and a certain degree of interdependence developed, to the extent that they not only traded with each other but also helped to build each others' houses.

The Serpent Mound

The most famous monument built by the Adena is inarguably the Serpent Mound, which is one-quarter of a mile in length. There is a circle in the snake's mouth that is believed to be the representation of a comet, corresponding to the radio carbon date of the early part of the eleventh century for the construction of the mound, and the fact that a comet is shown in a Norman tapestry corresponding to the same date. The Adena used the mounds to bury pottery and other valuable objects, such as jewelry, associated with burials in them.

Habitation

Unfortunately, the houses of the Adena people have not endured as well as the mounds that they are best known for. Archaeologists believe that the paucity of evidence of the way they lived is due to the fact that they did not form villages composed of clustered houses, but of dispersed units, so that no deep village middens or waste dumps that could reveal house forms have been left behind.[6] Another reason for the lack of evidence of settlement is, ironically, the mounds themselves, since the Adena scraped up any refuse from their shelters and put it in them, including the bodies of the deceased that were cremated. Since they lived in river valleys with high water tables and flood plains, much evidence has also been destroyed by ground moisture, so that all that has survived are stone implements, copper tools and jewelry, and mica ornaments.

Rock Shelters

But, the recent discovery of rock shelters at higher elevations in the foothills of the mountains in eastern Kentucky that have now been unmistakably attributed to the Adena have given us new insight into their culture and living patterns. These shelters have also preserved a great deal of the organic material in them, which has increased that knowledge a great deal. The shelters have protected the material from moisture, and the soil in the area is rich in nitrates, which has preserved the organic material.[7] These shelters were also high enough to not be easily accessible and were well hidden in the forest, so they were usually not disturbed. The floors of the houses are typically covered with a four-inch thick layer of ash, which has protected the refuse level beneath it. Thirty-eight shelters were found in this area, which extends across Indee, Menifee, Powell, and Wolfe Counties. These houses were apparently temporary, used by hunters as shelter on a seasonal basis in the winter. They provide some tantalizing clues about the construction methods and details used in their more permanent habitation, as a typological model. The ages of these shelters were confirmed by radiocarbon dating to be contemporary with the Adena mounds, with a date of about 2,600 years old, plus or minus 300 years. Their location, in eastern Kentucky, is within 150 miles circumference of Chillicothe, Ohio, as well as the Scioto River Valley, which is the heartland of Adena culture.

The houses were circular, with a timber frame of individual columns holding up a timber roof and stone used to fill in the spaces between the posts. Sometimes these columns were paired for additional strength. Prairie grass, which was used as bedding and which provided the radiocarbon dating of the houses, was found inside. Personal objects that have been found in the shelters, consistent with their use as camps for hunting parties, include flint blades, arrowheads, stone mortars and pestles, awes, spoons, pottery, and flint axes. Fabric in both plain and twill patterns has also been found in them, as were several graves, which included cremations and bundled inhumation burials.

The circular form, timber frame, and stone infill typology is consistent with that of a 45 feet diameter structure that was built of 68 pairs of columns around its circumference, found near a mound at Cowan Creek, Ohio. The paired columns were one foot seven and a half inches apart, center to center, and the distance between the pairs was four feet six and a half inches. Similar structures have subsequently been found after this site was excavated in the late 1950s. These have included circular houses with an outer and an inner ring of columns, with the second ring near the middle of the house, circling a central fireplace. This would seem to indicate a roof structure above the fireplace that allowed the smoke to escape through a hole, and the second circle was also necessary because of the large span involved. At Cowen Creek the houses were burned intentionally to make space for a burial ground, which was then covered over with a mound, and this pattern was later confirmed at Clough, Ohio, as well.

THE ANASAZI

Because it is the product of one of the most extensive, and in some phases the best preserved, of the ancient cultures in America, Anasazi architecture has been widely studied and published, accompanied by the inevitable level of scholarly debate that results from such a wide level of attention. The irrefutable facts that can be gleaned from all of the divergent theories, however, are as follows.

Pueblo Bonito, which is in Chaco Canyon, New Mexico, is usually identified with the Anasazi culture by the general public because of the level of publicity it has received. But they actually extended much farther south into lower Arizona and even across the border into northern Mexico, far beyond the Four Corners area around Mesa Verde that has conventionally been considered the place from which the Anasazi originated.[8] This society is a classic example of the relatively new realization that the agricultural "revolution," which took place somewhere between 4,500 to 5,000 years ago, was not as sudden and definitive as once thought. There was considerable overlap between hunter-gatherer and agrarian cultures competing in the same regions, or even occurring in the same society over a relatively brief period of time. The Anasazi went through phases depending upon the resources available to them and the wealth they could generate from them, starting and ending with pit house villages. These required less material than large aboveground Pueblo communities that were built at intermittent and more affluent periods in between.

One timeline that has been proposed is that aboveground pueblos began to appear in the Four Corners area, along with pit dwellings, about A.D. 750 or 800.[9] The Anasazi then continued to build up in cycles, predicted by a return to earlier, less resource intensive methods of habitation. As one archaeologist has described this cycle: "pit houses precede major shifts in settlement patterns and reorganization of Anasazi society at roughly 1150, 1220 and 1310—times when

The pueblos of the Anasazi represent a perfect adaptation to the natural environment. In Chaco Canyon that context is barren, hot, and dry for much of the year.   *Source:* Ken Breish

they would not have otherwise have been expected if one adhered to a neat, unilinear, architectural progression." [10]

This may be the best time to introduce another recent attitude shift, about the degree of environmental stewardship shown by preindustrial societies, which was previously thought to have been exemplary. There is no doubt that the Anasazi pueblos generally demonstrate an exceptionally high level of ecological awareness and adaptive skill, which will be discussed in detail further on. However, the cycling just mentioned was accompanied by the depletion of natural resources. The great pueblos were realized at the expense of water and wood, causing the depletion of both. Piñón and juniper trees were too twisted for general use, so ponderosa pine and Douglass fir were preferred. At an average of 40 beams per room, it is estimated that 250,000 wooden beams were used to build the pueblos in Chaco Canyon, which deforested an area of about 50 miles in diameter around it. [11]

Pit Houses

The pit house, which the Anasazi emerged from and returned to when they were forced to go into a survival mode, is reminiscent of a similar kind of structure used by prehistoric societies all over the world, such as the partially subterranean house of the Jomon culture in Japan. The advantage of this strategy is that the walls of the house are the sides of the excavated pit itself, which saves considerably on the amount of material used, requiring the construction of only a roof. The thermal advantages are also high, since heat and cold level off to an average 65 to 68 degrees Fahrenheit at 3 feet or more below ground level, regardless of climactic conditions. It is not such a good idea in areas where it rains frequently, for obvious reasons of

The Anasazi built in stone as well as adobe, or mud brick, specializing in walls without mortar that were constructed so well that they have stood the test of time. *Source:* Ken Breish

flooding, but makes good sense in the high desert where heat and cold can be extreme and rainfall is minimal.

Excellent Masons

The emergence of the Anasazi from beneath the surface to begin the construction of the pueblos, which evokes the image of a caterpillar larvae buried beneath the earth, pushing up and out to become a butterfly, began in earnest in A.D. 800. It started with fairly modest structures that were four stories high made up of about 200 rooms, before leading to the construction of Pueblo Bonito, which had 650 rooms. These were built of stone, wood, and clay. At Chaco Canyon the main material was either tabular sandstone quarried from a flat site above the Canyon's floor or bedded sandstone from the cliff's face. The advantage of the tabular sandstone was that it sheared off into sheets. Skill in masonry construction evolved fairly quickly into what has been referred to as "banded masonry."[12]

It was a natural progression from the use of mud brick within a wooden frame that preceded it, followed by one-story high walls that were only one stone thick, and then finally to the party wall construction that typifies the multistory blocks that archaeologists call the Pueblo I Period. This consists of a load-bearing rubble core faced with a veneer wall on each side. The veneer wall was laid up in several ways, as empirical understanding of what patterns worked best increased. One method was laying sandstone slabs horizontally in random courses on thick beds of mud mortar. A second method, which has since been discovered to provide more flexibility in the event of settlement, was to have rubble in between, predominating over mortar. A third technique used large and small flat stones laid up randomly and horizontally, with some mortar. A fourth technique was a dry wall of tabular sandstone laid horizontally.[13] The important thing about each of these techniques is that they make the best use of the natural characteristic of the sandstone, which is a sedimentary rock that is laid down in horizontal beds over time, and so works best in compression in this orientation. The random layering of the large stones, and the use of smaller ones in between, rather than just using mortar, also shows an intuitive understanding of the structural forces at work in a multistory building. This does not mean that the Anasazi builders were completely ingenious, since they sometimes simply butted walls together rather than interlocking them at the corners, and also used sandstone blocks placed vertically in walls, but the adaptations that were made over time were brilliant.[14]

The levels of the pueblos ascended on what is known as a platform frame, with each upper story set back from the one below. A series of parallel walls would be built first, followed by the individual roofs over each room. Pine or fir, or sometimes juniper, beams were laid between the walls, which were spaced to allow for fairly short spans. Pine, juniper, or cottonwood joists were then run in the opposite direction, running parallel to the walls. A willow mat woven with yucca lashing was then laid on the joists, topped by a thick layer of tamped clay, as a roof or a floor for the room above, taken from the alluvial soil of the Canyon's floor. As this clay dried, it showered dust down on the space beneath because no matter how tightly the roof mat was woven, dirt would find its way through the spaces between.

Room Finishes

The interior walls of the rooms were also plastered with clay mixed with sand, left natural. But, there have been discoveries of rooms that were coated with white gypsum plaster and decorated with a red wainscot made from iron oxide.[15] The ceilings of the rooms were sometimes up to 10 feet high, and so this wainscot would help to bring the feeling of the space down to human scale and to animate it. This would have been especially important since window openings were small, at best, for the rooms on the periphery, and those in the interior had none at all. Ventilation shafts were cut into the walls and the floor, with the supply vent placed just below the ceiling or the roof of each room. Access was by a ladder through an opening in the roof, which also served as a chimney for a fire pit, below. Doorways between rooms rarely had doors and were usually shut off with an animal skin curtain, stone slab, or reed blind, which could be raised or lowered with a cord. In several cases archaeologists have found the *metate*, which was used for grinding corn into flour, still in place on the floor, with the *manas*, or handheld stone used to do so, on top of it.

Researchers have also found evidence that some rooms in these pueblo complexes were designated as storage bins, and they have discovered huge amounts of refuse, human waste, and even human remains inside them. One team has painted a graphic verbal image of what this says about life inside the pueblos by saying: "the stench from these deposits, the inevitable swarms of bugs and rodents attracted to them, the unsanitary discomforts of close living in dimly lit rooms, stifling with human smells and the smoke of open fires, and the dampness trapped by heavy stone walls . . ." certainly made them no paradise to live in.[16]

Although research on the origin of the Anasazi is still ongoing, it is widely believed that their first houses were partially subterranean, and the underground *kiva* substantiates this belief. *Source:* Ken Breish

Life in the Open

This image supports the idea that this was basically a society that spent most of its time outside, working in the fields that were irrigated by the extensive canal system that they dug, living their lives on the plazas in the sky created by the terraced setbacks of the pueblo roofs, and sleeping on them as well, under the stars. This close connection to the sky is also evident in the siting of the pueblos, based on cosmological and astronomical criteria, as well as sun angle, to get maximum shade in the summer and the warm sun for as many hours of the day as possible.[17] When the compact ecological footprint of the pueblos as well as the use of local materials of high thermal mass are added to this, the destruction of the woodland and depletion of water resources mentioned earlier are somewhat offset in the environmental balance.

The Sacred *Kiva* as a Large Subterranean House

The Anasazi were animists, imbuing every element in nature with a life force. They also thought of the earth as their place of origin, believing that they began, as a people, in the womb, or the "shipap" or "sipa" of the earth mother.

The most overt architectural evidence of this mystical, animistic belief in a collective subterranean origin is the great *kiva* found in at least ten of the Chaco Canyon pueblos.[18] One of these was excavated at the Aztec Ruins in 1921. It is 41 feet in diameter, containing 14 arc-shaped rooms at ground level that each have doors to the outside and one large room below, accessed by two stairways. This large worship space was supported by four massive masonry pillars that demarcate a square in the middle of the space, which were each three feet square with a huge circular stone footing placed on a bed of lignite to carry the concentrated roof load.[19] The floor was coated with many layers of adobe plaster, with rectangular recesses in it that were covered by a trapdoor. These were presumably spaces where the shaman would hide and then magically emerge into the darkened room during the religious ceremony. Masonry benches, which were a luxury not found in the pueblo dwellings themselves, ran around the circular perimeter of the space. There was also a fire pit, from which smoke escaped from a hole in the roof. Another hole on the northern side of the circle was the symbolic connection to the *sipapu* or womb of the earth mother as well as what one researcher has described as "The point of contact between the natural world and the supernatural world, where the spirit people, the *kachinas*, live and where the dead return." [20]

To enhance the feeling of being below ground, even if the *kiva* was built on an upper terrace, the interstitial space between its outer circular wall and the rectilinear rooms around it was filled with rubble, to add to the feeling of solidity and privacy considered to be desirable for the ceremonies held inside. The roof over the *kiva* was usually also different from those of other rooms in the pueblo. It started with heavy timber beams that formed a square on top of the masonry piers in the middle of the circle and then a series of long beams placed at the midpoint of the square below, forming a "cribbed" or corbelled roof in a series of steps that rose up from the circular edge to an apex at the square center. Sometimes the roof was flat, projecting a considerable distance above the first pueblo terrace.

A Return to Subterranean Beginnings

One plausible theory that has been put forward is that the *kiva* was a commemoration, at a monumental scale, of Anasazi beginnings in pit houses in the distant past.[21] If that is the case, this society seems to have celebrated the cyclical pattern that it followed over the more than one millennium that it occupied this region, finally returning to houses in the earth when all of the resources that they had used up to build their magnificent pueblos were finally depleted.[22]

INUIT SNOW HOUSES

Indigenous shelter, regardless of the historical time period in which it is built or the society that builds it, invariably represents an ingenious adaptation to special climatic conditions and an efficient and appropriate use of local materials. But it is no exaggeration to say that the Inuit snow house, or igloo, is one of the best examples of such ingenuity. It is the result of basic human survival instincts, an adaptation to one of the most extreme climates on earth in the subarctic and arctic regions of northern Canada. There are many variations according to location and tribal group, but there are several generic characteristics that they all share.

The excellent environmental performance of the igloo is due to several simple formal aspects, most essentially its curved shape. Its main chamber, which is dome-like but not necessarily hemispherical, is perfect for deflecting high winds and wind-driven snow, and is also exceptionally strong, being able to resist polar bear attacks. The curved shape allows heat generated by its occupants and their fuel lamps to stratify inside, and it allows the moisture caused by this heat to run down its curved inner surface. It can also be built quickly, in less than an hour by a skilled craftsman, which is essential in such extreme conditions, and can accept appendages, through vaults cut in its sides.

The Perfect Form

The *igdluling*, or entrance, is frequently compartmentalized to hold the leather harness that is used for the huskies that pull a dogsled and includes a domed antechamber. The entrance, which acts as an air lock, is long, narrow, and often very low, requiring those coming in and out to crawl. The floor of the entrance is also about a foot lower than that of the igloo to prevent air filtration. A block of snow is placed at the entrance to prevent the wind from coming in, acting like a front door. Sometimes this snow block, rather than being loose, is built as a curved wall that extends out from one side of the *igdluling*, like an embracing, protective arm. So, the idealized plan of the Inuit igloo is much more complex than the pure, circular form that many imagine, starting with a hook-like baffle wall to block the wind, connected to the circular, small domed antechamber or *uadling*, followed by the elongated *igdluling* and then the much larger circle of the igloo itself, with semicircular side chambers for food storage attached to it, called *audlitiving*.

Construction Technique

The construction process of what has properly been referred to as the "Canadian Innuit spiral built snow block dome," rather than the igloo, is just as ingenious as its configuration, formal adaptations, and internal refinements.[23]

By mid to late November, with progressively colder weather, the thickness of the sea ice and the increasing accumulation of snow forced the Inuit to abandon their transitional houses and begin building igloos. These were typically built in clusters, with individual houses usually by a family or small group of hunters in an interim or emergency situation. If possible, the cluster was sited on the leeward side of a slope to avoid being covered by wind-driven snow. The consistency of the snow was also important in order to make the right size and shape of block needed, and probing to find just the right type could take the builders just as much time as building the igloo itself. After being satisfied that the snow was neither too soft or too icy, the builders, who usually worked in teams, with one person cutting the blocks and the other putting them in place, marked the circular foundation line of the igloo in the snow, and then began removing it from inside the circle to get to the level of ice that would be the floor. The cutter shaped each block so that it had a slightly rounded surface to allow it to fit into the curved perimeter of the dome, while the person placing them put the blocks making up the foundation row end to end around the circle, cutting each one as necessary to ensure a tight fit

After the first perimeter ring was complete, a diagonal slice was made through one of the blocks and a piece was removed so that the remaining rows would rise upward in a spiral, rather than simply making progressively smaller concentric rings from bottom to top. This may seem unnecessarily complicated, but it is the technique that made it possible to build the dome without internal support, or shuttering. It also gave it extra strength, since it would otherwise fail along its contiguous vertical joints, or latitudes. After the final cap block was inserted from the inside, an air vent was cut near the top and a rudimentary entrance was removed to allow the rest of the family to come in with the lamps and other household items to fit out the interior.[24] A rectangular opening was also cut above the entrance so that a slab of lake ice that had been carried along since fall could be inserted, to act as a translucent light source.

The next stage of construction was the building of the sleeping platform and the entrance tunnel. The sleeping platform was fairly straightforward, unless a storage space was incorporated into it, but the entrance was more complex, involving several interconnected chambers of various sizes as well as the carving of an inclined floor plane that would end up being lower than the floor of the main chamber of the igloo, when the two met, to prevent the flow of cold air from coming inside. In the case of clustered igloos, one entry passage would serve all, with a large, circular chamber ending the entry sequence and serving as a hub to which all of the igloos were joined. The builder might use an arched roof over the long narrow part of the entrance chamber or, just as often, use straight, rectilinear slabs of snow, which would span from one vertical side to the other if material of the right consistency was available.

The Living Area

The circular main chamber is divided equally by a central axis that differentiates between a lower floor, about one foot higher than that of the entry chamber, and a raised sleeping platform that is also made of snow blocks and covered with caribou hides for warmth and comfort. The whole family sleeps on this semicircular deck that is approximately three feet high on average, with their heads toward the entrance because there is more headroom toward the center of the curved interior. In some tribes, the level of the sleeping platform is placed higher to take advantage of the warmer air that rises in the igloo. This air is caused by convection of the heat caused by the inhabitants and the one or two, but rarely more, oil lamps that are placed inside, which burn animal fat. The height of the igloo in relationship to that of the sleeping platform also varies from group to group, as does the fuel in the lamps, or even the use of lamps, depending on hunting patterns and diet. Most Inuit subsist predominantly on seal during the winter, and so burn seal fat in the lamp, and the height of their igloos at the apex is about three times higher than that of their bed, which is generally covered with the caribou hides that have been collected during the hunting season in the warmer months. But other tribes have different diets and build their igloos in different ways. The Netschilluks, or Netsilik, for example, make the catenary curve of the igloo flatter, reducing the space between the top of the sleeping platform and the apex of the roof to increase the amount of heat from convection inside. They have decided to trade off headroom for thermal comfort.[25] This also makes it difficult to use lamps inside because the increased heat raises the dew point, causing condensation that drips straight down because of the flatter surface of the ceiling; so the trade-off for added warmth, which still hovers around freezing, also includes darkness and dripping water. While this applies to the Kinepeetoo Inuit, who live around and to the north of the Chesterfield Inlet, the Oo-quee-sik Salit, near Back's River, have dark interiors because they live on salmon, and so have little sea or walrus blubber for lamp oil.[26]

The Iwillil and Iglulik, on the other hand, who live along the northern edge of Hudson Bay, have a higher height ratio between their sleeping platform and the apex of the ceiling because they have larger supplies of seal oil. This makes it possible for them to stand up inside the igloo, to make it warm and bright, and to not have water dripping down on them while they are sleeping because the curve of the walls is steeper, making their lives more comfortable.

This dimension or ratio, then, of the height of the curve roof to the level of the floor, represents a fine line, or balance point, between interior warmth and being able to stand up inside, or not, depending upon the availability of lamp fuel and the willingness of the occupants to sacrifice convenience for warmth. It also depends upon the kind of snow available, since a flatter arch cannot be built with a softer variety.[27]

Fine-Tuning the Living Environment

Several ingenious refinements add to the overall intelligence of the Inuit as masters of environmental adaptation and show the amount of forethought that they give to small things that will immeasurably improve their quality of life at different times during the year.

The first and most important of these is the lamp that stays with the family when they move. More specifically it is the responsibility of the female head of household to care for the lamp, which is frequently given as a wedding gift to a young bride. In one description, the lamp, or *Gullig*, is equated with life itself since "whether warming the air, lighting the house, melting ice for water, drying apparel, or beckoning hunters homeward, the Inuit lamp literally created culture, transforming dark into bright, cold into hot, raw into cooked."[28] Its functional role as a source of survival also extends to the color of the flame, which when white indicates a normal level of carbon dioxide, but when yellow signals the need for more natural ventilation from a vent hole (*gibag*) that could be opened in the roof.

Two additional refinements related to the lamp are the drying rack and a soapstone cooking vessel, which also help to make life in this extreme environment easier. These are suspended above the lamp by ropes hung from the roof or are supported by poles. The drying rack is essential because moisture conducts cold faster, and so, as soon as men come back from hunting, they take off their outer garments to dry them. The rack, which is made in the same way as the Inuit snowshoes, has gut strung both ways across a large circular frame. In addition to the lamp, or lamps, the cooking vessel, and the drying rack, other small details such as an ice window, bed mat, and skin lining help make life inside the igloo more comfortable.

When it is first built, the igloo transmits some light through the snow blocks, but soot from the lamp or reindeer or seal skins attached to the inside of the dome to provide added insulation and to curb condensation and dripping soon block that source. So, at the end of their summer migration, the Inuit cut out a slab of fresh water ice to use as a window when they build their winter igloo, placed over the entrance passage. They do not use salt water ice because it is too murky. They also collect young birch or elm twigs during the spring and summer, which they weave together into a mat used under the reindeer hides that cover the snow platform they use as a bed to keep the hides dry and to provide airflow between the hides and the snow. The Inuit who hunt whales use baleen strips for the same purpose, since wood is scarce for this group.

On the Move

The Inuit have become so closely identified with igloos in the public consciousness that their nomadic lifestyle may come as a surprise. As with other groups that are still classified as nomads, they are dependant upon changes in the weather and the migratory patterns of their main sources of food. When spring arrived and temperatures began to rise, in April and May, igloos began to melt, but in spite of constant dripping their occupants tried to remain in them as long as possible. If the roof collapsed, or threatened to fall, they would trim the hole, or remove the weak part and patch it with reindeer hide to prolong their stay until their summer food source was abundant and they could move to be near it. Their summer house (or *tupig*) was a tent, constructed just as ingeniously as the igloo.

THE AZTECS

When the Spanish *conquistadors*, under the leadership of Hernan Cortes, arrived at the Aztec capital of Tenochtitlan in 1521, it was the center of an empire that stretched from Michoacan in the north and the border of the Tarascan Empire to the Mayan Empire in the south, and across the neck of the continent from the Pacific Ocean to the Gulf of Mexico. One especially evocative description of the capital, from which the last Aztec emperor, Motecuhzoma Xocoyotzin, ruled this empire, survives from one of the Spanish soldiers that conquered it, named Bernal Diaz Castillo. He describes his disbelief that a relatively small force could defeat such a large army, supposedly unaware of the myth of Quetzaquatl, a fair-skinned god, who would return to lead the Aztec people, whom Cortes was mistaken for. Diaz specifically mentions the canals, which made the Spanish advance difficult, lined with houses on each side with a monumental pyramid and public square in the center of this island city in the middle of Lake Texcoco. He describes in graphic detail the nightly ritual of the sacrifice of his compatriots who were unlucky enough to be captured. They were killed by the high priest at the top of this pyramid and then tossed down the steps, which Diaz describes as having been covered in blood.[29] Diaz also mentions the fact that the Aztec defenders threw clay tiles from the roofs of the houses down on the *conquistadors*, further hindering their advance. The pyramid, along with the other ceremonial and administrative buildings around the central square, as well as all the houses, was systematically demolished once the city was captured and the rubble was thrown into the lake, eventually forming the first layer of the foundation of the middle of Mexico City, as it is today. This destruction was substantially complete by the end of the sixteenth century, and the same process of the eradication of any evidence of the Aztec civilization was then extended throughout the rest of their empire.

A Few Records Survive

One of the few records of the history of the Aztec people that has survived the massive destruction that took place after the Spanish conquest is known as the

Codex Boturini, or the *Tira de la Peregrinacion*.[30] It describes an epic, nomadic journey by the Aztecs from an original island city called Aztlan that had six districts, of which only four decided to migrate. Their wandering ended at Lake Texcoco, in which they simulated their memory of Aztlan. They did this by creating floating rafts called *chinampas* woven of reeds that contained earth and plants and pushing them out into the relatively shallow lake. The plants sent down roots to the lake bottom, and as these became denser, small islands were formed, which eventually joined together to become the foundation of the new city, Tenochtitlan. In some cases, parts of the lake were exposed, using a rudimentary version of a cofferdam, and the foundations of the heavier stone movements, such as the great pyramid, were built directly on the bottom.

The city was divided into four districts, conforming to the four migrating tribes, named Teopan, Moyotlan, Atzacualco, and Cuepopan, with the Temple Mayor in the middle. It was connected to the encircling shore by three main roads and bridges, which all converged on the central plaza like the spokes of a wheel.

Daily Life in Village and City

Slowly, archaeologists and sociologists have been able to reconstruct both the character and type of dwellings in the capital and those in villages through the rest of the vast Aztec Empire, giving us a more complete picture of the daily life of the people before the Spanish conquest. As in other cultures discussed elsewhere here, the size and quality of construction of the homes depended on social status and economic level. In Tenochtitlan, the royal palaces were at the top of this hierarchical system, with that of Motecuhzoma being the grandest of all. It was the center of government as well as the emperor's residence, and it has been described as containing "court houses, warrior's council chambers, tribute storage rooms, two armories, rooms for bureaucratic officials and visiting dignitaries, a library, an aviary, a zoo, and various courtyards, gardens and ponds."[31] The life of the common people, or *macehualtin*, by contrast, differed drastically from the *pipiltin*, or nobility. They lived in small, individual adobe huts, with dirt floors covered in woven mats on which they worked, ate, and slept. Food and drink were stored in clay jars, food was served on clay plates, and corn or wheat was pounded with flour for *tortillas* in a stone *metate*, which is still used in this region today. This a basically a rectangular stone slab on which the corn kernels or wheat were placed and crushed with a stone rolling pin by someone kneeling at the short side of the slab. Finer seeds, for ground spices or sauces, were ground in a stone mortar and pestle, called a *molcajete*. The diet of the common people was very simple, consisting of *atolli*, a maize gruel, and one larger meal consisting of *tortillas*, with beans and vegetables. Fish was more plentiful than meat, which was rarely eaten.

Depending on economic circumstances, this single room hut might have been augmented with others of similar size, organized in a square or rectangle to surround a central courtyard. Because it is difficult to make an opening in an adobe or wattle and daub wall without using a substantial amount of wood, these rooms typically had no windows, and daily life, as in Chinese vernacular houses, was lived in the central courtyard, rather than in their dark claustrophobic interiors.

A Similar Pattern

This pattern was repeated on a reduced scale in smaller cities and villages throughout the remainder of the vast Aztec Empire, in which lesser kings ruled and delivered tribute in a pyramidal governmental hierarchy, to Motecuhzoma at its peak in Tenochtitlan. Local nobles came next in this hierarchy, and commoners were at the bottom. What has come as a surprise to archaeologists are their recent discoveries of higher population levels in this empire than originally thought, estimated to have numbered in the millions, with nearly one million in the Valley of Mexico, around Lake Texcoco alone, when the Spanish invaded.[32] Commoners were taxed, which all contributed to the tribute paid to Motecuhzoma each year, but, because of the higher population figures now being discovered, this tax was less onerous than previously thought.

A Typical Village

Excavation of a typical preconquest Aztec village called Cuexcomate near current day Cuernavaca has revealed what daily life may have been like for those living in outlying districts. This village was strung out in a line along a main road running through a shallow valley, terminating at a temple and plaza. It demonstrates a clear distinction between the enclave of the nobles on one side of the road and the more dispersed houses of the less privileged on the opposite side. The compound of the nobles, which was organized around a common square central court, was made up of individual rectilinear houses with entrances that faced inside, all built on a raised platform, or plinth. These houses may have been whitewashed, with gable roofs made of straw. The houses on the opposite side of the linear thoroughfare, however, were built on grade and were surfaced more roughly, creating a clear visual and physical distinction between these diametrically different parts of Aztec society.

This was a farming community, surrounded by fields and terraced planted plateaus, which was a technique commonly used to maximize the amount of arable area available, by using stone retaining walls to create raised beds for crops. Cotton was popular because of its use in cloth, and the production of it was a basic cottage industry. So, the houses here probably contained implements for hand spinning, and many ceramic and wooden spindles have been found, along with tripods used to hold them. Remnants of bark from the wild fig tree in other houses implies that paper was also produced here, confirmed by the discovery of basalt slabs used to beat it into fibers. The houses themselves were typically about 15 to 25 square meters in size, with a dirt floor. They had two doors, one in each of the long walls of the rectilinear enclosure walls, probably for cross ventilation. Straw mats were used on the floor for sitting and sleeping. The remains of clay figurines of deities indicate that houses also had a simple shrine inside, with incense burners on the wall nearby.[33] No hearths have been found, so cooking may have been done either in a separate structure to avoid smoke inside the house or in a common bakery as it is in traditional Greek villages today.

A Sharp Contrast between Classes

The houses of those living in the compound of the nobles were larger than those of commoners and contained artifacts that were imported and more costly, such as polychrome bowls. Artifacts found along the main street indicate that it was also lined with vendors or shops. The archaeologist excavating this site has described this trade by saying that the village

> teamed with vendors, buyers and artisans. Here commoners would trade craft goods made in their home—mainly textiles—for salt and painted pottery imported from the Valley of Mexico and other areas, obsidian blades from regions hundreds of kilometers away and needles and other bronze objects from Western Mexico. Local produce and goods such as woven mats, baskets, corn grinding tools and tortilla griddles were also displayed and traded.[34]

Along with the recently revised estimates of population levels throughout the Aztec Empire there is also a new realization of the extent and quality of the road system that made the variety of objects that were traded possible, like the Roman road system that sustained its vast empire. These also originated at the Aztec capital of Tenochtitlan.

LA GALGADA AND CASMA AND MOCHE VALLEYS OF PERU

Peru is perhaps best known historically for the glorious Inca civilization that existed there prior to the Spanish conquest, but that only represents the final episode in an extended sequence of civilization that preceded it in the region. This started with La Galgada, near Pedregal, Peru, located high above the Tablachaca River, which thrived from 2540 until 1400 B.C. and culminates with the Chimu city of Chan Chan, which played such a large part in influencing the Incas who conquered and assimilated Chimu culture.

La Galgada

La Galgada was primarily a ceremonial center that eventually was converted into a burial ground. It was chosen as the place to settle because of the configuration of the mountain range around it. It was considered to be sacred, and the river that supported this primarily agricultural community helped support this choice. La Galgada is reminiscent of many of the other civilizations of this age studied here since the residential needs of each strata of this society seem to have been a far lower priority than ritualistic and religious preoccupations.[35] The site of the settlement is dominated by two large ziggurat-like temples as well as a circular sunken plaza, with a constellation of small circular or oval houses scattered around them, with agricultural fields stretching out beyond. The two stacked temples, which were each accessed by a steep central stair, have been prosaically designated as the North and South mounds by archaeologists, who believe they represented "the personification of the mountains as divine beings" in which the

> terreform of mother earth conforms to the widespread ancient belief that west is the direction dominated by the feminine power of the earth, where all the celestial bodies are swallowed up by the earth, their setting taken as an analogy for death.[36]

This may explain why these mounds were eventually converted from temples to burial sites, to allow the deceased to be in the presence, or literally in the bosom, of their deity.

This walled city has much in common with the Anasazi Pueblos in that it also had subterranean ceremonial buildings, like the *kivas*, which had a central fire pit and a built-in bench running around their periphery, hinting at a fire cult that focuses on a circular plaza.[37]

The houses at La Galgada were either round or almost so, and were relatively small, at about 14 square meters on average. They were built of fieldstone laid in mud mortar and had thatched roofs. Cooking was probably done outside. Plaster was widely used in larger buildings and may have been used for the floors of the houses as well.

The Casma Valley

In the Casma Valley, at Pampade las Llamas-Moxeke, over 70 mound structures have been found, along with several large buildings that are up to 50 meters long and 5 meters high, and several hundred houses of various sizes.[38] These houses differ from those at La Galgada in being either square or rectangular made of stone cavity walls filled with rubble, and some of these may have been covered by a roof held up by wooden columns at the corners, standing free of the walls. There is also evidence of raised floors and round fireplaces in some of the houses.

San Diego

Another residential compound is the Casma Valley, now referred to as San Diego, which dates from between 500 to 300 B.C. It also has plazas, courts, and platform mounds and is unique in that the houses seem to predominate over the ceremonial spaces, with no monumental structures being predominant. Every building was oriented on an axis between 12 and 18 degrees east of north.[39] Rather than being built entirely of stone, some of the houses were built of wood, or wattle and daub, referred to here as *quincha*.

The Moche Valley

The Moche Valley is in a V-shaped plain that is the confined delta of the river that gives it its name, with the wide mouth of the "V" facing west, toward the Pacific Ocean. Conditions here were optimal for urban communities to emerge, and many did, between roughly 500 B.C. and A.D. 1480, in continuous sequence.[40] The first of these is Salinar in Cerro Arena, southeast of the Moche River. The second is Moche, with its prominent Huacas del Sol and de la Luna (or Pyramids of the Sun and the Moon), even closer to the river, as it bends toward the southwest, Galindo, near the base of the mountains to the northeast, and Chan Chan, which was the closest to the coast, to the northwest.

Salinar

The Salinar site, which dates from 200 B.C. to the early part of the first century A.D., is located high above the Moche Valley about 20 miles from the Pacific Ocean, positioned to control passage from the interior to the sea.[41] The settlement, called Cerro Arena, covers about 2 square kilometers and has more than

2,000 buildings, including many houses that sheltered both rich and poor. These have been classified into two types by prominent archaeologist Curtis Brennan. The first, which has several permutations, is a large mixed use house that has living spaces clustered around a courtyard, sharing access to it with other rooms that were obviously set aside for other purposes, all relying upon a single, offset entrance. These house shops were relatively large and angular, if not rectilinear.[42] In sharp contrast, the second type is very small and round, typically consisting of a pair of single semicircular rooms joined by an entry that acts as a hinge between them. Each has cooking areas inside the house, based on grinding stones found there.

Moche

A very large urban center was established 6 kilometers from the Pacific coast that lasted from A.D. 300 to 550 and takes its name from its proximity to the Moche River to the northwest. It is dominated by the Huaca del Sol, Pyramid of the Sun, and Huaca de la Luna, of the moon, with the civic spaces surrounding them being more advanced than in other sites in this region.[43] Also, unlike other sites, the houses at Moche have rooms designated for individual uses with cooking done in one and living in another. One investigator has noted that "this trend toward segmentation seen in the individual residential dwelling can also be clearly seen in the wider intersettlement plan, in which there are three classes of residential architecture designated by construction style, elaboration and room content."[44]

These range from small houses with walls made of compressed plant fibers at the lower end of the economic spectrum, through larger houses with plastered mud brick walls with stone bases, stairs, and furniture, to even larger houses with extensive storage areas inside them that imply a strategic difference between these and the houses of the lower social level elsewhere.

Galindo

After what appears to have been a major dislocation around A.D. 600, the locus of power shifted from Moche to Galindo, further inland. It was also quite large, with pyramids, a palace, and a new element, called a *carcadura*, which is similar to a theatre, as an enclosed performance platform. These civic buildings were flanked by residential areas on the northwest and southwest, with houses that are even more segmented, divided into cooking, living, and storage areas.

This pattern of divisibility culminates at Chan Chan founded by the Lambayeque dynasty in A.D. 1000. Rather than being an urbanized settlement in the conventional senses, it is a series of walled palace compounds, called *cindadelas*, more like citadels, which can each be identified with an individual ruler.[45]

THE INCA AND THE CHIMU

When Francisco Pizarro arrived in Peru, he and the nearly 200 *conquistadors* whom he led were amazed to discover an extremely sophisticated and well-organized civilization that was firmly established there. The Incas were led by a king who was supported by highly efficient governmental bureaucracy. The tightly structured society of about 12 million people that they ruled ran the gamut from a privileged nobility through a priestly class to merchants, artisans, warriors, and farmers. This burgeoning population was fed by a productive agricultural system that included advanced irrigation and terracing techniques that allowed farmers to plant on what would otherwise have been rocky, barren, inaccessible slopes. It was also joined together by more miles of paved roads than the Romans were able to construct at the height of their empire.[46]

Older Than Originally Thought

What is beginning to become increasingly clear, however, is that this kingdom was not only in decline when Pizarro subjugated it but that it is also much older than it was originally thought to be.[47] It began as a religious community, called the Chavin, about 800 B.C., which supported itself by fishing along the Pacific coast, rather than by agriculture, as it did later on. Even at the beginning, however, economic, military, and religious power was concentrated among an elite ruling class, who controlled the rest of the population by limiting access to the food supply.[48]

The Chimu

In a way that is similar to the Roman appropriation of cultural authority from the Etruscans who had preceded them in Latium, the Incas assimilated a great deal from the Chimu, whom they displaced. The Chimu, in turn, had done the same with the Mochica, or Moche, culture that predated them. Central to each of these appropriations was an advanced irrigation system, perfected by the Chimu, that allowed the Incas to dramatically increase the productivity of the land and support a population that was ten times larger than exists in the same region today.[49] The key to this ingenious system was the excavation of a series of parallel canals, spaced far enough apart to allow a long field to be planted between them. The factor that governed the width of these intermittent fields was the distance that the mist that rose up from the canals that flanked them could cover, since the canals and the fields worked together in a symbiotic relationship. Once they were dug, the canals were reinforced with battered stone sidewalls that projected up about 5 feet above the bottom of the canals. The fields between them were layered upward like a Roman road, beginning with a thick cobblestone base. This was then topped with a layer of clay to prevent canal water from percolating up and soaking the topsoil, and then layers of increasingly small sizes of gravel, ending with a 3 feet thick layer of topsoil for planting.

The water in the canals was used to irrigate the crops, but also protected them from frost during the cold nights that are typical in the Andean foothills, with average altitudes of 12,000 feet above sea level. The heat that the canal water had absorbed during the day radiated up and over the fields after sunset, protecting them like a warm blanket. The water to fill these canals was diverted by channels that were excavated to follow the contours of the foothills, to more efficiently capture the spring runoff from melting snow. This irrigation system was critical because of the arid climate with a very low average rainfall. Maize was the main crop grown in the raised fields used throughout the Inca Empire.[50]

Chan Chan

The Incas borrowed much more than this highly productive irrigation system from the Chimu, who had flourished from A.D. 1200 to 1400 along the northern coast of Peru in an extensive empire that extended 660 miles south from what is now the border with Ecuador. By the time the Incas cut their reign short, the Chimu controlled the entire coastline in this region, from their base in their capital city of Chan Chan. This city was located near the present day settlement of Trujillo in northern Peru and at its height housed about 100,000 people, in an area of about 12 square miles.[51]

Chan Chan had an orthogonal plan, which was a spatial representation of a clearly defined social organization, centered around large palaces for royalty and the nobility, administrative precincts, temples, and military quarters, as well as storehouses for grain controlled by the government.

Everything in the city, including the walls, the palaces, and the homes of the artisans, merchants, and farmers, was built of adobe, which the Chimu referred to as *tapia*.[52]

In addition to being orthogonal, the plan of Chan Chan is also distinctly additive with ten separate compounds being connected to the monumental, ceremonial center. The reason for these successive compounds, which were each surrounded by a wall, is not clear, but they were built sequentially and show the distinct evolution of the culture during the two centuries of its existence. Each had its own walled ceremonial plaza, consisting of a religious cluster that typically included a temple.[53]

Each of these centers was also built at a monumental scale that seems to have been inspired by the vast expanse of the Pacific Ocean nearby, providing an eastern architectural counterpoint to it. One theory put forward for the reason behind the ten separate citadels of Chan Chan, now named Chayhuac, Vihle, Tello, Labertino, Gran Chima, Bandolier, Lekarde, Rivero, Tshudi, and Squier, is that they were built by successive kings of the Chimu Dynasty to represent their individual power. This theory is strengthened by the discovery of separate tombs near the ceremonial plazas in each of them. Labertino, however, lacks a tomb, but has the most extensive area of housing for nobility found in any of the ten, followed by Gran Chimu, which is the largest of the citadels. Gran Chimu has the remains of a royal palace as well as an extensive precinct of large homes nearby, and a more organically organized area for houses and workshops that may have accommodated artisans or merchants.

Adobe

The Chimu raised the skill level of building in mud brick to new levels. They sculpted the walls of each citadel, as well as those of their houses, using geometric motifs, such as squares and swirling circles in addition to representations of fish and birds. But the repetition of these conventions in each of the citadels over time indicates a rigidly structural political system as well as aesthetic standardization at a level that is reminiscent of Egypt during the Old Kingdom.[54]

The Inca Ascendant

Rather than confronting Chan Chan directly, the Incas cut off its water supply at its source in the foothills at the Andes, bringing the two-centuries-old Chimu dynasty to an end. The Incas learned quickly, readily adopting the governmental and bureaucratic structure that the Chimu had used as well as adopting several of the urban planning strategies that they saw in Chan Chan for their own capital of Cuzco. Quite wisely, they also relocated all of the Chimu metalworkers to Cuzco as well, to teach their weapon-making skills to their own artisans, which also thwarted any attempt at a revolt. The Chimu had perfected special techniques of annealing, casting, molding, and hammering bronze weapons, and their *tumi* or sword was highly prized.

The Incas were also innovative builders, considerably improving upon the architectural skills of their predecessors. This is especially true in their adaptation of the use of stone masonry rather than mud brick. Contemporary engineers are still trying to determine how they were able to move stone blocks weighing between 20 and 300 tons, and then fit them together very precisely, without clamps or mortar.[55]

Machu Picchu

These masonry skills are especially evident at Machu Picchu, which was part of the royal estate of Emperor Pachacuti and was a religious compound relocated from Cuzco to an ancient temple of the sun. It was located high in the mountains above the Urubamba River and was so inaccessible that it remained hidden until archaeologist Hiram Bingham, who served as the inspiration for the film character Indiana Jones, uncovered it in 1912. The settlement he found occupied 21 acres (8.5 hectares), had nearly 170 buildings, and was surrounded by agricultural terraces that cascaded down the slopes around it, toward the valley far below. He determined that most of these structures were either temples or houses, divided into distinct groupings.

The steep slope on which Machu Picchu is located has a flat space, or swale, in the center, which seems to have acted as a main court around which the rest of the settlement was organized. This may possibly have also been an important reason for the selection of the site, since it is the only flat space on the entire Urubamba canyon wall.[56] A monumental stair connects this *pampa* to one of the most important temples in the settlement.

Houses

The houses of Machu Picchu are clustered together into several compounds grouped around open central spaces, with a single entrance into each one. Bingham felt that these must have been allocated to various groups or clans. Each of the houses has a rectilinear plan, with relatively low walls on the long sides and steeply pitched gable ends, all built as one continuous masonry structure. A single door, which was wider at the base than it was at the top, was placed in the middle of the front façade and was capped by a massive long stone that served as a lintel. The Incas solved the problem of how to build a roof on the steeply pitched stone gables of these houses by inserting five equally spaced stone bars between the stone courses. These had a hole drilled into the end that projected up beyond the

21

Inca House at Machu Picchu.   Courtesy of Shutterstock

coursing, so that the girders, which were made of square cut alder wood, could be tied down to the gable ends with rope. Joists were then run in the opposite direction, parallel to the gable ends, and these were then tied to the girders before reed grass thatch was placed over the entire roof structure.[57]

Some houses, in a compound on the southeast side of the site, have more than one door, and those in another have niches cut into the stone walls that are large enough for someone to have stood in them. Bingham speculated that these niches might have held mummies brought to Machu Picchu after the evacuation of Cuzco, perhaps being those of Inca emperors. A house near the Principal Temple has a finely carved built-in bench that seems to have been especially intended for this purpose.

In each case, however, the interiors of the stone walls were covered with lime plaster placed over clay mixed with fine stones, then painted with yellow ochre. The floors were also covered with plaster placed over an 8 to 12 inch thick (20 to 30 cm) bed of gravel and sand. An elaborate drainage system, mostly concealed below ground, kept the entire settlement dry.[58]

THE IROQUOIS LONGHOUSE

Many Native American tribes are now commonly known by the names that Europeans gave them, which were not always complimentary; the Iroquois call

Flowers and terraces at Machu Picchu.   Courtesy of Shutterstock

themselves the Haudenosaunee, which means "the people of the longhouse." They are technically part of what was originally the Iroquois Confederacy, which also included the Senecas, Cayugas, Onondagas, Oneidas, and Mohawks, and was later opened up to also include the Tuscaroras in 1725.[59] Foundation myths often say much about the character of a people, and the foundation story of the Iroquois revolves around the legendary Peacemaker Deganawida who, along with Hiawatha, or Ayenwatha, first forged the confederation in A.D. 1142.[60] This was initiated after a total eclipse of the sun, which was taken as a "sign in the sky" leading to the Great Law of Peace, which is believed to have been in August 1142, based on eclipse tables.[61] This preference for peace, for the sake of maintaining a confederacy, was to have important repercussions later when the French and the British were battling for supremacy over the eastern Great Lakes Region and were each trying to recruit the Iroquois to their cause. Realizing that by taking sides they would threaten each of the other of the Six Nations, they negotiated an agreement of neutrality with the French, called the Grand Settlement, in Montreal in 1701.[62] There was a direct benefit to matrilineal control, in addition to the fact that clans stayed together in individual groupings within each village. As one historian has described it:

> women of the same matrilineage or clan segment shared the same structure along with their husbands and children. When a man married, he moved out of his mother's (or sister's) longhouse and into the one in which his wife is living . . . matrilocal residence

has the effect of moving men around, physically splitting up brothers and other male relatives. This is a pattern that tends to prevent disputes between groups of related males and provide instead for the mobilization of large group[s] of men . . . .[63]

Village Structure

The criteria for the selection of a site for an Iroquois settlement reflected their transitional place on the timeline from periodic nomadic relocation toward seasonally dependant agricultural domesticity, with a violent history of intertribal warfare as part of the equation, prior to unification by the Peacemaker Deganawida. The mixture of a hunting-gathering and farming lifestyle to ensure subsistence meant that villages were always located on defensible terrain, such as the top of a hill and were surrounded by a wooden palisade. They were placed near a freshwater source with relatively flat land nearby that could be used to plant corn, squash, and beans, which were the main ingredients of the Iroquois diet along with the meat that was made possible by hunting.[64] There was an average of 2,000 people in a village, and it occupied 8 to 10 acres after the 1500s. Cedar swamps in the vicinity were also favored because wetlands were a good source of migratory birds as well as for fish and plants.[65]

The Garoga site, which was a Mohawk village in Fulton County, New York, provides a useful example. It was located on the top of a hill, with about a dozen longhouses dispersed on it in various orientations intended to make the best use of the land available. The preferred axis used to build a longhouse was east-west, to prevent the long sides from prolonged exposure to the rising and setting sun. But at Garoga, three longhouses, oriented on a southeast-northwest axis, bisect the village on a diagonal line through its center to take advantage of the width of the hilltop there.[66] The mixed orientation may also have been used for defense purposes, to reduce easy access to the center of the village and confuse an invading enemy running along the 10 to 12 feet wide spaces between the houses that served as the streets and lanes of each village.

In addition to habitation, these villages also had structures that served other uses, such as circular longhouses for cribs for the storage of corn, sweat lodges that served a ritualistic as well as purgative purpose, and outdoor hearths, used for cooking during the summer.

Because of the slash and burn technique of farming, Iroquois villages were relocated after about ten years because the land was played out. The difference between this pattern and the colonial practice of plowing and using cow and horse manure for fertilizer, which allowed them to remain on one plot of land, is often cited as a decisive factor in the displacement of native Americans by European settlers.[67]

The Longhouse

The weather in New York State, where a majority of the Haudenosaunee lived, is hot in the summer and cold and wet in the winter, with heavy snow being typical. Various kinds of wood were prevalent in the forests that covered the area when the Iroquois Confederacy was in full spate, and each type was used in a way that maximized its innate characteristics. Cedar was preferred for the vertical posts that were inserted in the ground at regular intervals as the main components of the long side walls of the longhouse because it is resistant to rot.[68] These posts were spaced

Iroquois longhouse.   Courtesy of Shutterstock

about two feet apart. Holes were dug first using a pointed stake made out of a harder wood before the white cedar columns were inserted, and these were then shimmed with their stone wedges. An extensive sampling of 63 Iroquois long-houses by noted scholar of Iroquois settlements Susan Prezzano has provided an average width of 6.5 meters (or about 24 feet), although wider houses have fre-quently been described elsewhere. The cedar posts were either forked or notched at the top to hold a horizontal beam that tied the two sides together and also acted as the bottom chord of a roof truss, with a curved arched member acting as the top chord, which supported the roof. Elm bark, called *ganasote* by the Senecas, was stripped and kept wet by laying it out in a stream bed, which also made it easier to work with. Cedar bark was also used, but elm was preferred because it did not burn as easily.

The length of each longhouse depended on the number of families that lived in it. Families occupied a 2 by 6 meters (about 8 by 20 feet) space on either side of a center aisle, which was used for circulation and for the hearths that were shared by each pair of families flanking it.[69] Each family was made up of four or five peo-ple. An average house might then have ten families, or about 50 people in it, di-vided up into five bays, with a hearth in each bay and with each bay housing two families separated by the central aisle. Houses could get much longer, especially those of chiefs, who used the size of their longhouses to convey their power. These were also used for meetings and ceremonies.[70]

Such an arrangement had advantages and disadvantages. The linear sequence of living quarters and provision of a single door at each end of the longhouse meant that it could be more easily defended, especially when the men were away on hunt-ing or war expeditions. If oriented correctly, the shape of the house also provided maximum heat in the winter and coolness in the summer, when flaps in the outer bark skin were opened to allow cross ventilation. The major disadvantage was the lack of privacy since people were constantly walking up and down the middle aisle through each of the pairs of family quarters, although lack of privacy was offset to some extent because the house belonged to the one clan. Each family lived on a wooden platform that was raised about a foot off the ground to prevent sleeping directly on the ground, which was cold and damp in the winter. The ends of each longhouse were used as storage areas, which served as an additional layer of insulation, preventing the wind from blowing in. A porch also extended out from each end to provide shade for the entrance, as well as a covering during rainstorms. There were holes in the roof of the longhouse above each hearth to let smoke escape, and these holes were covered with flaps that could be closed with long poles when it snowed or rained.[71]

Unhusked corn was hung along the entire length of the longhouse, along with clothing put out to dry and smoked fish, which, along with the smoke from the fire pits and the lack of openings, must have made the interior very pungent.

The average ten-family house would have used about 500 bushels of shelled corn a year, and a large bark silo was used to store 80 bushels, requiring six or seven silos for each longhouse. The processing of this corn into flour was a basic part of the domestic routine since it was a major component of the Iroquois diet, along with beans and squash, the smoked fish mentioned above, and roasted meat, including bear, beaver, muskrat, squirrel, and wild turkey. The corn kernels were boiled with wood ash and then washed in a basket to remove the hulls. The ash, according to one source, enhanced "the nutritional quality of the maize, increasing the amount of lysine as well as niacin that can be metabolized."[72] The corn was then pounded into flour using a wooden mortar and pestle. Early European observers have recorded how the Iroquois prepared the corn; Lewis Henry Morgan wrote, in 1851, that the husks were braided and the corn was hung "on the cross poles near the roof." He also wrote that "charred and dried corn and beans were generally stored in bark barrels, and laid away in corners."[73]

As Long as the Sun Shall Shine

Consistent with their role as peacemakers, 21 representatives of the Iroquois Confederacy met with the Continental Congress in Philadelphia in May 1776, staying in Independence Hall for about a month. When they met with delegates there on June 11, they were assured that the "friendship between us will continue as long as the sun shall shine and the waters run."[74] But their diplomacy was not able to preserve their traditional way of life in the face of the cataclysmic change that followed.

THE MAYA

The various Kingdoms of the Maya, which reached the height of their power between the early fourth century A.D. and the invasion by the Spanish *conquistadors* in the beginning of the fifteenth century A.D., were concentrated in a 125,000 square mile area that included Yucatan, Campeche, Tabasco, Quintana Roo, and part of Chiapas in what is now Mexico, as well as much of Guatemala.[75] This civilization that effectively spanned between the Pacific Ocean on the west, the Gulf of Mexico to the north, and the Gulf of Honduras and the Caribbean to the east emerged relatively quickly and disappeared just as fast, in historical terms. This occurred through four distinct phases generally agreed to be the Formative Period, or Old Empire, followed by the Late Formative, Proto-Classic, and Post-Classic Periods. The earliest recorded date of this civilization is September 18, A.D. 320. There is the usual divergence of scholarly opinion about its beginnings, since it seems to spring up out of nowhere, split between those arguing for an indigenous source and those who believe in an external influence. After the Classic Period, roughly placed between A.D. 700 and 800, the decline of the civilization was rapid and the remnants of it that the *conquistadors* under Cortez encountered were not as vibrant as the culture was at its height. What caused it to rise up and become so brilliant? Where did it come from? Where did it go? Part of the mystery surrounding it has been its alphabet, which remained undeciphered until recently, as well as the fact that many of the books that the Maya wrote were burned by the Spanish. Only three of these survived and, once their writing was decoded, these have opened up a treasure trove of information about them, including the most minute details of their daily life and a complex system of ritualized behavior, based on their calendar. A central feature of this system was the idea of a cycle of creation and destruction. These cycles were long, measuring 13 *baktuns*, or a little less than 5,200 years. The Maya believed that the final cycle would be the thirteenth, which, according to one calculation, places the first of these at 3113 B.C. and means that the last "Great Cycle of the Long Count" will end on December 24, A.D. 2011.[76]

A Stratified Society

Mayan society was clearly hierarchical with a theocratic hereditary elite at the top of the pyramid. This was headed by the king, *Ahau*, or *halach uinic* (true man), followed by the nobles, or *almehen*, meaning "he whose descent is known on both sides." This refers to the naming system used, which included the mother's name first, transmitted through the female line, and the father's second. As historian Michael Coe explains, "there is now abundant evidence that these two kind of names represented two different kinds of crosscutting and co-existing descent groups . . . the matrilineage and the patrilineage . . . they were strictly exogamous, all inheritance of property was patrilineal." [77] This landed gentry under the *Ahau* was the foundation of social power, followed by the military, the merchants, the clergy, the farmers, and the common people, or *milpas*. While their destruction of the records the Maya kept on their own culture is a disaster, the Spaniards did make helpful observations of their own about the daily life of the Maya, including descriptions of the houses of the *milpas*, which sound very similar to those found in Maya villages today. In fact, one of the most fascinating things about this culture is that the upper part of the social hierarchy, which was responsible for building the tall stepped monuments, plazas, ball courts, palaces, and administrative buildings that we have come to identify with it and which also dictated the pattern of constant warfare that is now believed to have been the major factor in its demise, seems to have vanished as quickly as it appeared. The social strata that supported it, however, as well as their way of life, houses, diet, and means of subsistence, still remain the same. In this, it is similar to many other cultures included here such as the Khmers, the Indus River Valley and Mesopotamian civilizations, and the Egyptians during the Pharaonic Period, in which the way of life in the rural areas has remained substantially the same for millennia.

Trade

Because of the extensive coastlines that bordered their empires, as well as their ability to build seaworthy ships and their engineering skill in planning excellent roads, which they called *sakbehs* (sometimes "*sacbeah*") or "white ways" because they were coated in white stucco, the Maya were able to trade with neighbors near and far. We often have a preconceived notion of them as being stationary, tied to the cities that they built in the middle of the rain forest, and so it may come as some surprise to imagine them as accomplished road builders and sailors. The downside of this was that their *sakbehs* also made it easier for their enemies to attack them. It is now understood that there was almost constant warfare that took place between rival city-states, which probably contributed to the ultimate collapse of the entire collective civilization.

Through their ability to trade extensively with other cultures around them, however, the Maya were able to enrich their lives and to give distinct character to their civilization through the exchange of such exotic items as cacao, copal, rubber, *balche*, salt, cotton, flint, quetzal feathers, obsidian, and jade. Of these, cacao, which was highly sought after by royalty, was so valuable that the beans were used as a means of monetary exchange, and copal, which is a resin similar to frankincense and equally rare, was used primarily for religious ceremonies. *Balche*, which is a fermented beverage similar to beer, certainly must have improved their quality of life, as did their salt, which was made from evaporated seawater and highly regarded for its quality.

The Mayan House

The Maya, like so many other ancient societies that have been included here, built large ceremonial centers, while the people who built them lived in modest and temporary shelters on their periphery. The first house that a couple built after they were married was near either one of their families' houses, until they could manage to build a larger one elsewhere. Although there are several examples of nonrectangular plans, the typical form of the house of a common person was long and narrow, with rounded ends, technically referred to by one historian as "apsidal."[78] It was built by firmly securing thin, flexible saplings in a stone foundation and then bending them to support a gable roof, which was covered with thatch. The spaces between the saplings was then interwoven with smaller branches and covered with adobe. The interior of the house, which has a smooth hard clay floor, was divided by a wall running across its narrow width, which separated the cooking and eating area from the sleeping quarters. Fray Diego de Landa, whose keen observations written shortly after the Spanish conquest are the source of much of our knowledge of the everyday habits of the Maya, has written that the beds in this area were also "made of small saplings laced together by withes which gave way to the movement of the body like a mattress."[79] He observed that this framework was covered with a flat grass or reed mat. Cotton fabric was then placed over this as a covering.

The entrance to the house was in the center of one of the long sides, and there was rarely more than one of these. There was no door, probably because the thin wattle and daub wall could not support the weight of more than a thin wooden gate, and the vibrations caused by constant opening and closing would have cracked the adobe surface near the hinges. The entrance was covered by beads or bells or strings, or by a curtain instead, giving some idea of the sense of security that the family must have felt.

Victor W. Von Hagen, who has attempted to give an insight into the daily life of the Maya in the 1960s long before it was easy or popular to do so, has made the interesting point that, since this house type has survived, relatively unchanged, for more than 2,000 years, the Maya names for several of its parts may also have remained the same over that time. This may be thought of, he says, as "linguistic paleontology." In it, the roof purlin is called "the road of the rat," the entrance is "the mouth of the house," and the main roof post is "the leg of the house." [80]

The burial practices of the Maya are also similar in many ways to those of other societies discussed here in that, as Landa also records, they buried their dead under the floor of the house, designating one of the apsidal ends for that purpose. When that area was fully used, usually within 20 to 30 years' time, a new house was built and the plot used for the previous one was designated to be a sacred space.

Houses of the Nobles

The houses of the nobles, on the other hand, were made of stone rather than wattle and daub or adobe. They were covered with stucco and painted with frescos, which were very colorful. This technique of covering stone structures with lime-based stucco gave all Mayan buildings, other than the houses of the *milpas*, a dazzling appearance that is difficult to imagine when looking at the raw stone ruins that survive today. They developed a stucco-making process, which is still prevalent, even though it is resource intensive in that no kiln is required. Wood is first stacked on end in a pile, and the limestone is placed on top of it. The trick is to use just the right amount of wood and to position it in such a way that there is a minimum amount of waste product at the end once the lime is slaked. Once the burning is complete, it is left to cool for several days, before water and a mixture of finely crushed limestone particles called *sascab* were added as temper.[81] A great deal of wood was needed to burn the lime, and the Maya used stone headed axes to cut it, which gives some indication of their wood-cutting and tool-making skills and their high level of energy and strength. Since the stone walls were covered with gypsum stucco, the masonry joints were less than perfect, unlike the stonework of the Incas, which is known for its amazing precision. This was not true of the roof structure of Mayan stone buildings, however, in which an arched form, typically referred to as a corbel or a vault was used. As one expert on Mayan architecture, Tatiana Proskouriakoff, has explained, however,

> the course of this new development is so sharply in contrast with the evolution of Old World style that we find it difficult to speak of Maya buildings in traditional architecture terms. The so-called "vault" of the Maya, for example, is neither a vault in the true

sense nor a true "corbel vault" as it is often called. It is a unique form of construction, taking advantage of principles of stone arrangement, while at the same time relying heavily on the strength of mortar for its support.[82]

The end result of the use of what must be called corbel vault for want of a more accurate term, however, is that spans were severely restricted and rooms were very long and narrow. A good example is the Palace of the Governors at Uxmal, which is generally considered to be one of the most excellent monuments of this civilization. This was, more accurately, built in the *Puuc* style named after the hills nearby, in western Yucatan, in which an L-shaped stone was used to add strength to the corbelled vaults, so that it could also be used as a doorway.[83] The surfaces of *Puuc* architecture are also much more sculpturally ornate and deeply carved, giving it an unmistakably textured quality. The Governor's Palace is a long narrow structure built on a high platform that originally had battered walls and a single wide staircase leading up to it in the middle. It is organized in three joined segments, with the longest in the center, flanked by two nearly square pieces at the ends. These are all unified by a richly carved, 11.5 foot high and 320 foot long frieze, which acts as a datum at the top and which also covers 75 percent of the horizontal composition of the surface elevation. The remaining 25 percent of the horizontal surface of the elevation on the bottom is plain, interrupted only by a series of small doorways, with the central entrance being square. The Palace of the Governor was commissioned by King Chaak, who was the last ruler of Uxmal before it was deserted at the beginning of the tenth century.

It is difficult to imagine how this house, or palace, might have been used since the interior spaces are so small and dark, due to the structural limitations imposed by the corbels. If this is the case in what is widely considered to be the most beautiful existing Mayan residential building, it seems to confirm the image of a society that valued a life of action, lived outdoors and organized around ceremonial public rituals and patterns, rather than one that was sedentary and fond of domestic comfort.

2

Africa

AL QAHIRA, EGYPT

Cairo was established by the Shiite Fatimids, who swept across North Africa and inaugurated the new city, Al Qahira (the triumphant) in A.D. 969. It was laid out in a grid plan by the Fatimid general Al-Jawhar (the Sicilian) presumably inspired by the rectilinear configurations of Roman cities he had seen while marching eastward along the Mediterranean coast. The main north-south street, replicating the Roman Cardo Maximus, was named after the Fatimid Caliph Al-Muizz, who built his palace on an east-west cross street near the middle, called the Qasaba or Bien Qasrean.

Islam had spread into Egypt from the Arabian Peninsula nearly three centuries earlier, in 696, and the port city of al Fustat, which had replaced the Byzantine fortress of Babylon, was prospering when the new Fatimid city was founded. The two urban areas were intended to function symbiotically, with al Fustat, which was more exposed and had far better access to trade, as the gateway to the outside world. It acted as an economic hub for the general populace, and Al Qahira, which was more protected by both its inland location and fortifications, served as a royal, judicial, and ceremonial enclave.

Al Fustat

What is now known about the physical configurations of the houses in al Fustat has only come to light relatively recently due to the fact that the area has been used as a landfill for the rapidly expanding Cairo metropolitan area as well as because the river Nile changed course. Excavations by archaeologists Ali Bahgat, Albert Gabriel, Wladyshlaw Kubiak, and George Scanlon, in combination with historical accounts, increasingly provide a more vivid, if still incomplete, picture of how the general populace of various economic levels outside the princely city of Al Qahira lived. The materials used varied from mud brick to stone depending upon social level, from rich to very poor. They also varied in height for the same reason, ranging from what were described in 1191 as mud shacks to multistory apartments,

Cairo was founded in A.D. 969 by Sultan Al Muizz and was laid out by his leading general Al-Jawhar on a grid system, similar to that of the Roman cities the Fatamids had seen on their way across North Africa toward Egypt. *Source:* James Steele

clustered in neighborhoods. According to contemporary accounts, the height of the housing blocks increased to 14 stories or more in the central district, giving the city the appearance of a mountain.

Regardless of the number of stories, the houses of the lower middle class and above shared several common characteristics that are also typically found in other houses throughout the Middle East from the beginning of the agricultural revolution around 400 B.C., such as those in Ur, in the Chaldees. These common attributes were to be later refined in Cairo itself, as the political situation changed over the next four centuries to become specifically identifiable as belonging only to this city. The way that they evolved, from being generically Middle Eastern to uniquely Cairiene, provides an instructive case study in the cultural adaptation of common residential prototypes.

Common Characteristics

There are typical features that the al Fustat houses share with those in other parts of the region from earliest times. The first of these is an inner courtyard, which helped to compensate for the compressed conditions that started to exist when houses began to share perimeter walls. The courtyard was a quiet inner sanctum offering a refuge from the bustle of city life as well as a temperature regulator, moderating the intense heat in the area by acting as a reservoir for cooler nighttime air and providing natural ventilation to each of the spaces around it. The courtyard also facilitated the second common feature of the Middle Eastern house, which is privacy, offering protection from prying eyes. The third feature is an offset entrance, which does not allow outsiders to see into the house when the front door is open. The fourth characteristic, which is a refinement on internal privacy, is zoning to selectively allow outsiders to enter, in a careful compartmentalization of public and private spaces. These are further divided to effectively allow the segregation of the sexes, with male visitors relegated to one reception hall and female guests to another. A fifth characteristic is the flexible nature of interior space, with each placed in the optimum location to take advantage of the environmental benefits available at the time of day it was used. An open, south facing second floor balcony, for example, was used by the family for a late afternoon gathering, for example, because the sun angle and prevailing breeze at that time of day made it the most comfortable place to be. A sixth and final similarity relates to an extension of the internal orientation and order of the open spaces within each house out into the alleys, streets, and plazas beyond, creating a deliberate pattern of openings oriented to facilitate airflow and heat convection.

Saladin

Under the Fatimids the bivalent cities of al Fustat and Al Qahira prospered, so that, as experts Richard Ettinghausen and Oleg Grabar have described it,

> The whole area to the south and southwest was transformed so that by the year 1000 Cairo, with the old city of Fustat, had become one of the largest and most cosmopolitan urban complexes of the medieval world, with its markets, mosques, streets, gardens, multi-story apartments and private houses.[1]

After the Fatimids were displaced by the Ayyubids from Syria, however, under the leadership of the legendary Sultan Salih Najm al-Din Ayyub (Saladin), the urban configuration of Cairo changed dramatically. This was due to Saladin's decision to move the royal residence to the Citadel, outside the city walls, and to open up the nearly square walled enclosure to the common people. The legal changes that this precipitated, to facilitate access to new religious institutions related to the ideological difference between the Fatimids and Ayyubids, as well as trade within various quarters and the major caravan route through it along the Shariah al-Muizz Li Din from the Bab Zuwailah in the south to the Bah al Futah in the north, led to a dramatic alteration of street patterns. This change has been identified in other urban areas throughout Asia, in the Middle East, and in Europe as well during the beginning of the Middle Ages due to an expanded, market-based economy based on wider trade. It was "epitomized" as a historian of the Chinese walled city of Suzhou has noted, "by the collapse of the old system of the enclosed marketplace and walled residential wards and by their replacement with a fairly free street plan in which trade and commerce could be conducted anywhere with the city or its outlying suburbs."[2]

The change that occurred in Cairo, however, was profound, affecting both the street and house configurations inside the roughly one square kilometer walled enclosure. It reaffirms recent work by anthropologists and sociologists regarding the specialized refinements that can take place within a regional typology due to political, social, or religious differences. The shift that took place in Cairo, from the Fatimids, who were Shiites from North Africa, to the Ayyubids, who were Syrian Sunnis, is traceable in the influence that spatial organizations derived from the Ayyubids' Mesopotamian heartland began to have on the basic and ancient domestic features common to this area, described earlier.

The torturous street patterns and unique houses of Arabic cities such as Cairo, which fascinated the first Western travelers able to enter them in the seventeenth and eighteenth centuries, were described by Orientalist observers in purely formal and phenomenological terms as recently as the early 1980s. This ended when pioneer researchers such as Jameel Akbar and Besim Hakim began to apply legal and religious precedents on a case-by-case basis to show that formal changes occurred primarily due to potential social or economic advantage. Although many Western writers still maintain that many spaces in the middle and upper-middle class houses of Cairiene merchants in the Middle Ages are exotic, mysterious, and indecipherable, keen observers such as the late Egyptian architect Hassan Fathy have done much to explain the uses and trace the origins of spaces that have been the subject of much speculation by others.

The *Qa'a*

By far, the most remarkable transition was that of the generic reception hall for male guests, typically called *a majlis* throughout the Arab world, to the *qa'a*, which is different from anything seen previously in that region. It migrated, once perfected, to the Hijaz region of the Arabian Peninsula.

In several well-researched articles, Egyptian architect Hassan Fathy has described how the *qa'a*, which is usually easily accessible from the main entrance to effectively isolate male guests from the rest of the house, slowly evolved from its first appearance in the Ukhaider Palace in Iraq, built by a *gazi* warrior prince as a fortress palace on what was then the front line of the Islamic push northward. The Ukaider Palace is aligned on a north-south symmetrical axis, running through an open rectangular walled central court with an entrance at one end and the formal, official place and throne room at the other. The bedrooms for each of the prince's four wives were arranged along the two long east-west sides of the rectangle. They were each the same, based on an open square central courtyard, flanked by an *iwan* or covered alcove opening up to the central courtyard on both its north and south sides. Even though Iraq is relatively warm for most of the year, there is a winter season, during which late afternoons and evenings can become quite cold. Summers, by contrast, are very hot, and so these opposing sets of *iwans* were intended to allow the occupant to take advantage of the warm sun by facing south in the winter and the cooler breezes by switching to the north facing *iwan* in the summer.[3]

In its transplanted, Cairiene version nearly three centuries later, this square central courtyard with flanking *iwans* was converted from a bedroom into a public social configuration with the court recessed by one step and covered with a wind tower roof, called a *shuksheika*, to cool it. The tower acted in concert with a second vertical projection, a *maalkaf*, which was oriented toward the prevailing breeze, directing it down over a fountain to cool it further and then into the *qa'a*. As this air heated, due to transpiration caused by the occupants of the space, it rose up into the *shuksheika* directly above the small central court and out, completing the cycle and providing a constant supply of cool fresh air for the space. The opposing *iwans*, freed from seasonal occupation, were also no longer tied to orientation and so could be more flexibly located in the house plan, within the constraint of family privacy. The opposing configuration of the *iwans* made them ideally suited to the formal requirements of social etiquette, with a guest or guests on one side and the host on the other, facing each other across the recessed central zone, which could also be used by domestic help when serving food and drinks. The *qa'a* became an internal oasis of gentility and calm.

The *Taktaboosh*

The prevailing breeze in the medieval quarter of Cairo comes from the desert to the northwest, and at dusk and after dark this is invariably cool throughout the year. Through observation, those building houses learned that planted areas and gardens retained this cool night air blowing in from the desert on the shaded surface area of leaves, which also filtered out sand and dust and that, as the day progressed, this cool air would rise as it heated. They also observed that a paved area, when placed in tandem with this planted area, would accelerate and direct the flow of cool air sideways rather than straight up due to convection; the sun would heat the unshaded paved surface faster as it rose, especially if this portion was slightly wet, drawing the cool night air trapped in the leaves of the adjacent garden toward it. Many other cultures have made use of this simple physical principle as a cooling device, such as the *lanai* in Hawaii, but builders in medieval Cairo capitalized on it further by creating a special second-story room that bridges over an opening between the paved and planted gardens. The room and the shaded area beneath it are called a *taktaboosh*, and it was the preferred space for the family to meet for a midday meal because the cool air rushing from the garden below, on the north, through the shaded space below it toward the paved courtyard on the south, was channeled up and into it, through vents in the floor: the medieval equivalent of air conditioning. The use of materials that did not absorb heat quickly, such as stone and Isnick tiles from Turkey, in this room helped to make the *taktaboosh* comfortable at the hottest time of the day and, coincidentally, added to its elegance.[4]

The *Maqaad*

The final adaptation of the second story *maqaad*, which faced onto the paved courtyard, also relates to orientation, since this open, *iwan*-like porch was developed to take advantage of the prevailing breeze coming in from the desert in the early evening. It was a favorite meeting place for the family at that time, and the evening meal was often served here before everyone retired to their respective bedrooms on the upper floors after dark.

The evolution in Cairo of the *qa'a*, *taktaboosh*, and *maqaad*, based on preexisting regional and then specifically Mesopotamian models, demonstrates the ingenuity of local builders in adopting generic, time-tested spaces to uses more appropriate for this place. They also show that the Cairiene family, at this economic level, was willing to be flexible in their use of these spaces, moving to them at the time of day at which the environmental purpose they were designed to benefit from was at its best. Architects specializing in sustainability and ecological sensitivity today call such movement "diurnal zoning," meaning that the various spaces in a house or other building are designed for optimal environmental performance based on orientation and heat gain or loss at a certain time of day. The medieval builders in Cairo understood this concept very well.

CARTHAGE, TUNISIA

Carthage, which was the early rival and omnipresent scourge of ancient Rome, was originally settled by Phoenicians who established a city around the Bay of Tunis, with the earliest Punic occupation being dated to the end of the fifth century B.C. It has been difficult for archaeologists to determine both the form and the extent of this city, given the absence of defensive walls and the ferocity of Roman determination to eliminate it. The oldest settlement seems to have been clustered in an arc between the base of two dominant hills later known as Juno and Byrsa and to have spread out in a southeastern direction along the Bay.[5]

A Rational System

What can be determined about the houses in the Punic city is that a very logical system was used in their layout and construction, making them very different from those of their Roman counterparts built at the same time. There was a standard lot size and several different typologies that were used alternatively in each block. Each plot was as deep as the block was wide, and there were six equally wide plots.[6]

The Basic House Types

The typical 9 meters wide by 29.5 meters long housing unit exactly spanned between two streets. It had a narrow corridor running the entire length of the unit along one wall connected to a rectilinear courtyard in the middle. This corridor was only 90 centimeters wide, and access to it was provided by a door at each end opening onto the street. There was a wooden screen that divided it from the central courtyard for privacy. The floor of both the courtyard and corridor was *pozzolana* with a mixed aggregate of marble chips and broken pottery, giving it the appearance of *terrazzo*.[7] There was a channel let into the floor of the corridor, running along the outer wall for sewage that directed it outside to "soakaways," so that, in this detail at least, the houses of Punic Carthage were less hygienic than those in Rome at the same time.

At the beginning, this house, which is small, had only two rooms flanking the central courtyard. One had a portico over windows looking out to the courtyard, shading them from the direct sun coming in from above, and an entrance from the corridor, as well as a window onto the street on that side of the house. The second room on the other end was an *oecus*, which had an entrance both from the courtyard and directly to the street. The *oecus*, or living area, was the formal reception room, and its elevated status is obvious in the mosaic flooring used there. It also typically had a pair of doors on each end, and an elegant stone threshold beneath them, which is indicative of its status.

What these houses lacked in sanitation they somewhat made up for in water storage facilities, since the courtyard was used as an *impluvium*. The roof pitched inward on all sides, directing rainwater into it and then into a large circular drain that led to a deep, oblong water tank beneath the floor. This pitched roof may have projected slightly over the inward edge of both the *oecus* and its partner at the opposite end of the house, as well as the face of the side walls, and it may have been supported by slender columns to keep each of these walls dry, forming a *peristyle*. The side walls were about 52 centimeters wide, since they were structural.[8]

Somehow, stairs also must have been included in this tight plan, due to Roman descriptions of the houses as being more than one story high when they invaded the city, but archaeological evidence of these stairways has yet to be found. The modest size of the ground floor rooms as well as the estimated capacity of the cisterns, however, imply that there must have been more than one story in these houses. There was a hierarchy of street widths, and where two of the wider streets intersect, as well as in the space between houses when they do not, there was enough room for market stalls. This raises the prospect of commercial activity along these edges and at these intersections. The excavation of the various stones needed to grind grain into flour near one of these squares lends credence to this idea.

The Punic city existed for more than 600 years before Scipio Africanus declared to the emperor and the Roman Senate that "Carthage Delenda Est" ("Carthage is destroyed"), and its ruins were plowed under with salt, following the battle of Zana in A.D. 201.

DEIR EL MEDINA AND TEL EL AMARNA, LUXOR, EGYPT

Any attempt to describe the circumstances in which the average person lived during the Pharaonic Period in ancient Egypt is complicated by both the many phases of what is one of the oldest civilizations in history and the impermanence of the materials that people other than royalty or nobles used to build their houses. Egypt is matched only by China in duration, with the Pharaonic Period beginning its early Dynastic phase about 3000 B.C. and lasting until the Ptolemaic Kingdom was brought to an end by Octavian at the battle of Actium and the death of Cleopatra on the August 12, 30 B.C. During those 2,970 years there were also three interregnums or intermediate periods. These occurred between what are now known as the Old Kingdom (2686–2125 B.C.), the Middle Kingdom (2055–1650 B.C.), the New Kingdom (1550–1069 B.C.), and the Ramessid Period (1295–1069 B.C.) when the civilization reached its height.

An Incomplete Record
Because the homes that were not part of the royal enclave were typically built of mud brick, many have not survived, leaving us with very little information about them. The scant evidence we do have comes from representations of houses on tomb paintings, as well as the remains of several villages where the artisans who painted them lived, or from those who built the new city of Tel El Amarna or the pyramid of Sesostris II, because these were in relatively remote areas that were left undisturbed. Tel El Amarna has been especially helpful, even though it was primarily a royal city, built as the new capital of King Amenhotep IV, who changed his name to Akhenaten, or "the manifestation of the sun god."[9] The isolated location of the city in a natural amphitheatre on the east bank of the Nile, halfway between Memphis and Thebes, was selected because it provided the ideal place

from which to observe the rising and setting of the sun, in a place that has no associations with the priestly bureaucracies that had been established around existing deities in the Egyptian pantheon, such as Amun.

Common Characteristics

By comparing all of the sources available, it has now been possible to identify several consistently occurring characteristics of the residential architecture of the average Egyptian during the most representative phases of the Pharaonic Period. It has been noted that such houses might more accurately be referred to as "Kamitic," due to the fact that the ancient Egyptians referred to their land as *kemet*.[10] This name has great significance for both their lifeview and their attitude toward their houses because *kemet*, which means "the black earth," also implies the sharp division that exists between it and *deshre*, "the red land," or desert alongside it, graphically symbolic of life and death. The flooding of the Nile each year was caused by the spring thaw of snow on the mountains around its source at Lake Victoria, in Tanzania. This created an annual cycle that had always been a part of Egyptian life until a series of dams were built to control it, beginning in the nineteenth century and ending with the Aswan High Dam in the mid-1960s. The inundation of the land around the Nile meant that it was enriched by the soil that the river had picked up on its long passage through Africa and carried with it in suspension, dropping it on its banks, in various widths depending on the geological formations and topography, once it receded. The inundation, which lasted for months, meant that the houses in that zone had to be abandoned each year and rebuilt when the flood was over. Mud brick was the best material to use for this because the land was replenished, and the soil that had been left behind was viscous and rich, making it perfect for molding bricks.

This dichotomy of *kemet*, or the black land of fertility and life, and *deshre*, or "the red land" and death, is central to the ancient Egyptian concept of a cycle of renewal and of life after death, finally expressed in the construction of the pyramids that were intended to preserve the body of the Pharaoh for this regeneration.

The Mud Brick House

The rectilinear mud brick house, which may be identified as being typical throughout the Pharaonic Period, represents the final stage in a long evolution of forms that mirror those in the traditional residential architecture of Africa. These can be classified as tent structures, followed by clusters of circular huts, before the development of a rectangular mud brick house with a courtyard.[11] In its final form, the Kamitic house had either a vaulted or flat roof, faced with a ribbed configuration of reeds on the inside. These reed mats, which are still used as floor and wall coverings in the rural houses of the *fellahin*, were also represented in stone inside the Old Kingdom funerary complex of King Djoser at Saqqara, which provides a vivid image of what they looked like. The houses also typically had angular wind catches that channeled the prevailing breeze into the interior. Kamitic houses did have secondary towers that let hot air escape. They had external stairs leading to the roof, which, on houses in which this was flat, was used as an outdoor room and a sleeping platform at night. This was especially advantageous because, even though a thick mud brick wall prevents solar heat gain from penetrating into the house during the day, it eventually reaches a saturation point just before sunset, after which the heat stored in the wall radiates into the interior all night long. Since the nights in Egypt are fairly warm and dry for most of the year, sleeping out in the open is a pleasant option, which allows the house to be used during all of the daily and seasonal temperature cycle that it accommodated.

The use of the roof as a sleeping platform at night as well as for many other purposes during the day, when canopies were raised to protect people from the sun, made a permanent stairway to it necessary, which was located outside the house in a rear courtyard. This external stair and the courtyard it was placed in then become the final two typical features of this house type. To save material and labor, it was not built of solid mud brick all the way up, but was supported by an arch, which also allowed for a storage space beneath it. It is remarkable that this feature also survives in the mud brick houses of the *fellahin* today, and this arched opening under the stair is typically used as the place where a clay jar holding drinking water is kept in a tripod-shaped stand. As a breeze passed over the surface of the jar, which is porous enough to allow condensation to form on it, the temperature of the water in it was lowered by evaporative cooling. The courtyard was also a very versatile component of the house, providing a protected area for family use as well as playing a critically important role in keeping the house cool.

Deir El Medina

The shift from burial in singular pyramids like those on the Giza plateau to rock cut tombs like those in which Tutankamen was found spawned a new industry, requiring artisans to both carve them and paint their interiors. The Valley of the Kings and Queens near Thebes, now known as Luxor, became the preferred necropolis of royalty, who chose it in the hope that their tombs would finally escape the attention of grave robbers. It was also believed to be auspicious that a prominent mountain there had a top shaped like a pyramid, which is called "Alqurn," or the horn, today. Rock cut tombs also required less time to build and were less expensive. Because of the numbers of burials there, requiring generations of artisans to carve them and create the exquisite wall paintings that accompanied them, it was necessary for the workers to build a permanent settlement nearby, and this evolved naturally over time within the confines of the shallow valley in which it was located.

Extreme Conditions

This community, which is now referred to as Deir El Medina, is on the way from the Nile to the Valley of the Kings and Queens, in a slight depression flanked by low hills that are 100 feet high at most. It is a desolate moonscape of barren rock and sand with very little vegetation; it is hot and dry in the summer and cooler in the winter with the frigid nights that are typical in the desert that surrounds it. The transformation of this inhospitable place into a thriving settlement that endured and grew over many generations is a testament to the human capacity for enduring hardship and providing ingenious solutions to extreme environmental conditions.

Deir El Medina ruins, Luxor, Egypt.   Courtesy of Shutterstock

Unlike similar workers' compounds that have been found at Kaheen, which housed the builders of the pyramid of Sesostris II and Tel El Amarna who built the new city of *Akhetaten* for the Pharaoh Akhenaten and Nefertiti, the village of Deir El Medina was not standardized or built to a regular plan. And yet, the houses seem to have each conformed to a predictable pattern, based on the evidence that has been found, being compartmentalized into a series of consecutive spaces, or rooms, from the entrance from the street in the front to the less formal service areas at the back. Each of these, except for the courtyard, was covered and was relatively high, to allow the natural ventilation introduced in the first of these rooms to flow easily through the entire linear arrangement of spaces and then rise up and out through the courtyard in the back, which helped draw the air through. The first of these spaces, which contained a small enclosed chapel that protected an effigy of the household deity, had a floor that was several steps lower than street level, accentuating the feeling of a threshold by adding the experience of moving downward at the start. The intention of using this entry area as an intermediate, preparatory place prior to the central living space that followed it was that of an architectural equivalent of shaking the dust off one's feet, as the living area was raised up an equal number of steps. A post hole found in the middle of this nearly square central hall hints at a central column that must have seemed like a presence in the room, which was probably loti form, with capitals like closed lotus or

Deir El Medina ruins, Luxor, Egypt.   Courtesy of Shutterstock

papyrus buds, like those in the rock cut tombs at Beni Hasan carved during the Middle Kingdom, about 2000 B.C. This probably supported a girder, which held joists running in the opposite direction, making the span of between 15 and 20 feet possible. Stairways found in many of these rooms have been formed, leading down to small basements carved out of the rock floor of the valley, with indications that these were covered with a trapdoor, hidden by a dais.[12] The next room was the bedroom, which was raised up one step from the living space and had a corridor running along one side of it that connected the living area to the courtyard in the back. This room, which must have been used on nights when the heat was not oppressive, had a built-in raised platform on which a cotton mattress and cover could have been placed, and it was rather low compared to the rooms that preceded it. The courtyard, which followed, had a mud brick oven and tone sink as well as a place for grinding grain into flour to make bread.[13]

While the walls of these houses were made of mud brick, they were built on stone stem walls, or foundations, since stone is plentiful in this valley and the people who lived here were certainly adapt at carving it. The facts that these stem walls are so high and the village was outside the annual inundation zone of the Nile in this area have both contributed to the preservation of the plan outlines of the houses and have made it possible to reconstruct what the village looked like.

Tel El Amarna

Known as *Akhetaten*, or the Horizon of the Aten, when Amenhotep IV ordered it built in 1348 B.C., during the latter part of the New Kingdom, Tel El Amarna is located in a natural, semicircular curve in the face of a low cliff facing the Nile, which bends slightly at the same point creating a harbor. The site is halfway between the previous governmental centers of Memphis and Thebes, deliberately chosen as neutral territory that would be free from the influence of the priestly establishment surrounding the deity Amun and the extensive temple complex dedicated to him, now known as Karnak, in Luxor. After the death of Amenhotep IV, who took the name Akhenaten, or "the creative manifestation of the Aten," and that of his successor, Neferneferuaten, who some believe was his wife Nerfertiti, in 1336, the city was abandoned. The couple's son Tutankamen, most famous for the astonishingly beautiful contents of his tomb discovered in 1922, returned to Theban orthodoxy, as indicated by the suffix chosen for his name, but it is suspected that he was assassinated anyway just to ensure that the Amarna heresy had ended.[14]

Innovative Techniques

Because of the revolutionary aspect of the theocratic apostasy that Akhenaten had initiated, his new capital city had to be built quickly and also had to embody his principles and ideals. When he took the throne, Egypt was at the height of its power and the Kingdom stretched from Nubia to Syria. Much of the center of the city was built in two years, due to the innovation of using smaller stone blocks for the public structures and royal palaces. These were about three hand lengths long, or 60 cm, making it easy for one laborer to carry them, and are now referred to as a *talatat*, which is Arabic for three, because of the manual method of measurement used.[15] The organization of the city plan, like the art for which this period is famous, broke with previous conventions and was much less formal. It has been accurately described as "a cluster of small villages centered around loosely grouped houses both large and small, each with its own subsidiary buildings." [16] The central part of the city where the Royal Residence Palace and Temple were located, was bisected by the Royal Road, along which Akhenaten and Nefertiti would ride in a chariot to demonstrate solidarity with their subjects.

The palace, which was on one side of the road, was raised up so that it had an unobstructed view of the temple and the extended shoreline of the Nile beyond it. The royal couple would cross over the road on their way to the temple everyday by using a covered bridge dedicated for their use. They would frequently stop at an opening in the middle and shower money down on their subjects who were waiting below. The residence, palace, and temple were each organized around large, open courtyards, with the buildings themselves supported by many rows of columns. The Maru-Aten, dedicated to the couples' daughter Meritaten, was located at the southern end of the Royal Road, grouped around a lake, with a pavilion near it.[17]

An Egalitarian Order

The openness that Akhenaten and Nefertiti encouraged in urban planning and artistic style also extended to the houses of their subjects, since the villas of the rich were interspersed with the smaller houses of the poor. The large villas typically had one large central hall with dependencies such as bedrooms and the open courtyards associated with them organized around it. This cluster was surrounded by a second rank of servants' quarters and service functions such as the kitchen and gardens. There was a separate settlement of the workers and artisans who actually built

Akhetaten, consisting of about 70 small houses organized in a roughly square block, clearly distinguishable from houses in the rest of the city.[18]

GREAT ZIMBABWE

A walled city was built in Zimbabwe about A.D. 1100 and was a political economic powerhouse for the next 500 years. The stone walls that remain today testify to a high level of masonry skill, standing 37 feet high in some places, with 4 feet wide gates cut through them at strategic locations.[19] The settlement, which covers an area of 1,779 acres, included three separate zones: the Hill Complex, the Great Enclosure, and the Valley Ruins. The Hill Complex, which is the oldest part of the settlement, was obviously selected for its value as a vantage point and its ability to be defended. There are houses, called *daga*, inside its 328 feet long and 148 feet wide walled enclosure that are either round or oval mud brick huts covered with thatched roofs. These vary in size and shape, creating an organic pattern in plan that covers the hilltop. The Great Enclosure, which is on the southern side of the valley that separates it from the Hill Complex, is about 650 yards away from it and is about one-quarter of its size. It has a high, roughly elliptical wall capped with open work known in Arabic as "sixes and sevens," because the alternating V-shaped stones represent those numbers in the language. The Great Zimbabwe is known as *Imba huru*, or "house of the great women" in Karanga, which is a Shona dialect.[20] It has a 30 feet high, 18 feet diameter conical tower built into the wall, which one historian has taken as a symbolic portion of its purpose, which he believes to have been a royal palace, in which the grooves in the walls perhaps represented the female anatomy and the conical tower a phallus, so "the compound was used for adolescent initiation rites or for other important ceremonies" and "it may also have housed the many wives of the ruler." [21]

Control of the Trade in Gold

Great Zimbabwe was strategically located as a control point on the main route between gold fields to the north of it and the Indian Ocean, which seems to be the source of its wealth, and as its prosperity increased there are indications that the three separate parts of the city grew also, which explains its organic form. The Valley Ruins are also evidence of this expansion, since they were the last to be built, hinting at a binuclear arrangement of a high fortress and second settlement below it at first, followed by overflow housing as the population grew.

House of Stone

Dzimbabwe, from which the name of the country where this walled city was taken after it was changed from Rhodesia after independence from the United Kingdom in 1980, means "houses of stone" in Shona.

THE NUBIAN HOUSE

Nubia is a geographic region concentrated along the Nile, divided almost evenly by the border between Upper Egypt and the Sudan so it is an ethnic rather than

43

a national designation. The second cataract of the river at Wadi Halfa acts as a more natural dividing line between the Egyptian and Sudanese Nubians than the border itself.

Nubian culture is very diverse. The only consistent link is the Nile, and yet the landscape around it constantly changes. In Upper Egypt, huge sand dunes come down almost to the edge of the riverbank, but near the Wadi Halfa the banks flatten out into wider areas strewn with large boulders, and acacia groves begin to soften the plains beyond. The Kanuzi Nubians, faced with the challenge of a harsh, treeless environment, and the problem of roofing over spaces without wood for beams or supporting members for centering of scaffolding, have perpetuated a building technique that has been used in Egypt since at least the thirteenth century B.C. It has been identified as having been used to build the Ramesseum, the mortuary complex of Ramses II, which is across the Nile from Luxor. This was the utilitarian storehouse part of the temple, holding the provisions for the Pharaohs' afterlife. The mud bricks used in the construction of the granaries still bear the finger marks of the masons who built them.

An Ingenious Technique

The technique used by the Kanuzi was published at the beginning of the twentieth century by several noted scholars, but was brought to public attention most dramatically by Egyptian architect Hassan Fathy, who proposed it in combination of a set of spatial typologies borrowed from the medieval houses in Cairo, described earlier here, as an inexpensive solution to the critical housing shortage facing the Egyptian peasant. In brief, this method of construction shows a great intuitive understanding of the laws of statics and resistance of materials by utilizing the compressive strength of mud brick, while avoiding tensile or bending stresses, which it cannot resist. The vaults that form the basis of the system are made in a parabolic shape that will keep the material in compression only.

Typically, the vaults begin with the erection of an end wall to the desired height of the space to be constructed. The masons, usually working in pairs, make a free-form outline of the parabolic vault in mud on the end wall as a guide. The proper shape of the curve is crucial for structural success, and learning how to lay it out without surveying tools of any kind requires long hours of practice, with skills often passed from father to son.

After this mud guideline has partially dried, the masons trim the rough edges of the parabolic arch with a sharp adze before applying the first course of mud bricks to it. The bricks used for the vault have a higher proportion of straw to mud, which makes them much lighter than those used for the walls, and each brick is scored with two finger grooves while still wet in order to give better adherence to the mud mortar.

A starter brick is laid straight up at the base of the vault line on both sides, and mud mortar is packed on it to form a wedge that is thinner at the top of the bricks and wider at the bottom. This sets the angle for each of the vault courses to follow, so that they incline toward the end wall in compression rather than remaining perpendicular to the ground, which would make them collapse. As each course of bricks is added, the masons stagger the joint lines between each row of bricks to assist in resisting structural stresses related to bending moments and gradually continue to make the mortar thicker at the base of the arch than at the peak so that the entire assembly leans on the end wall.

This purposeful inclining of the vault as it is put into place accounts for the characteristically massive vertical end wall and sloped front edge of the vaults that are usually found in these mud brick houses. The recommended span for vaults built this way is 3 meters, and 5 meters is the maximum diameter for domes using vaults as buttressing, which limits the width of the rooms that can be built using this method. Aside from favorable aesthetic considerations, the vault also has the advantage of allowing more natural air ventilation in the higher space that it creates. If the ends of the vault are provided with open grilles, a convection cycle can be created that is difficult to achieve in the flat-roofed, wood-beamed houses farther up the Nile, keeping all the rooms of the house cool during the hottest times of the day.

Domes Are Symbolic

The use of dome forms that architect Hassan Fathy adopted for his houses has been restricted by the Nubians to buildings with religious functions, such as mosques and the tombs of saints. There are exceptions, however, where more conical shapes are used over purely utilitarian structures, but care is taken in these instances to avoid a hemispherical outline.

The religious connotations of the dome form may come from its symbolic connection with the sky vault, as indicated by the Arabic word *qubba* for dome from the Aramaic *qubtha*, the vault of heaven. The use of the dome for tombs in particular has been ascribed to the Shiite influence of the Fatimids who entered Egypt from North Africa in A.D. 969 to found Cairo.

Clearly Designated Functions

Nubian house forms were also affected by the conversion to Islam, mainly in ways related to privacy and the separation of the sexes. Archaeological excavations near the Wadi Halfa have shown that the houses of the Christian era consisted of a string of rooms grouped around a single entry space with no central open area being used. The courtyard, as a device for protecting private family areas from the view of guests, eventually appeared as a standard feature in the houses of all the Nubian groups, although both the size and the function of the rooms surrounding it vary greatly from Egypt to the Sudan. In the village of Abu al-Riche, near Aswan, for example, two rooms that are always a common denominator are the *mandara* and the *khayma*. The *mandara*, which is set aside for guests, is usually located close to the main entrance and placed in such a way that the view into the interior of the house is blocked. All windows from the room face the street only, and it is normally vaulted and spacious compared to the other spaces of the house, indicating the importance of hospitality in this society. The *khayma* is a flat-roofed loggia, covered over with palm leaves for coolness, that is located on the private side of the courtyard and used as a sitting and sleeping area for the family, especially during the summer when the temperature in Upper Egypt can reach 55 degrees Celsius.[22]

In the Wadi Halfa region there may be rooms given over to guests, where a *diwan*, or sitting room, is reserved for wedding receptions only, a *diwan hasil* is used as a social space for women, and the *mandara*, which serves the same function as in Aswan, is provided with an additional antechamber, or *dahliz*, to insulate it even further from the private family areas.

In addition to the innovative construction methods and spatial forms and organizations used by the Nubians, their method of exterior decoration in painted scribed earth is unique and shows a high level of empathy for the plastic and artistic potential of the material, using mud plaster as a protective as well as a decorative medium.

A Cultural Disaster

The construction of the Aswan High Dam, which began in 1960, led to the flooding of the majority of the Nubian homeland, obliterating most of the traditional villages where this style of architecture existed. Prior to the flooding, the Egyptian Minister of Culture Tharwat Okasha, in an enlightened gesture acknowledging the rare beauty of the work, invited a group of architects, artists, photographers, writers, poets, and musicians to visit this area to record what they saw before its destruction. Hassan Fathy was part of the group and was greatly moved by this farewell visit to the heartland of a people whose architecture had so greatly influenced his own, both technically and intellectually. As a result of the trip, he produced an extensive survey of the buildings he saw.[23]

3

Asia and Australasia

ZHOUZHUANG, A CANAL VILLAGE IN CHINA

Zhouzhuang is located in the Taihu district of the lower Yangtze River basin in the Jiangsu Province of China. This small village is more than 1000 years old and is one of 200 similar townships located in what is known locally as "water country," because of all the streams, ponds, lakes, and canals that crisscross the area. This region lies between the major cities of Shanghai, to the east, and Nanjing, to the northwest, and is bounded by the Yangtze River to the north. It has four distinct seasons and the climate can generally be described as temperate, although snow is typical in the winter, and summers can be very warm and humid. This has a direct bearing on the design of the houses that have evolved there over time. Because of the high water table and the proximity of the Yangtze, the soil is very fertile, so it is among the most productive agricultural regions in China, to the extent of also being referred to "*yu mi zhi xiang*," or "the land of fish and rice."

Ancient Heritage

Zhouzhuang was founded in A.D. 1086 by a wealthy landowner named Zhou Di, who established it as a settlement for farmers. He eventually donated his own house to the town, along with an additional 13 hectares of land that was dedicated for the construction of a temple complex for the community, which was then named in his honor. During the Song Dynasty, from A.D. 960 to 1279, this entire region thrived and Zhouzhuang was a direct beneficiary of its prosperity, becoming a major cultural and economic center. This growth was fueled by the construction of the Grand Canal from Beijing to the southeastern part of China, which made trade between the richest of the eastern regions more efficient and was far less risky than exposing trading vessels to the vicissitudes of traveling along the coast.[1] Major stretches of this Canal have now been replaced by highways and urban development or filled in for agricultural use, but Zhouzhuang is a vivid reminder of what life must have been like along its shores. Drawings and paintings of it that have survived depict it as a liquid lifeline that fed a bustling, thriving society along its edges. These idyllic images portray a way of life that is far different from the increasingly polluted industrial wasteland that is now replacing it. Zhouzhuang is one of the last remaining remnants of a far more peaceful way of life, but is itself increasingly threatened by the drastic changes taking place around it.

The wealth and importance of this densely textured water village continued to grow when the Emperor Gaozong moved his capital from Kaifeng to Hangzhou, which is relatively close to Zhouzhuang and is famous for its beautiful central lake. Prosperity continued when a rich entrepreneur named Shen Wansan established a business there during the Yuan Dynasty (from A.D. 1271 to 1368). This mixture of wealthy inhabitants, farmers, traders, and fishermen is legible in the house types seen throughout the village, which run the gamut from palatial residential compounds to simple row houses connected by party walls along each of the twisted, narrow walkways, which are typically only wide enough for two people to pass.

An Organic Organization

While it seems chaotic to a pedestrian who has never experienced it before, Zhouzhuang does have a roughly grid-like pattern of canals, organized around two main waterways called the *Nanshihe* and the *Beishihe*. These form the major thoroughfares for the long, slender rowboats that are the local equivalent of gondolas that move up and down them, with women, rather than men, traditionally acting as the gondoliers. There are many small bridges crossing over these two major canals and their smaller tributaries, but the most recognizable of these, due to its elegant design, is the Fu'an Bridge. It was built in 1335 and is now one of the most prominent focal points in the village. This canal system is fed by four major lakes that surround the town, and nearly one-quarter of its area is covered by water. The plan of the village is the serendipitous result of a skillful and sensitive reading of the position and flow of the original water bodies on the site and the need for an efficient movement system through them, based on the recognition that waterways would be essential to the health and growth of the village over time. Main streets, which are really little more than alleys, generally run parallel to the rivers and canals. Zhouzhuang also follows the pattern found in other traditional water villages in that its houses are designed to face the street in the front end and to open up to the water in the back. There are two main advantages to this alignment. From an economic standpoint, this made it easier to run a business at the ground floor level, since customers and clients could have access to trading houses from the street, and goods and merchandise could be delivered from the back. From an environmental point of view, the street, which was paved with flat stones, serves as a perfect convective generator, drawing the cool air from the river or canal in the back of the house through the entire length of it on all levels, as it heats up during the day and the warm air from it rises. In the winter, this cycle would reverse, bringing warmer air through the house in the other direction, because the water would act as a heat sink. In the houses of the more well to do, courtyards were added to this linear sequence to help accelerate the process, as well as to help control the public/private division that running a business on the ground level necessitated.[2]

A Distinct Character

Because of the humid conditions Zhouzhuang evolved in, and the modest lifestyle of most of its hard-working inhabitants, many of the houses that line the canals of the village are simple, two story timber frame structures, with whitewashed brick walls and gray tiled roofs. Although this creates a largely black and white palette, there are accents of rich colored woodwork and deep red window frames that add subtle visual cues to enliven it. Other components of the village, such as bridges, streets, river banks, wharves, and water plazas, are faced with local stone, which is plentiful. Bridges are an important feature in Zhouzhuang, connecting seven islands in 19 different locations. These not only serve as connections over waterways, but their placement also marks a historical event or a focal point in the social, economic, and artistic life of the community.

Coping with Capitalism

The quiet water town of Zhouzhuang was initially brought to public attention when Chinese painter Chen Yifei put 38 of his paintings, some of which depicted the village, on display in a gallery in New York City. This has initiated a large tourism industry

There are six so-called "Water Villages" located within the farming region west of Shanghai. Ihouzhang, which is one of the most accessible of these, is now flooded by tourists. *Source:* James Steele

in the town, which generated nearly $40 million in 2006. While there are apparent difficulties involved in maintaining its traditional architecture and culture, Zhouzhuang has managed to make the most of this drastic change. Its mayor has worked to implement a preservation plan put forward by Tongji University in 1985, which acknowledges that changes are inevitable. Part of this plan involves the relocation of nearly half the population, along with schools and other noncommercial activities, to open space outside the village to make room for shops and restaurants. Restoration efforts have been made, but in many cases do not follow traditional construction methods, such as the substitution of concrete where stone would have originally been used. Government officials justify this by pointing out that concrete is more durable and resistant to moisture and that the craft of making bricks from the local clay has now died out.

Over time the commercial center of the town expanded westward, and it reached its peak of growth and prosperity in the eighteenth century when a population of approximately 3,000 residents was recorded. In contemporary times, the village population has varied around 4,000 in 1953 to only 1,800 in 1986. In addition to permanent residents, in 1986 nearly 3,000 transient workers commuted daily to Zhouzhuang to fish or work in one of the village's 15 factories. Also at the time of the 1986 census, the average age of a resident was 61, signifying the migration of youth to the cities. The Tongji University scheme takes these changes into consideration by proposing new teahouses, restaurants, shops, and galleries mixed in with the houses that line the pedestrian walkways that run along the canals. Since this proposal was put forward, however, the village government has started a public relations campaign to attract tourists, proclaiming Zhouzhuang to be the "number one water country village in China." It now requires visitors to buy an entrance ticket to get into the Old Town section, and in 2006, nearly two and a half million visitors patronized the nearly 500 shops and restaurants that have been added to this small area. The growth that has taken place in Zhouzhuang focuses attention on the challenge that those promoting the preservation of a rich national heritage now face in China, where urbanization has grown so quickly and people are so eager to accumulate all of the modern conveniences that were unavailable to them for so long, causing a decline in an appreciation for heritage and craftsmanship.

THE DAI AND THAI HOUSE

Background

Thailand is located in the southeastern part of Asia, bordered by China to the north, Laos to the east, Myanmar to the west, and Malaysia to the south. It is roughly 200,000 square miles in area, with a diverse topography that varies from forested mountain ranges in the north to dry plateaus and fertile river plains in the middle to tropical beach areas in the south. Since it is primarily a tropical country, it is subject to monsoon rains from May through September. Otherwise, the weather is hot and humid from March to May and cool from November through February.

The predominant religion in Thailand is Theravada Buddhism, just as it is throughout the rest of this part of Southeast Asia, with the exception of Malaysia, which is officially a Muslim nation. Theravada is also known as the "greater vehicle" because it maintains that enlightenment is not only possible for a select few, who emulate the physical deprivation practiced by the Buddha, but for anyone, with the help of a guru or *bodhisattva*. The Mahayana school or the "lesser vehicle" is far more acetic.

Thailand was previously known as Siam until 1946, when the name of the country was officially changed during the reign of King Rama IX. The Thais themselves refer to it as Prathet Thai, which means "free country."

Different Theories of Origin

There are several conflicting opinions about the origins of the Thais. One theory is that they emerged about 4,500 years ago as a nomadic tribe in the northwestern part of the Szechwan Province of China and slowly migrated southward from there, splitting into two distinct groups. One of these settled in the north and eventually established the Lanna Kingdom, while the second moved south. The second group was conquered and subjugated by the Khmers, but eventually became independent and formed the Kingdom of Sukhothai.

Lanna

The Lanna Kingdom, which covered eight regions in northern Thailand that include Chiang Mai, Chiang Rai, Lampang, Lamphun, Nan, Phayao, Mae Hong Son, and Phrae is known for its cooler climate because of its higher elevation in the mountains that now separate it from Myanmar and Laos. Lanna, which means "a million rice fields," was founded in A.D. 1296 by King Mengrai who captured the Mon stronghold of Haripunjaya and established his capital at Chiang Mai on the Ping Riva. Lanna culture, which had its own dialect and distinctive architectural and artistic style as well as its own legal and literary tradition, flourished for over 200 years, reaching its peak during the reign of King Tilokorai in the fifteenth century. After his death, Lanna was weakened by wars with Sukhothai to the south, as well as by internal conflict and the Burmese invasion. It was annexed to Siam in 1892.

The Lanna House

Each of these phases had an impact on the style of the Lanna house, as well as on the religious monuments with which it shares a common architectural heritage within Theravada tradition. The house, in addition, exhibits decorative elements based on animism, which predates Buddhism, especially forest and animal motifs, such as *khrue thao*, which represents vines and *kalae*. *Kalae*, which are indigenous to Lanna houses, come from the *khrue*, meaning "glancing crow," presumably because of the "V" that is formed by extending the large boards of the roof about three feet above the apex of the gable, looking like a crow's eye. A *ruen*, or *hevan kalae*, refers to several gable-roofed houses with these horn-like extensions placed together to form one residence, connected by a terrace.[3] Like the Dai and the Malay houses, the Lanna house is based on a precut wooden frame on or into which the side walls are inserted, sloping outwards rather than being straight or sloping inwards, as they do in the traditional houses farther south. To keep the rooms as free of clutter as possible, a wooden bin called a *khwan* is suspended from the rafters and is used for the storage of kitchen and other household items. The raised terrace, which connects the units together, typically has a balustrade around it with a shaft around the perimeter, called a *ron nam*, where water jars are placed.[4] Since teak wood was abundant during the Lanna period, and is strong and resistant to infestation and moisture, it was the material of choice for house construction, as well as by the artisans who carved these images into it. But much of this has been lost.

Sukhothai

The second strand of Thais, who migrated south, confronted the Mon civilization (also called the Dvaravati), who shared common lineage with the Khmers. Dvaravati was influenced by Indian culture, at its strongest in Nakhon Fathom,

Khu Bua, Phong Tuk, and Lopburi. In 1238, two Thai governors, Khun Bang Klang, who is also known as Si Inthrathit, and Khun Pha Muang, organized a rebellion against their Khmer overlords and established the first purely Thai kingdom of Sukhothai in this area. It is remembered as a time of peace and prosperity, commemorated in a popular saying that there were then "abundant fish in the water and rice in the fields." The borders of the Kingdom of Sukhothai eventually expanded to just below Lamphan in the north to Vientiane, in present day Laos, in the east, and into Malaysia in the south. During this period, strong diplomatic ties were established with neighboring rulers, and there was a free exchange of ideas and cultural influence, especially with the Chinese, the Khmers, and the Indians. After the death of Khun Pha Muang in 1279, King Ramkhamhaeng, the third son of Si Inthrathit, ascended to the throne. Under his rule, Sukhothai was even more closely aligned with China. He also devised a new writing system, which eventually evolved into the modern Thai alphabet.

The Dai and the Thai

There is a striking similarity between the religious structures and the traditional residences of both the Thais and the Dai, which is one of the 56 different ethnic groups in China, and still exists directly across the border in southern Yunnan Province, which seem to strongly indicate a common ancestry.

But there is also a theory, which challenges this diffusionist view, that argues for indigenous origin, based on excavations in the village of Ban Chiang in the Nong Han district of Udon Thani Province in the northeastern part of the country. Evidence of early bronze metallurgy that has been discovered there has led archaeologists to conclude that migration alone may not account for the ethnic origin of the nation.

Physical, social, and cultural similarities aside, the argument will now be put forward that the Thai traditional house is an extension of a Dai predecessor. Domestic architecture is the major focus of this book, but to the extent that religious structures have influenced house design in Thailand, it must be briefly mentioned here. The similarities between Thai and Dai religious complexes further strengthen the case for a single origin, which is relevant to a discussion of their common housing type.

The Temple as a Large House, the House as a Small Temple

Theravada Buddhism entered Thailand from China, in the sixth century A.D. As one historian describes the sequence:

> The Theravada school of Buddhism ... entered China from the south during the sixth century A.D., having traveled from India from Sri Lanka, and its trading partners in the states and kingdoms of the era in the Southeast Asian peninsula, especially in what are now Burma and Thailand, as well as into the Dai regions of Southeast China who were converted.[5]

A temple is referred to as a *wat* in Thai and is typically both a place of religious worship and a monastery for monks, which are referred to as *sangha* and are typically male. Traditional Thai temples, like those of the Dai across the Chinese border, do not simply consist of one structure, but are a compound made up of many buildings. These include a *chedi, bot, viharn, sala, haw-trai,* and *mondrop.* The *chedi* is considered the most sacred of all of these because it contains a relic of the Buddha. It is thought to have been derived from the Indian *stupa,* which is a domical structure serving the same commemorative purpose, but in China and Japan evolved differently into the pagoda form. The *bot* (or *ubosot*) is an ordination hall, where the monks worship and meditate, separate from their living quarters. It is not open to the public and faces east. It is preferable for the *bot* to be near water if possible, because the Buddha is thought to have achieved enlightenment while facing a river. The *bot* is typically rectangular with a tall, narrow door at one end and a distinctive multilayered and gently curved roof, which is thought by some to have been derived from a similar roof form in both the Dai and Thai houses.[6]

The *viharn* is similar to the *bot* in that it is a prayer and assembly hall but differs in being open to the public. People gather here to listen to the monks chant and read from Buddhist scriptures. The exterior of the *viharn* is also similar in appearance to the *bot.* In both Thai and Dai villages, the *viharn* is given a prominent place of honor, so that it is easily recognized and dominant in the horizon. It may not always be in the center, but it is always given the most advantageous siting.

The similarities between these two cultures continue in the remaining parts of the temple compound: the *sala,* for public assemblies that do not relate to sacred ceremonies, the *haw-trai,* or library, and *mondrop,* or bell tower. They also extend to decoration, although after the Thais migrated, their temples evolved different kinds of imagery. Decoration includes wooden carvings, mother-of-pearl art glass, tile, and even paint, as well as images that include mythological serpents and monsters like the *kala,* which is a fanged creature that guards the temple compound.

The Dai and Thai Traditional House

Finally, then, to the main issue: the basic aspects of the traditional house of these two groups. The traditional Thai house was initially designed in direct response to Thailand's geographical climate conditions, and today it is respected for its architectural beauty. Records of the houses can be traced back to as early as the eighth century with its depiction on Dvaravati stone reliefs. Also known as *ruen Thai derm,* the traditional Thai house in general, like the Lanna house, is characterized as a wood dwelling raised off the ground on posts with a gabled, elegantly tapering roof. The design functions in harmony with the tropical environment, which has abundant rainfall, often leading to flooding. In addition to the Lanna in the north, there are three geographical areas in Thailand: the central, the northeast, and the south regions, each with its own subtle variations on the Thai house.

Village Types, the House in Context

Before modern times, the traditional Thai house operated as an integral part of the village community and served a way of life that has now all but vanished. One of these village types is the ribbon, which developed along rivers and roads. Growth occurred in a linear way, with houses located along the river that was essential for domestic and agricultural use, as well as for communication. Directly behind the houses and other village facilities, fruit orchards and rice fields would typically be planted.

Wat Chai Wattanaram Temple, Ayuthaya, Thailand.   Courtesy of Shutterstock

Cluster-type villages developed in areas away from waterways, usually on high ground above rice fields. The villagers built their dwellings in close proximity and then spread outwards to work the fields. Water was provided by a community pond that was replenished by the rains and annual floods. The third village style was the loose village, which consisted of scattered houses on personal plots of farmland. These houses may have originally developed from rice huts, and their physical isolation prevented close-knit community growth.

While different village types arose out of varying geographical locations, types of the traditional Thai house differed according to family structure. The most basic organization occurs in the nuclear family single house, with a mother, father, and unmarried children. The *sork* is the unit of measurement used in the construction of the house, with one *sork* being the span of an adult's elbow. The sleeping room, for example, is 6–9 *sork* wide and 15–18 *sork* long, which is divided into three spans, one for an open hall and two for the bedroom. A living area is created by connecting a covered verandah, which is connected to the front of the bedroom, to the terrace. The terrace serves as an outdoor living area, as well as a space for bathing and washing.

When children get married, the nuclear family expands since Thai custom calls for a married man to live with the family of his wife. At this point the family typically built a second house next to their own, if possible, to avoid taboos relating to adapting buildings and to ensure a degree of privacy for all family members,

The Dai and Tai House.   Courtesy of Frans Devriese. *Source:* Flickr

creating a clustered house. The new house was oriented with the gabled ends facing in the same direction as the old, if the site allowed, and is usually filled in on only three sides, leaving the side adjacent to the parents' terrace open.

The raised floor. One of the most prominent characteristics of the traditional Thai houses is the elevated position. They are typically raised above the ground to just above head height, and many houses will integrate varying levels determined by differing spatial functions. The highest part is the bedroom floor, which is approximately 260 cm above the ground, followed by 40 cm drops for the verandah and then the terrace. These 40 cm height changes allow for floor surfaces that act as benches. There are several reasons for the raised house design with the primary concern being floor evasion. During the rainy season, all regions of Thailand experience flooding, which can sometimes last several months. When the ground becomes inundated with water, people, animals, and equipment are able to stay dry.

In China, the raised dwelling is called the *gan lan* or "house on stilts." It is a very old typology, having been discovered in ancient settlements along the Yangtze River basin and farther south and developed as a defense against flooding, malaria, reptiles, rats, and insects. It is obviously different from the urban *hutong* house, which is on grade and consists of a series of rectilinear blocks strung around the perimeter of a site to create two, three, or more internal courtyards, which was favored by the Han Chinese. The Dai and Thai houses also differ from the Han courtyard house in being less axial, more open and overt, less private, less permanent, and nonadditive. That is, rather than adding another room onto the *hutong* house to include new family members, newly married Dai and Thai sons and daughters leave and build houses of their own.[7]

Shaded ground level. Raising the house on columns provides a shaded area under it. This area is well ventilated and cooler because it is shaded, and it is a popular place for the family to sit during the day. In wealthier households, this open area between the ground and the first floor may actually provide living quarters for servants, as well as a place for the family to live during the day. There will typically be a hammock here for resting or for rocking a baby to sleep, and grandparents may sometimes take care of children here if their daughter or daughter-in-law has to go to work in the fields or elsewhere. Sometimes cottage industries, such as metalworking or basket weaving, are performed here too. In rice growing areas, the ox cart, which is an important implement that is still widely used for carrying the rice sheafs from the field to the house or the milled rice from the house to market, will be stored here, as well as other farm implements, like the sickles used to cut the rice, and sometimes the generator used to run the milling machine itself. Although automation and larger conglomerates are taking over some of the farms in Southern China and Northern Thailand, as well as in Laos, Cambodia, Vietnam, Malaysia, and Indonesia, as has already happened in Japan, most of the backbreaking work of planting, harvesting, shipping, and threshing rice is done by people working from sunrise to sunset. The water buffalo, which may seem like an anachronism to outsiders, is still a vital part of this process, and is used to walk on the sheafs of rice to separate the grains from the stem. It is also used to plow the land after each harvest, which can be three times a year if the soil is good enough and there is enough water available. Much of this replanting is still done in the ancient slash and burn way, since cultivating machinery and fertilizer are too expensive. After the rice is hand cut and the sheafs are taken to the house to be winnowed on a rattan mat spread out underneath it to catch the grains as they fall, the stubble, which can still be up to two or three feet high, is burned. When the fire stops, the field is flooded by whatever means possible, and once it is wet enough to work, it is plowed by a man walking behind one or two buffalo. Then it is flooded again and hand planted with fresh shoots of rice. The water buffalo, as well as assorted cows, pigs, and chickens are kept in stables under the house, protected from mosquitoes by net screens. Their waste is collected by hand daily in a wedge-shaped basket to be spread on the garden as fertilizer. The burned rice stubble, when plowed under, acts as fertilizer as well, as it is high in nitrogen.

So, the space under the house, which may be as little as 6 or as much as 10 feet high, depending on the module the builder has used, is an important, multipurpose area that facilitates many parts of daily life in this part of the world.

The stair. One steep stair provides access up to the main living floor of the house, and the number of steps used in Dai communities of Yunnan Province, as in northern Thailand and in the traditional Malay house, has deep symbolic significance as a protection against evil. Ghosts are considered to be unable to negotiate an odd number of stairs, as well as angled passageways.

The veranda. The stair leads to a covered porch-like balcony attached to the house and open on three sides, which in Malaysia is called the *dapur* and doubles as a reception space for visitors. Because it is still outside the main living area of the house, family privacy is preserved. This can be used for larger gatherings, such as wedding receptions, for visitation to offer condolences or pay respects after a funeral, or for other major family events.

Living, eating, sleeping. Since the perimeter of the house is usually nearly square, or at least the raised floor is, the interior is simply partitioned into a living, dining, and kitchen space on one side and a sleeping space on the other, usually on the left side of the entry. Dai and Thai houses differ in this regard from the Malay house, in which the kitchen is usually located outside to avoid burning the house down. Yunnan Province and northern Thailand, especially in the mountains near Chiang Mai, Chiang Rai, and Mai Hong Son, also get much colder than anywhere in Malaysia, which is closer to the equator, and so the cooking hearth also serves as a source of heat, as it also does in the rural *minka* of Japan.

The spirit house. An animistic holdover in these provinces is that the spirits in the earth that are disturbed and displaced when a house is built must be appeased by the provision of another "spirit house" for them. This is usually a smaller replica of the house placed on top of a pillar somewhere in the corner of each property. These used to be much more ornate than they tend to be today, made with as much care as the house itself, rather than being mass produced in garish colors as many of them are now.

A complex set of customs and rituals apply to those living in or visiting a Thai house, developing upon an individual's stature within the family or relationship to it. The plan configuration of the house is also a spatial manipulation of those unwritten codes. Visitors, for example, are confined to a room located closest to the house ladder or stair (*han dai*) and the *saan*, which is that part of the connecting raised terrace that serves as an open entrance platform. This guest room, also known as "the little house," faces south toward the entrance terrace, as the first of a series of rooms organized on a north-south axis. If conditions allow it, the kitchen or *khrua* is an extension of the guest room, in its western end, and a small open court separates guests from the main family area, or *huean yaai*, also known as "the large house," even though it may be the same size or even smaller than the guest house. A bathroom, or "wash place," *haung noam*, is usually located on the western side of this small dividing courtyard, contiguous to the kitchen, on its northern end. The rectangular family area is further divided down the middle into two roughly square parts, with the eastern part occupied by the parents and the western half by the children; and each half has a door to allow separate entry if a partition is built down the middle, as it usually is. When a daughter marries, her husband moves into this western half of the family area, occupying the section along the wall, while the unmarried children sleep against the dividing partition.

Position Is Everything

In such open surroundings, privacy and decorum are assisted a great deal by the place each family ensemble occupies on the floor. In a Thai house, the father sleeps on the right side of half of "the large house," along the east wall, related to a small head of the household. His wife sleeps closest to the middle partition, and daughters sleep to the left of her. Sons occupy the space between the female children and the married daughter until they reach puberty, after which they move into a part of the "little house" set aside for them. When the married daughter's husband moves in, his position to her left against the wall has been identified by ethnologists as expressing "the fact that he is an intruder into the family and isolates him from the other women, particularly unmarried daughters in the middle of the room."[8] This same source eloquently describes the important associations that directions have for the Thais, which also apply to the Dai, in which

> the north and east are auspicious orientations, south neutral, west inauspicious. North is related to the elephant, a royal animal important in Buddhist mythology and when facing north the east is on the right—the dominant hand, and that associated with the male sex. The east-west axis also relates to the rising and setting of the sun, thus east is life giving while the west is associated with death. For this reason, people normally sleep with their heads to the east, while a corpse is laid nit with its head to the west.[9]

This attention to orientation also means that the "large house" should never face west, while the washing room must always be on the western side of the house because it is impure.

HUTONG

The Chinese word *hutong* translates roughly into residential district or quarter but has come to imply a special configuration of dwelling characteristics of older, walled Chinese cities like Beijing, Nanjing, and Pingyao. To understand this house type, it is necessary to first discuss the urban context related to it, since it is so closely connected to the urban fabric.[10] The *hutong* of Beijing are a representative example of the type. Beijing has been continuously inhabited in different forms since the first millennium B.C., due to its strategic location at the crossroads of several important trade routes and mountain passes. The historical city we see today was established by Genghis Khan after his imposition of a Mongolian Empire in the twelfth century. He made it the northern terminus of a grand canal that he ordered to be built, running roughly parallel to the coastline and ending in Nanjing. It is as much of an engineering marvel as the Great Wall, but not nearly as well known because much of the waterway has now disappeared under urban development. Because of this additional economic impetus, added to that of the Silk Route, which also ended there, Beijing, or Khanbaliq as it was known, prospered beyond belief.

Strict Organization

After a relatively brief hiatus during which the capital was moved to Nanjing at the beginning of the Ming Dynasty, it was relocated back to Beijing at the end of that period. The Manchus, who followed, did not change the city plan, which conformed to a gridiron pattern first established at Chang'an and institutionalized there. It refined that compartmentalized layout by stratifying social classes even more clearly in four successively exclusive zones, which were each surrounded by a wall and a moat. Moving from south to north, as these zones would be experienced by any visitor who was privileged enough to be brought into the throne room of the emperor, these are the Outer City, the Inner City, the Imperial City inside the Inner City, and finally the Forbidden City, where the emperor's palace was located. Beijing also differs from the strictly rectilinear pattern of Chang'an in its adaptation to a natural watercourse, which flows down from the mountains to the northwest and penetrates the wall of the Inner City at that corner. It finally ends up as an organically shaped lake that forms the western edge of the Forbidden City. In addition to its strategic location as a trading city, Beijing was also chosen because it has good *feng shui*, a Chinese concept based on geomancy that literally means "wind and water." Although *feng shui* has now become much more obtuse, it originally referred to good orientation, and the best site for a city was considered to be below the south-facing slope of a mountain with water nearby. Rather than simply being based on aesthetically driven criteria, these factors ensured protection from cold winter winds coming down from Manchuria, to the north, and cool breezes when the direction of the flow changed during the summer, since the temperature of the air drops as it passes over water.

Feng Shui in Houses

This preference for southern orientation carried over to the houses, which are organized on a north-south access in Beijing, aligned with the walls of each of the four districts. They are strictly organized according to socioeconomic level, but all follow a typical planning format, based on the *sibeyuan*, which is a central courtyard surrounded on each side by a single-story rectangular building, with the entrance being on the southernmost side adjacent to the street. This front door, or *chuihuamen* ("festooned gate"), was covered by a gable roof that was higher than the rest of that portion of the house, usually occupied by servants, because it was the most vulnerable. Its street side was completely windowless as were those of the houses adjoining it, creating a blank 10 to 12 feet high wall to the public. Since the streets giving access to the *hutong* had no sidewalks, they have a forbidding, unwelcoming aspect, which was intentional, since the protection of family privacy was an utmost concern.

The whole concept of public space, in fact, in Beijing and throughout China during the Manchu, Ming, and Qing Dynasties when the historical core was at its height, was quite different from that in the West at the same time. Women rarely left the home, and the custom of foot binding, which was common at the time, was partially intended to ensure that they physically could not do so. So the house was their entire world, from birth to death. The house often also served as an office or shop, so the owner himself may have only rarely ventured outside. Commercial areas and shops were located in specified areas, and servants usually did the shopping or vendors made deliveries directly to the entrance. There were specific times during the year when the emperor performed certain rituals, in which upper social echelons could participate, according to rigid etiquette. Important research has been done recently showing how closely the size of the main open spaces in the Forbidden City matches the number of people allowed to participate in these annual rituals, indicating that they are far from being random as are, for example, the size of plazas in Europe, since they have grown organically by accretion, over time.

The front door to the *sibeyuan* compound was massive and studded with huge metal rivets to emphasize its role as the first line of defense against the public invasion of family privacy. After it was opened, a visitor would be faced with the "spirit wall" as a second line of protection, to prevent direct access or view into the interior. Its name refers to the belief that evil spirits could also enter if not impeded, but that they cannot turn corners. This wall is found in many other cultures, especially throughout the Middle East. In the medieval Cairiene house, for example, this bent entrance is called a *magaz* and serves the same purposes of preserving family security and privacy and blocking direct public view into the courtyard when the front door is opened. The front gate was also built on a raised platform to block the flow of water into the *sibeyuan*.

The buildings on the east and west of the courtyard were allocated to married sons and their families or unmarried children, while the main wing, which took pride of place along the northern edge of the courtyard and had a floor that was higher than the rest, was occupied by the parents. This hierarchical organization of both the home and the city mirrors Confucian teaching about the triangular relationship between the emperor who is at the apex and his subjects, which Confucius considered to be the same as that of the father, mother, and their family. These *hutong* houses also accommodated extended family, including grandparents and grandchildren, and would have a second, third, or even fourth courtyard, if necessary to do so. These additional segments were once again subject to strict rules, according to social and economic status.

Courtyard Life

There was no kitchen component in the *sibeyuan*, and all cooking was done in the courtyard, as was the washing. There was also typically one small bathroom attached to the wall next to the servants' quarters, accessible to the street so that it could be cleaned out daily by someone who collected "night soil," which was then spread out on the fields to fertilize them. Daily life really took place in the courtyard, or courtyards, as well as under the extended eaves of the raised arcades that surrounded them, if weather permitted. These open spaces served as a children's playground, conversation area, living room, kitchen, and dining room all in one, although there was typically always a study incorporated into the parents' wing. Temperature in the various wings could be controlled by inserting or removing rice paper screens, which were inserted into masonry lattice-work grilles built into the side walls, and portable charcoal burning furnaces were brought inside in the winter time for warmth.

JOMON AND YAYOI HERITAGE IN JAPAN

Two parallel traditions with ancient roots exist in Japanese residential architecture. One contentious, but highly plausible and extremely persuasive, explanation for the reason for the difference between these traditions is that one belongs to the indigenous population of the islands and the other was introduced and nurtured by others, who displaced them. The preexisting culture is called Jomon after the cord-like patterns found on the pottery it produced.

This culture predates the Neolithic Period and sustained itself until about 300 B.C. when it was challenged by outsiders, called the Yayoi who have been described as "invaders who crossed into western Kysuhu by the straits from

Korea."[11] The Yayoi were assisted in their competition with the Jomon people in being faster to adapt to working with iron, so that "with the Iron Age, the inheritors of Yayoi culture emerge into proto-history as the 'Yamato,' the half-legendary hero ancestors of the historic Japanese."[12] Jomon houses were pit dwellings similar to those described as being used by the Long-shan and Shang cultures. Like them, they were buried in the earth to about shoulder height to take advantage of the natural capacity of earth to balance out the temperature swings that prevail at grade. If superimposed on a map of the United States, Japan would extend along its entire eastern coast, with Hokkaido in the north corresponding to Maine and Fukuoka in the south aligned with Houston, Texas. While most of the archipelago is temperate, it does have the subarctic and tropical extremes associated with those comparisons, and even in the temperate zones summers are known to be extremely humid and winters frigid with lots of snow. Although they do mitigate temperature swings, pit dwellings, with their wood frame structures and sloping thatched roofs that extended all the way down to ground level, are especially adapted to cold climates. Because their walls and floor are literally the earth

The Yayoi and Jomon traditions represent two divergent directions in the history of vernacular architecture of Japan. *Source:* James Steele

itself, they are not as exposed to wind as their ground level counterparts. The rice straw used for the heavy thatched roof is also highly insulative since the air inside the center of each piece of straw prevents the transmission of cold into the interior.

Jomon Houses

Jomon pit dwellings are concentrated in the central and eastern parts of Japan, usually grouped in clusters near a dependable water source, but sited well above the flood plain. In spite of the images of them that have usually been published, they were not always circular, although this shape must have been the easiest to build. Rectilinear and elliptical plan forms are also evident, with compactness to avoid exposure being the primary criteria. Diameters of the circular forms or the longest dimensions of the rectilinear ones do not exceed 12 to 15 feet, and depths of the pits vary from very shallow to 3 to 4 feet deep. There was a hearth in the middle of the earthen floor, ringed by stones to provide a harder surface.[13]

One of the most visible and important structures that still exists in Japan, which allows us to understand the transition from Jomon to the Yayoi residential tradition, is the Ise Shrine, near Nagoya.

The Ise Shrine

The Ise Shrine is technically known as *Jingu*, which refers to a compound consisting of the inner shrine, or *Naiku*, and the outer shrine, or *Geku*. *Naiku* is dedicated to the sun goddess Amaterasu Omikami, who is revered as the divine source of the Japanese Imperial Family line and the deity that protects the entire nation. The outer shrine, or *Geku*, is dedicated to the deity of fertility and sustenance, *Toyuke*. Amaterasu had originally been worshipped at a residential temple near the Imperial Palace at Nara, but during the reign of Emperor Sujin this dwelling was moved to the village of Kasanui. In the following dynasty of Emperor Suinin, the responsibility for the care of this sacred residence was given to Princess Yamoto-hime-no-Mikoto, who selected the present location after a long search. The style of the *Naiku* shrine is very similar to representations of houses that have been found that date from the time that the 20-year cycle of its reconstruction first started in A.D. 478.

There is significance in the location of *Naiku* and *Geku*, since Amaterasu, who is the ancestral goddess of the Imperial Family, and its Yamato tradition takes pride of place in the center of the sacred site. *Toyuke*, the goddess of food and agriculture, who represents a more ancient and indigenous deity, was displaced and relegated to an outside location.[14]

Before the Yayoi infiltration, each region and the families living there adopted a guardian deity of fertility, with each district using different names for the focus of their worship as well as sacred zones and ceremonies dedicated to it.

By concentrating each of these individual deities into one that was also identified with the Imperial House, the fledgling Yamato government discovered an effective political means of uniting the people behind them, using potent architectural symbolism to do so.

The house form for the deities of the sun and of abundant food or sustenance seen at Ise today represents the third phase of development of the way that Shinto has designated a site as sacred. In the earliest phase of Shinto, no buildings were used, since, in a belief system based on animism in which everything seen and known in nature is considered to have a spirit, no architecture is necessary.

In the first phase, a sanctuary rope, or *shimenawa*, was placed around an object or site to designate it as being sacred. The second phase of recognition was the construction of storage buildings that were used to protect valuable offerings that were made to the deities or precious objects used for worship. The third phase was the form seen at Ise today.

The *Naiku* Shrine

Naiku consists of four rectangular buildings located on a level clearing in a dense forest. The clearing measures 55 yards wide by 127 yards long, is oriented on a north-south axis, and is surrounded by a high three part wooden palisade. Worshippers approach up a hill along a winding path from the south, echoing a similar orientation used in the Imperial Chinese Palace architecture. The main building, the dwelling of Amaterasu, or the *Shoden*, is located in the center of the clearing, and it, like the other buildings around it, is built of Japanese cypress, or *hinoki*, which is distinctive for its even texture, gray-green color, and fragrance. No glue or nails are used since they would defile the natural purity of the material, so that *Naiku* and *Geku* are held together simply by a series of mortise and tenon joints, which take a carpenter a long apprenticeship to master. The ancient column and beam system that is used, which has no diagonal structural members, meant that the traditional Japanese house, which evolved from this Yayoi / Yamato prototype, could have nonstructural wall partitions and wide openings. This would allow for the combination of two spaces into one or the opening of the demising wall to establish a connection between inside and outside. This system is also ideal for earthquake-prone areas like Japan because it is very flexible. The bases of the cypress columns at the *Jingu* shrines come in direct contact with the earth, with no intermediate stone footing to protect the wood from ground moisture and rotting. This is especially important with the large vertical columns placed at each end of the shrine residence, called *munamochi-bashira*, which carry the ridge girder that supports the entire gable roof. The *munamochi-bashira* are considered to be the direct natural conduit between heaven and earth through which the *kami*, or spirits, pass, which in the case of *Naiku* and *Geku* are Amaterasu and *Toyuke* both designated with the suffix "*Omikami*" or "meta-spirit."

The roofs of the shrine are steeply sloped, rather than curved upward in the Chinese fashion, and have deep eaves, which underscore their ancient lineage. The proportions are identical, but are larger than a typical residence at the time they were initiated, using what is called the "*shinmei zukuri*" or monumental ceremonial style instead, since a superhuman scale was considered to be more appropriate for the earthly residence of these deities.[15] The roofs are thatched with *kaya* grass (*Miscanthus sinensis*) and have distinctive extensions of the final gable rafters called *Chigi*. The roof is protected against the uplifting force of typhoons, which Japan is subject to, by weights called *katsuogi*, which are placed at regular intervals along the ridge girder. All of these details also appear on clay models of houses that date from the fifth century that have been uncovered near Tokyo.

Minka Heritage

Except for the obvious fact that the typical Japanese farmhouse, or *minka*, has its foundation at grade, there are many similarities between it and the Jomon pit house. The most generic of these is the thatched rice straw roof, which is steeply pitched and extends down very close to the ground. Because the plan of these farmhouses is rectangular, the gable ends of the *minka* are not protected by the thatch, but the exposed surface area of the ends is kept to a minimum. There is also a strong similarity between the hearth areas of some of the Jomon houses and the *moya* of the *minka*. In each case it is the center of the house, both literally and figuratively, because it is the only place that is warm in the winter. Although the roof structure of the pit house usually projects upward from the perimeter, four columns have been placed around the hearth as the type has evolved

to hold up the apex of the roof, with one at each corner of the fireplace. In its later stages, as one historian has observed,

> The most advanced type may have looked like a small, clumsy forerunner of the traditional farmhouse. One may imagine a central area like the later *moya* room, bounded by four main posts; a rectangle of substantial beams above; and a thatched gable roof with open ends to discharge smoke.[16]

Minka, which vary widely from region to region, all conform to the typology of this timber-framed configuration, with the steep heavily thatched roof and central hearth that has just been described. But they are much larger than Jomon pit houses were. *Minka* typically also served as a barn as well as a house, with space allowed for the livestock at the ground floor level, and the first floor was used as a storage area for their feed and bedding. By raising the wooden floor of the area used as living space by the farmers to a foot or so above the dirt floor of the stables, it was possible to retain a certain degree of cleanliness. In addition, the body heat of the animals helped to raise the ambient temperatures of the interior during the winter. A fire was usually always kept burning during the coldest months, and even though there were openings in the gable

Before the Yayoi culture entered Japan, the indigenous people built houses that were partially dug into the earth, which had heavily thatched roofs like the *minka* farmhouses today. *Source:* James Steele

ends to let the smoke escape, instead of having a chimney, which was thought to allow too much cold air to infiltrate, the interior of the *minka* was always smoky. Cooking was done in a pot suspended by a chain from a beam above the fire, and its distance from the fire was adjusted by a counterweight. Bedrooms were in the several stories that were tucked under the steep eaves, with their width diminishing toward the top of the steep gable, and were accessible by ladder.

Minka farmhouses, like their pit house predecessors, were well adapted to winter weather and heavy snow, but they were dark, smoky, damp, and claustrophobic in the thick humidity of a Japanese summer. Representations of an alternative type of lighter house, with a floor raised up above ground level by columns, began to

The Jomon tradition persists in the heavy wooded and thatched roof *minka* farmhouses in Japan, and the Yayoi strain is most evident in the raised floor and light frame house most commonly associated with that country. *Source:* James Steele

appear as early as the Bronze Age in Japan. A bronze mirror from the fifth century A.D. shows elevations of four houses that look remarkably like the Ise Shrine.

In spite of its general similarity to the Jomon pit house, the *minka*, which means "houses of the people," differs widely from region to region and family to family.[17] It is clear also that the *minka* farmhouse shares the same architectural heritage as the Jingu shrines at Ise as well as the storehouses that were used in the past to keep rice dry and free from rodent and insect infestation, and are still common in a far less sophisticated form throughout Southeast Asia today. The Ise Shrines are built in almost the same way that they were 15 centuries ago, and they open a remarkable window for us into the distant past. While they honor Shinto deities rather than being the houses of mortals, they do provide a substantial clue to the way in which the transformation from the Jomon pit dwelling and its *minka* descendant to the light frame house that we now associate with Japanese traditional architecture took place.

THE KHMERS IN CAMBODIA

There is exquisite irony in the fact that some of the most powerful civilizations in history, in China, Mesopotamia, Mesoamerica, Cambodia, and Egypt, which also have the most impressive monumental remains, only survive today in the everyday habits of the common people whose architecture was the most expendable. When media tycoon Rupert Murdoch was asked the secret of his success, he said, "I keep doing what works and I stop doing what doesn't." In considering each of these cultures, it can be seen that the monumental phase of their history, in which grandiose stone pyramids, temples, and tombs were produced, was unsustainable because of the vast extent of the resources required to perpetuate it, but social patterns honed by evolutionary effectiveness were able to survive. Cultural memory is a potent force that encompasses far more than nostalgia for the way things have been done in the past and goes to a continuing respect for what works best.

Daily Life Virtually Unchanged

In Cambodia, this is especially true. Speculation continues to swirl around the question of what happened to the people who built the beautiful temple cities around Siem Reap between A.D. 770 and 1295. But the answer is simple; their descendants are still there, living in the same way they lived when these grand cities were at their height of power, before they collapsed from the inability to meet the demands of food production and defense that a rapidly increasing population placed on them.[18] In a way that is startlingly similar to other cultures, such as the Maya in particular, the houses of Khmer farmers today are virtually the same as they were 800 years ago.

Origins

The origin of the Khmer people, as well as that of their kings, is still a mystery, but mention of them begins in the records of the Chinese, with whom they traded, in the seventh century. The earliest inscription in Khmer script, which was based on Sanskrit that appeared on Angkor Borei, is dated A.D. 612.[19] The Khmers are believed to have migrated south from Vat Ph'u, in Laos.[20] Their first kin of record was Bhavavarman, followed by Isanavarman and Jayavarman I during the seventh century, but the next King Jayavarman II, who ruled from A.D. 770 to 834, is widely regarded as the founder of the Khmer Kingdom. He declared Khmer unity and independence from the suzerainty of any other external power at Mahendra Parvata in A.D. 802.[21] He established his capital at Lolei, several miles southeast of Siem Reap, with the Rolos group of monuments that still survive there being a visual reminder of his rule. These were augmented by Indravarman I (A.D. 877–890), who built the Preah Kan and the Bakong there.

The monuments built by Jayavarman II and Indravarman I established a tradition that was followed by subsequent rulers, described best by two historians of this period as "a pattern that was to recur often in the quest for legitimacy: a group of shrines to previous rulers and their wives, and then a pyramid representing a mountain of the gods, destined to receive the kings own relics ... after his death."[22]

The model for this divine residence, like Olympus for the Greek pantheon, was Mount Meru in Java, with the most famous architectural representation of it being the Borobudur Temple in Yogyakarta, nearby. In the case of Borobudur the way to nirvana is physically represented by three distinct levels, which are an analogy for the individual struggle for enlightenment, with the last of these, at the summit being circular, rather than rectilinear, to indicate the transition from the secular to the sacred realm.

Rather than constructing his own version of Mount Meru, King Yasovarman chose a real mountain for his capital north of Siem Reap and built Phnom Bakhang on top of it as the center of his royal city of Yasod Harapura, ruling from there from A.D. 890 to 912. As at Borobudur, roads radiate out from the cardinal points of this artificial mountain to the four corners of the Khmer Kingdom.

This begins to occur more ostensibly at Angkor Wat, which is the most famous of these monuments, built by Suryavarman II, from A.D. 1113 to 1150 and in the Bayon at the center of Angkor Thom, built by Jayavarman VII between A.D. 1181 and 1218.

Angkor Wat

Angkor Wat was a largely ceremonial city as well as a religious shrine surrounded by a wide moat. The palace of the king and various governmental structures were inside its 815 meters by 1,000 meters enclosure. This barrier had a main entrance causeway on its western side, related to the original connection of the city to the Hindu god Vishnu, the god of creation and destruction symbolized by the cosmic serpent Amanta and the bird Garuda, which was his protector. These are commemorated in a temple at the top of its central tower, which is surrounded at each cardinal point by additional towers dedicated to other deities and, by extension, the royal predecessors of Suryavarman II that are associated with them.

Hindu Influence

The complex layering of Hinduism and Buddhism, which is a consistent feature of Khmer culture, is extensively evident at Angkor Wat. Indian culture began to penetrate into Southeast Asia in the fourth century A.D., during the Gupta Dynasty.[23]

Like Borobudur, Angkor Wat also rises up in three distinct increasingly smaller stages, which are each also surrounded by galleries, just as they are in Yogyakarta. The most descriptive of these are carved on the inside wall of the first gallery, mixing mythological scenes, such as the Ramayana, with those of daily life. While there are similar scenes carved on Mayan pyramids and stele, they are not nearly as informal and informative of the habits of the ordinary people of their society as these are. These carvings give us a clear idea of how the Khmers led their lives.

Khmer Houses

The Khmer Kingdom was based on agriculture, and there were strict laws that governed how people of various classes would live, what they could own and wear, and what their houses could be like.[24] Life in a farming village was carefully circumscribed by these laws, the unforgiving cycle of the seasons, the hot humid climate, and the relatively poor quality of the soil. The houses shown in the gallery carvings at Angkor Wat and elsewhere are very similar to those found in farming villages throughout Cambodia today. They are raised up on columns, to a level that seems to be generally higher than that of similar houses in neighboring Southeast Asian countries, such as Thailand, Laos, and Malaysia. Elevating the house on posts is primarily done to allow an air movement up, under, and through it, since the climate is hot and humid most of the year. Unlike southern Thailand and all of Malaysia, however, Cambodia does get cooler for a few months of the year, around December and January, but when it gets hot, it is really oppressive, and the flow of cool air up through the heavy wooden floor boards, from the shaded area beneath the house, is very welcome during that time. The height of these lower supporting columns varies according to the economic circumstances of each family and is a status symbol, to some extent. Based on archaeological evidence, people were smaller at the height of the Khmer Kingdom than they are today, so a 6 feet high open area between the ground and the living floor would have been adequate, but the controlling factor, then as now, was the oxcart, which is stored there. This cart, which is primarily used for transporting rice from the field to this covered space that is also used as a threshing floor, and the oxen that pull it are possibly the most valuable possessions that farmers have, since the oxen are also used for plowing the rice fields, and they are also stabled under the house. In the Khmer bas-reliefs at Angkor Wat and the Bayon, troops are shown being transported to the front of the battle with the Khmers' arch nemesis the Chams, who occupied the area around what is now My Son in Vietnam. The carts that are depicted there are reassuringly similar to those seen in use on Cambodian farms today.

The rice sheafs are spread out on a large woven rattan mat under the house so that none of the grains are lost, and these are separated from the shaft by walking on them, or treading them lightly under foot. The same kind of rattan mat is used as a floor covering on the main floor of the house above because it is cool underfoot and light, and it lets the breeze enter unhindered. There is usually a steep, narrow stairway, sometimes a glorified ladder that provides access up into the house, with an odd number of steps used, based on the superstition that this will confound evil spirits.

The Spirit World

This belief in spirits still persists in parallel with organized religion. In a sense there was a discontinuity between the formal, abstract objective religious concepts and rituals of royalty and the highly personalized, subjective, and superstitious beliefs of the villagers who were their subjects. The Khmers, as one source describes,

> came from the forest; the forest remained, never very far away, as paradigm and symbol of the dark, chaotic, and dangerous world of nature from which civilization was born. No Khmer could even be completely at ease alone in the dark forest. Practical fears of physical dangers certainly contributed to their unease, but there was more. The invisible being[s] that dwell in the wild inspire dread.[25]

The list of these spirits is lengthy, but persists in a contemporary fascination with ghosts in the same region, the restless spirits of the departed that still haunt the places where they lived under the collective category of *nakta* or ancestors. There are also the spirits of the earth, including the *naga* serpent, which fall into either benevolent or malicious categories and which must be appropriated, especially when a new house is built. To do this, a small spirit house is usually placed near the new one, to be occupied by the earth force, which the construction has disturbed and displaced. Newborn babies are considered especially vulnerable to possession by evil spirits. In Thailand, for example, it is common for babies in rural areas to be called something other than their given name, such as "bird" or "bee" to confuse the evil spirits and prevent them from taking the babies' souls.

In spite of its adherence to well-established religious forms, Khmer rulers were not completely impervious to such animistic, supernatural beliefs. *Linga* shrines were usually placed at the cardinal points and center of each of their capitals, in recognition of Siva, and its earlier basis in fertility cults. These consist of a stone shaft, representing a phallus, placed vertically in the middle of a square basin, representing a womb. This basin had a trough cut into it that drained the water that was ritually poured on the *linga* and had an obvious symbolic reference to impregnation, as well as life-giving rain falling on the earth.

The Bayon

The Khmer Kingdom reached its furthest extent spreading into the Mekong Delta, Laos, and Thailand under Jayavarman VII, who ruled from 1181 to 1218, during a time in which Buddhism was dominant, and its iconography prevailed over the rival forms of Hinduism, which surfaced again soon after his reign. The Bayon, the centerpiece of his capital at Angkor Thom is evident of this dominance with its towers carved with the face of the Bodhisattva Lokesvara, who looks north, south, east, and west on each of them, as if he is surveying the vast kingdom that Java VII ruled. But, within 200 years, Angkor was abandoned and this glorious period of Khmer civilization was over. The bas-reliefs on the Bayon walls, like those on the Galley of Angkor Wat, are all that remain to remind us of the complexity of social levels of this great civilization.

THE MALAY HOUSE

Commonly referred to as the *"rumah ibu"* or "mother house" by the Malays, the traditional residential form that is recognizable throughout the archipelago is similar in many ways to houses in Japan, Cambodia, Laos, Thailand, and Vietnam in its three part vertical division into raised, columnar base, mid-level living area and large overhanging roof. The similarities relate to the following elements.

Anthropomorphic Dimensional System

The Malay house, like those in the countries just mentioned, is based on human proportions, to an extent that is only recently becoming apparent, due to the research that has been done by Dr. Syed Iskandar and several other investigators. It has been well known for some time that these houses are laid out by master builders rather than the owners themselves, although the people in the *kampung* or village collectively participate in the actual construction. The master builder measures the primary wife of the family, since the Malay Archipelago is primarily Muslim and there may be more than one, and uses key dimensions from her, such as the length of her forearm, to develop a module. This feature, of individuality within a systematic framework, is also the essence of traditional Malay society, in which a network of cultural norms governs behavior, but in which each person is valued as an individual. Such measuring also brings to mind a tailor, who custom

Malay house.   Courtesy of Shutterstock

fits a uniform to each person, taking anomalies into account, but striving for conformity nonetheless.

The builder is itinerant in that he moves from village to village as needed. He is considered to have magical powers, and the entire process of planning, preparing, and building a house is viewed as a spiritual act. The house is believed to be a living thing, as an extension of nature, since it is made of natural materials and is a manifestation of the people who inhabit it, so there is a mystical aspect to it that extends to numerology and orientation as well. This relates to the *tiang seri*, meaning central (or navel) post, which is the first structural member erected, symbolically establishing a cosmological link between heaven and earth. The word *seri*, which translates roughly as "aura," has connotations of radiant beauty and spiritual energy, transcending the purely functional role of the column as the central structural member. This aspect of an "axis mundi" is also common to the cultures mentioned earlier. In Japan, for example, this central column is called the *daikokubashira*. In the Ise Shrine, which is an important Shinto site near Osaka and is considered to be the earthly residence of the sun goddess Amaterasu, it is also erected first, and is felt to be the conduit through which her spirit or *kami* moves from heaven to earth. In the Malay house, a coin is placed under the *tiang seri* to ensure good fortune for the inhabitants in the future.

Natural Materials

Although metal has replaced wood and thatch to some extent, especially for the roof, where corrugated tin has now been substituted for the woven mat of *atap* or mangrove leaves because it is more durable, the structural members are all wood, precut on site to have interlocking joints that make nails unnecessary. To put this into context, it is important to remember that metal nails, which were first hand cut before being mass produced as they are now, are a relatively recent development in the long history of this indigenous residential typology, which started long before they were available. Nails were very expensive when they were hand cut, even in the Western industrializing countries where they were first produced, and so were prohibitive in undeveloped areas. Even now when they are machine made, their price is comparatively exorbitant in countries in which one bag may represent a day's wages. The use of interlocking joints, then, is not a conceit, or an issue of nationalistic pride and a desire to remain free of external influence, although this is a partial subtext in stylistic revivalism, but simply an economic necessity.

Chengal, rather than teak, is the wood of choice, because it resists rot and termites, but it is now becoming very scarce and expensive in Malaysia. In one recent instance, in the Salinger House designed by Jimmy Lim, for a site that was once part of a rubber plantation near Kuala Lumpur, the master builder had to apply to the state government in Selangor to purchase the trees he needed to build a sensitively conceived reworking of the traditional Malay prototype, created by an architect known for his originality. Because of the rarity and expense of the trees, the builder reduced the number he used to three for the entire house, which also shows how massive they are. The nature preserve from which they were culled was delivered to the site, and the builder set up his workshop near the drop-off point to avoid having to move them. He then cut them into the various framing pieces needed, wasting as little of the precious wood as possible.

The Malay house is identified by a raised floor supported by columns and a thatched roof with wide overhanging eaves. Instead of having fixed individual rooms, the Malay house has open spaces reserved for specific functions. *Source:* James Steele

Orientation

The symbolic and spiritual aspects of the construction process also pertain to orientation, going beyond purely environmental considerations of heat gain and loss, or natural ventilation, although these are also of critical importance. The east, the direction of the sunrise, is considered to be the side of life and brightness, and so it is preferred. The west, the sunset, is the side of death, darkness, and the devil. This idea is not new and is not confined to Malaysia. During the Pharaonic Age in Egypt, pyramids were oriented using the same criteria, and many indigenous cultures, including several described here, follow the same belief. If these conditions, which are primary, happen to coincide with climatic factors, so much the better, but if not, spiritual concerns take precedence. The preference of east over west also extends to the idea of a front and a back to the house, with each façade treated differently. The front, where the main entrance is located, is usually more ornately carved than the back and is more formal. By contrast, the service spaces are located at the back.

Daily Life

The front entrance, which is accessible by a narrow staircase leading up to the raised main floor, is covered by a roof to protect inhabitants and visitors from sun and rain, which are both abundant in Malaysia. The stair may be further protected by carved side panels, which allow only a minor amount of dappled light to guide people up to the front porch, or *serambi*. This space, which is covered by the roof but is open on three sides, is much more important than the prosaic designation of the front porch would indicate, being a place for social gatherings, family meetings, and relaxation, in turn. In his doctoral thesis, completed under Paul Oliver at Oxford Brooks University, Dr. Syed Iskandar has shown just how intensively the *serambi* is used and how its patterns of use have contributed to its long and narrow dimensions.[26]

His work, as well as that of his tutor, has provided considerable insight into the ways in which behavioral patterns and social conventions contribute to house form, and Iskandar's suppositions about the *serambi* are especially compelling. He maintains that its size is determined by the dimensions of a woven palm leaf floor mat (*tikar*), based on a 405 centimeters by 405 centimeters module, and the round *dulang* or dining tray used to serve guests, who are usually confined to this space to maintain family privacy inside the house itself. The size of the floor mat allows four people to sit around the dining tray, with their backs into the corner of the *tikar*. One row of these mats is placed against the side of the house and another along the outer railing of the *serambi* with an equally wide 405 centimeters space left open through the middle as a service corridor; and this determines the width of the space. Iskandar does not speculate on the possible relationship between mat placement and the width of the house, but his illustrations indicate that the same cause and effect condition pertains to it, as well. The proportion of the rectangular *serambi* is usually 1:5.

A Floor Oriented Culture

One obvious determinant in this relationship is that traditional Malay culture is based on living on the floor, rather than having furniture, as the Chinese did. In this way, they are similar to the Japanese, whose residential proportions are also based on a floor mat, the *tatami*, which is woven from rice straws, to a module called the *ken*, just over a meter in length. There is enormous significance to this difference related to sensory perception of the interior, the way the outside is seen from the inside and the overall worldview. Sitting and sleeping on the floor means that it must be kept very clean, so shoes are removed before entering the house. Before socks and stockings, this meant, and still means to a large extent, that bare feet came in contact with the floor boards, which are smooth, wide plank timber, providing a tactile and olfactory as well as aural and visual way of experiencing the interior. Unlike the *tatami*, which is thick and heavy, the *tikar* is rather thin and rough, but serves the same purpose of helping to keep the floor smooth and clean. It is also a sign of status, since, during large celebrations such as wedding receptions, there may be more guests than mats, and preference is given to those who are most important in deciding who may sit on them. Sitting and sleeping affects many other things as well, such as the size and location of windows. The sill height, or bottom of the window, which is usually based on someone sitting on a chair in Western cultures, must be much lower in the Malay house, if those inside are to see out. It can then vary from neck height at the very least, to allow this view, to lower, depending upon the amount of privacy desired.

Like the Japanese house, the Malay equivalent has a very flexible interior, with rooms being able to serve many functions. Once inside, past the *serambi* and into the *rumah ibu*, or mother house, which is the core, there are rarely compartmentalized divisions, in the Western sense, into living room, dining room, and so on, but rather areas that can accommodate these functions through customary use. The kitchen or *dapur*, which is usually relegated to the back of the house or even into a separate structure because of the risk of fire, is an exception to this flexibility.

Regional Differences

Within this basic framework of *serambi*, *rumah ibu*, and *dapur*, there are many clearly recognizable regional differences, primarily related to the way the house can grow to accommodate an extended family. In Malacca, for example, growth is dealt with by using a long, narrow central courtyard placed between the *rumah ibu* and an addition that is equal to it in size, to house more people, creating a symmetrical arrangement. The big advantage of the modular, prefabricated system that the core house is based on is the freedom it allows for growth and change, easily permitting the permutations seen in each region.

The Malay *Kampung*

The Malay village, known as a *kampung*, has usually begun near the source of the villagers' livelihood. *Kampungs* near the coast are supported by fishing, and inland villages are usually located near paddy fields. Governmental emphasis on modernization, urbanization, and industrial growth have sharply reduced the number of *kampungs*, and this valuable resource of tradition is now an endangered species.

Kampungs do not typically have one founder, but usually one family is dominant and the leader, or *Penghulu*, is selected from it. The *kampung* usually has a mosque (*masgid*), a village cemetery (*kubur*), the village leader's house (*Rumah Penghulu*), as well as the houses (*rumah*) of the people living in it. The *Rumah Penghulu*, in addition to being the headman's house, also serves as a bank, since he makes small loans to the villagers, courtroom, and jail, which usually occupies the space that is open under a typical Malay house, except in this case it is surrounded by bars. The layout of the *kampung* is based on hierarchical land ownership patterns, and buying or selling a property is difficult since it requires the agreement of all other inhabitants. All decisions affecting the village are based on consensus. The population of each *kampung* grows because of marriage between members of the various families rather than settlement by newcomers.

Arrangement of Houses in the *Kampung*

The rectilinear shape of properties owned by families means that houses in a typical kampung are arranged in a roughly linear way, with a space between them that acts as a pedestrian "street." There are examples of random placement, but local property-ownership laws are the key determinant of spacing. The cost of living in a typical *kampung* is relatively low, since many residents own their own houses and pass them on to their children. Since the 1960s, water and electricity service has improved, which is a minor expense, and sanitation systems became the norm after legislation in Malaysia was passed to make it mandatory, which adds another.

The open layout of the houses in a Malay *kampung* makes social interaction easy. The practices of *takbir*, or visiting neighbors on festive occasions, and *gotong-royong*, or sharing work, such as the building of a new house, with others in the village are encouraged by both the placement of the houses and their form. This spirit of cooperation, which is absent in urban areas, is called "*muhibbah*," or goodwill.

In the typical *kampung*, it is not possible to be a loner, and no household exists as an isolated unit. Weddings are always communal affairs, and everyone in the village takes part in preparing to celebrate these events. A musical ensemble, usually including drums (*hadrah*), is often part of each *kampung*. One of the other major festivals celebrated in the *kampung* is *Hari Raya*, observed by Muslims on the tenth day of the last month of the Muslim calendar at the end of the *Haj*, or pilgrimage in Makkah. A sheep, cow, or goat is sacrificed to commemorate Abraham's test of faith when he was asked to sacrifice his son. Since Malays are Muslim, religious homogeneity is a major unifying factor, and so the *masgid*, or mosque, and a smaller prayer hall, *sarau*, are not only reserved for religious activities but also become social centers for the entire village. In addition to *Hari Raya*, known as *Aid il Adha* elsewhere in the Islamic world, communal dinners are held there every night during the month of Ramadan, during which Muslims must fast until sunset. Religious classes also take place there.

Subtle Boundaries

While openness is a distinct characteristic of a *kampung*, and there are no ostensible physical boundaries between the houses, there are symbolic boundaries, such as plants and trees that act as a subtle demarcation of territory. But there is no concept of a front or back yard, simply an area that each household has the responsibility to keep clean. So, while there is the general impression of a lack of barriers and openness, there is a certain degree of ambiguity between public and private territory in a *kampung* and a tension between community intimacy and personal privacy, including a high respect for *adat*, which is an informal legal system based on the precedents of customs and traditions. People unfamiliar with this ambiguity, when studying it as outsiders, may bring their own predetermined social considerations of proper lines of demarcations to it, but understanding it requires a different and a new sensitivity to the way the inhabitants of a *kampung* interact with each other in this setting. There is an invisible but distinct overlapping of territories.

Dying Tradition

The house just described was once very prevalent, whether built individually as a small holding or as part of a *kampung*, or village, throughout Malaysia. The phenomenon of rural-urban migration, which is so prevalent throughout the developing world, is also affecting Malaysia to a large extent, with families moving off the farms to the cities. The hard labor required in single family agriculture does not appeal to the younger generation, who are attracted by the glamour and higher salaries of careers in "intelligence technology," and large conglomerates are buying up rural real estate. *Kampungs* are being rapidly depopulated and the houses are falling into ruin. Those that remain are also being adapted, with the most typical change being the use of concrete block to fill in the open ground floor level to provide more enclosed living space. This destroys the aerodynamics of natural ventilation that helps keep the house so cool and also introduces an alien industrial material into the traditional natural construction palette, completely changing its character. Several conservation efforts have begun, aimed at preserving this vital part of Malaysian heritage, but, sadly, have mostly resulted in dismantling old houses and rebuilding them in museum compounds.

MOHENJO-DARO AND HARAPPA, PAKISTAN

Relatively recent excavations that began in the 1920s in what is now Pakistan have uncovered one of the greatest civilizations in the ancient world. Its extent and complexity now allow it to unquestionably be ranked with China, Egypt, and Mesopotamia in both venerability and importance. Because of the brevity of the period of study involved, there is still much to be learned. The writing system of this civilization, for example, has yet to be deciphered. But every indication points to a very rich and complex culture that took maximum advantage of its proximity to the Indian Ocean. Since the excavation of two major sites in the Punjab and Sindh Provinces little more than 90 years ago, more than 1,500 settlements of smaller size but with similar characteristics have been discovered in an area that is more extensive than either Egypt or Mesopotamia. This culture was strategically located between the Arabian Peninsula, the Greek Islands, and the northern coast of Africa, and the people benefited from trade with all of these areas. The Indus River civilization was a thriving, politically well-organized society that lasted for ten centuries, from 2600 B.C. until its destruction by Aryan invaders from the north. It stretched from Karachi to the Gulf of Bombay to the southeast and northeast to Lahore, following the ancient course of the Indus and Saraswati Rivers, which have changed location today.

The Indus River civilization escaped attention for so long because of its location on an alluvial floor plain, since it lacked the stone to build large monuments like the pyramids of Egypt or bitumen with which to strengthen the mud brick as the Sumerians in Mesopotamia did, which made ziggurats possible. The presence of baked brick, jewelry, and clay tablets that all required firing, however, shows that they had wood and were able to maintain the high temperatures needed to create each of these things over a long period of time, indicating that they could have built large monuments if they had wanted to. One of the main questions occupying the archaeologists who are studying this culture is why they chose not to do so.

The Mound of the Dead

The two major settlements that have been excavated and the two major cities that seem to have bracketed the region were Mohenjo-daro, or "Mound of the Dead," near Karachi to the southeast, and Harappa, 400 miles away near the northeast. A third city, named Kalibangan, which is 100 miles south of Harappa, has also been discovered, but it is not considered to have been as important as these first two.

Mohenjo-daro and Harappa, which were roughly circular, were each about three miles in diameter and very similar in plan. Both of these cities also seem to have served as bivalent administrative rules and model settlements for each of the other settlements in the region as well.[27]

The picture that is emerging as excavations continue and both local and international interest mounts is one of well-planned cities and a focus on the fabrication of luxury items for export, produced from materials traded from both near and far.[28] The fact that no temples have been found has led some to think that this was a society that was preoccupied with worldly things. Others have noted, however, that this absence does not preclude the existence of organized religion, since images that appear to be of deities have been found on the exquisite fired clay tablets that have been found. One of the most recognizable of these is a tree of life symbol as well as a figure that looks like the ubiquitous "Mother Goddess" found elsewhere about this time. There are other figures that seem to prefigure Hinduism, such as a three-faced male god that could be seen to be a prototype of Shiva, lord of the beasts and all living things, and an elephant seal reminiscent of an image of Ganesh.[29]

The absence of monumental temples or cult centers and the lack of evidence of a priestly hierarchy may simply mean that people worshiped in their own houses, and the discovery of domestic shrines seems to support this. Based on the number of seals that show representations of animals, such as tigers, zebra, goats, rhinoceros, gazelle, bulls, and buffalo, it may have been human animistic religion, like Shinto in Japan today, which revered nature and in which people worshiped at open altars under the sky.[30]

Intriguingly, what has been found on Mohenjo-daro instead has been a large bathhouse, as well as a high terraced citadel with thick walls faced in baked brick and a large gate. The houses in this area were clustered around interior courtyards and were at least two stories high. They are believed to have been for a rich merchant class based on the ownership seals that have been found and the presence of storerooms for goods or merchandise. The streets in this area had a very advanced clay pipe sewage system, with drainage from the bathrooms in each of the houses, which also had rubbish slots that emptied into bins along the street, indicating organized garbage collections as well. The sewers ended in the surrounding fields to fertilize them. The less fortunate, on the other hand, lived in small two room huts clustered together near the granaries outside the walls.

Mohenjo-daro and Harappa

The peak of activity in the Indus Valley civilizations lasted for about 700 years, from 2600 to 1900 B.C., with estimates of residents ranging from 40,000 to 80,000. The discovery of stone weights based on a different size than those found in Egypt or Mesopotamia but obviously used in a local system of weights and measures, as well as the lack of weapons or a military, supports the theory of concentration on trade. As one historian has described the bounty available:

> The presence of raw materials and finished goods from Afghanistan and Central Asia indicates that merchants from these areas came to the city bringing lapis lazuli, tin, gold, silver and, perhaps, fine woolen textiles (which have since vanished). Traders would have carried back to the highlands cereal grains and livestock, as well as fine cotton and possibly even silks, but these items are not well preserved.[31]

The most important aspects of the city of Harappa relative to its houses are the street layout, the drainage system, and the citadel, which seems to have served a different social stratum.

The Streets

The streets serving the residential quarter in Harappa were laid out in a gridiron pattern. Main streets were about 45 feet wide with smaller lanes at right angles to them dividing the urban fabric into blocks. Some streets have been found to have been paved with identically sized terracotta blocks placed on a base of crushed ceramic pottery.[32] Different types of streets were designated to serve different functions. The north-south street, which was the widest, is believed to have served oxcart traffic based on the cart tracks etched in the paving blocks and several terracotta models of oxcarts that have been found.[33] Narrower streets, running east-west between the houses, provided pedestrian and service access to them, as well as having a secondary environmental function of allowing cross ventilation to cool the entire quarter. All residential lanes were provided with clay trash bins just like those found in Mohenjo-daro. This waste was collected regularly and deposited on the fields or in trash heaps.

The streets were also laid out according to cosmic considerations, with the main street aligned with the North Star, in order to bring visible order to the plan. Unlike Egyptian cities, such as Tel El Amarna, which was established by the monotheistic Pharaoh Akhenaten as the center for worship of the sun god Aten along the Nile in the middle of Egypt, however, it does not appear that the main north-south street in Harappa terminated at an important monument, such as a palace or temple, but only served a functional rather than a ritual purpose.

Remains of house and well shaft in Mohenjo-daro. The tall cylindrical structure is not a tower but a well shaft. *Source:* Amrit MacIntyre; Flickr

Harrappa had three elevated terraces, which were each ringed with a thick brick wall, areas identified by gates. Multistoned houses fronted onto the main north-south and east-west streets, which were more than 30 feet wide and had brick dividers in the center to separate two-way traffic.

The Drainage System

In addition to the efficient arrangement provided for the removal of domestic waste, a drainage system was used throughout Harappa that is one of the most comprehensive networks found in any ancient urban settlements. A brick-lined channel was placed under every main street, which had tributary drains that emptied into it from the house on either side. This main drain and the secondary conduits had slabs that covered them, laid a few inches below street level, which were segmented so that they could be lifted up easily when it became necessary to clean the drain.

The Citadel

Like Mohenjo-daro and Kalibangan, Harappa also had a citadel, surrounded by a 40 feet high wall that fortified a 600 feet by 1,200 feet area.[34] There is a 20 feet high and 1,000 feet square building located to the north of this walled area, near what used to be the river, that archaeologists believe might have been a granary. It consisted of two rows of storage bins with a 23 feet wide aisle down the middle, protected from flooding by being raised up on a 4 feet high mud brick platform covered with fried face brick.[35] The approach to the granary connects it directly to the river bank as is also the case at Mohenjo-daro and Kalibangan. The long galleries of storage bins also had slots at the ends to allow air to circulate into a channel beneath the floor, to prevent the grain stored in them from rotting.

Houses in Harappa

Each of these well-planned systems, for transportation, waste management, and food storage and delivery, when taken together provided a smoothly functioning network that served the residential quarters of the city. Those living there seem to have led comfortable, prosperous, and well-ordered lives, with a high level of domestic and urban sophistication. The logical layout of the streets and the waste collection and drainage system indicated a high degree of civic organization.

Houses in Mohenjo-daro

The houses in Mohenjo-daro and Harappa also run the gamut from the very modest to the very grand, and interestingly these often seem to be mixed together. They are also organized within a logical, hierarchical street system composed of wide main streets oriented toward cardinal points that service much narrower alleys or lanes that are raised up a few steps from the main roads to prevent flooding, which branch off from them and link them to the secondary streets.[36]

One residence in Mohenjo-daro, described by an archaeologist as an "average upper class house" and named house No. 8, reveals several design strategies that are typical of many other houses in Mohenjo-daro, even though they were occupied by families of a different socioeconomic background. It is located off a main thoroughfare labeled "First Street" by investigators, with its entrance on a branch

Ruins of house at Mohenjo-daro. *Source:* Amrit MacIntyre; Flickr

pedestrian pathway designated as "High Lane." The first thing that is obvious, upon coming into the house, is the effective use of the indirect entry that is so evident in many other urban areas throughout the West Asian region, up through the late Middle Ages. It is referred to as a *magaz* in Islamic architecture and is used to prevent direct physical or visual access into the private domestic realm, the sacrosanct domain of the family. The indirect entry at No. 8 is ingeniously arranged so that a visitor would first be confronted by a doorkeeper, who had a little alcove to sit and sleep in, before being allowed into the central court at the heart of the residence. If the person entering was a guest, he or she would then have unhindered access to guest quarters on the left side of the house behind the gatekeeper, without disturbing the permanent residents, and would also have discreet access to a bathroom and a source of water without entering the main part of the house. The owners, on the other hand, occupied the quietest and most protected part of the compound upstairs, having direct access to one of the extended legs of the L-shaped central court, which had servants' quarters and a kitchen at ground level. The mud brick walls of the house also vary in thickness according to the need for privacy, being widest when they are adjacent, or common to, other houses, as party walls, or when it is necessary to buffer noise such as in bathrooms and the master bedroom, and thinnest when privacy and noise are less of a concern, as in the guest room. The floor of both the bathrooms and the well chamber were paved with bricks, and there was an opening through the wall separating the house from High Lane to allow waste water to escape. The house had a stairway on the north side of the courtyard, giving access to an upper level.[37]

The whole approach to privacy and the division of areas into service and nonservice categories is very deliberate in this residence and is consistent with strategies used in other urban areas throughout this region at a later date. Service uses, such as the kitchen and servants' quarters, are relegated to the ground floor, while the family takes pride of place in the most privileged and private position on the upper level above. The open courtyard, as the main device for temperature regulation and spatial compartmentalization, helps make this strategy of public-private segregation possible.

THE MINANGKABAU HOUSE

The Minangkabau are an ethnic group in Australasia, an ethnographically defined world that extends from Madagascar on the west to Easter Island on the east, including Southeast Asia, Micronesia, Polynesia, Peninsula Malaysia, South Vietnam, Taiwan, and New Guinea. They originated in the central part of the island of Sumatra, forming the majority of the population of *Propinsi Sumatera Barat*, or West Sumatra Province. This is one of 33 provinces that make up the Republic of Indonesia.

The traditional Minangkabau village in this part of Sumatra is made up of a number of distinctive dwellings called *rumah gadang* or great houses in addition to the mosque or *surou*, the *balai adapt*, or *balairung*, which is a village hall where the representatives of the people living there meet to discuss issues related to the village and the *rangkiang* or *lam buong*, which are rice farms. Of all of these, the

The Minangkabau house has a unique profile related to both its social function and the history of the people. The Minangkabau are a matriarchal society and have a foundation legend based on the story of a duel between buffalo.   *Source:* Ezrin Arbi

rumah gadang has become most closely associated with the Minangkabau people because of its metaphorical form and the fact that the house is a direct extension of the social structure of the people.

The *Alam Minangkabau* or Minangkabau World

The Province of West Sumatra, which is the homeland of Minangkabau, has a coastal border formed by the Indian Ocean, along its western edge, and is contained, on its other three sides, by Sumatra Province on the north, Riau Province on the east, and Bengkulu Province on the south. West Sumatra Province is diagonally divided by the Bukit Barisan highlands, which span the equator. A mountain range, Bukit Barisan, which runs the length of West Sumatra, defines the territory of the Minangkabau, acting as a backdrop to the east, confining their group between it and the sea on the west. Mount Marabi is the most impressive peak along this ridge. It has three valleys that extend outward from it, called *Singgalang*, *Tandikat*, and *Sago*. These have been historically known as *Kuhak nan Tigo*, or the three districts, or simply as *darek*, the interior, and are the heartland of Minangkabau culture. Mount Marabi was once an active volcano, and so the soil in the valleys is very fertile. There are also several streams that originate in the foothills, which, in combination with the quality of the soil, make this an excellent area for the cultivation of rice. Because the altitude of the majority of the region is relatively high, except along the coastal plain, the temperature is mild. In the Agam district of West Sumatra Province, annual daytime temperatures average 69 degrees Fahrenheit or 26 degrees Celsius, in spite of the fact that it is right on the equator. It also has ample rainfall. But today, Agam is only one of eight *kabupaten* or districts in the Province of West Sumatra that are each administered by a *bupati*, or district head. The other seven are Pasaman, Padang-Pariaman, Tanah Datar, Limapuluh-Koto, Solok, Sawahlunto Sijunjung, and Pesisir Selatan. In addition, each district is subdivided into smaller units called *kecamatan*. The Minangkabau foundation legend is based on the story of their ancestors, who came across these mountains and down onto the coastal plain to settle there. They divide this territory into "the land" (*Darek*), "the coast" (*Pesisir*), and "the outer lands" beyond the mountains (*Rantars*). To the north, Bukit Tinggi, which is one of the highest peaks in the mountain range, is of special importance as a landmark for this group.

A World Apart

Because of the unique and relatively isolated geographical conditions in which their society has originated and evolved, the Minangkabau have developed an identifiably different culture, quite separate from that of the Malays of the lowlands along the east coast of Sumatra. From the seventh century until the beginning of Portuguese incursions into the Straits of Melaka, this area was a center of trade because it is on the main sea-lane connecting India and China, creating a cultural *entrepot* that fostered a strong and unified Malay civilization and identity. The Minangkabau had iron ore and gold, mined from relatively small and scattered deposits in the highlands, as well as rice to trade, but generally remained untouched by foreign influence from the Straits. Because of this relative detachment, the Minangkabau way of life has remained virtually unchanged for centuries, making the *rumah gadang* an especially valuable anthropological artifact. The Minangkabau, referred to locally simply as *Orang Minang* or *Orang Padang*, using the name of the capital of the province, are the fourth largest ethnic group in Indonesia, following the Javanese at 47 percent, the Sudanese at 15 percent, and the Madurese at 7 percent. But still, according to the 1990 census, they make up only 3 percent of the population of Indonesia.[38] This very small percentage is not just confined to the Minangkabau heartland, but is scattered throughout Indonesia and the remainder of the Malay Archipelago as well.

The Minangkabau House

The Minangkabau houses in Indonesia and Malaysia fall into the general category of Southeast Asian vernacular. They conform to a traditional typology, found throughout the region, with all having a similar design solution to the hot, humid climate that exists there. This solution involves the distancing and orientation of houses to allow for maximum ventilation, the raising of the main floor on columns to also encourage air flow and to keep the occupants safe from animals and reptiles, the practice of directly opposing openings to encourage airflow, and the inclusion of a broad overhanging roof for shade. The walls are also located to help direct air flow, and outside verandas and porches are used as living spaces to free up interior space. Local materials, such as wood and palm fronds or mangrove leaves (*atap* and *nipah*), are used for structural members and roof thatching, and wood is precut in modular units before being assembled on-site, with only interlocking joints (and no metal fasteners) being used to erect it. The rules used for the orientation of the house differ with the Minangkabau, however, due to the overriding importance of group identity in their society. Minangkabau houses also are among the most symbolic of all vernacular types, representing both the mythical origins of the group in external form and the reproductive life cycle and social ordering system in the room arrangement inside.

A Matriarchal Society

Women have always played an important part in Malay society, but the Minangkabau are unusual in that even after the advent of Islam in the sixteenth century, which puts great emphasis upon male authority within the family, they have remained matrilineal. That is, lineage is traced through the women, who own all of the property and control family finances and possessions, including the inheritance of houses.

Prior to the prevalence of Islam, Malay society used customs or traditions, agreed upon by consensus, called "*adat*," as rules of law. Once Islamic law was introduced, *adat* still remained intact, currently providing a dual set of laws. In Minangkabau society *adat* is referred to as "*perpateh*," or matrilineal rather than the "*adat temenggong*" or patrilineal legal traditions that prevail elsewhere in other Malaysian and Indonesian family structures. The way that the dominant role of the female members of this society has contributed to the development of the *rumah gadang*, or great house, makes it an important resource for studying how social norms affect house form.

The Minangkabau Great House or *Rumah Gadang*

Minangkabau houses are long and narrow, with the main entrance on one of the long sides. The position of the entrance is specifically related to the type of *adat* practiced in the village and house, of either the autocratic (*koto piliang*) or democratic (*bodi camiago*) form, based on the way final decisions are made in each residence. In the former, the entrance is in the middle of a central axis with the house stepping up in each direction toward elevated alcoves at the end, while the entrance is asymmetrically placed, usually toward the right. If the *bodi camiago* system prevails, the floor remains flat. Wherever it is placed, the main entrance leads directly into a semipublic space called a *ruang*, which is similar to the *serambi* of the Malay house in that it is intended for the reception of visitors and guests as well as daily use by the family; but here it is more of a large hall in which social activities occur and family meals are shared. There is a room, called the *anjuang*, which takes up one entire end of the rectangular house, that is directly accessible from the *ruang*, where the most recently married woman in the family and her husband live. This couple is then displaced by the next daughter to get married, moving clockwise to the next of a series of *billak*, or rooms arranged in a line along the long back edge of the house, shifting step by step toward the *dabu*, or kitchen at the end opposite the *anjuang*.

The matriarch of the family occupies a space near the *pangkalan*, or central post, which holds up the main roof girder, designating her status as the head of the family. In the Malay house this central post, called the *tiang seri*, is also important, as it is the first structural member installed, accompanied by a ceremony in which a coin is placed under it for good luck. In each instance, the dimensions of the central post, which set the module for the remaining structural members that are used, are derived from the height of the woman of the house. The central post is typically near the main entrance to the Minangkabau house, putting the senior matriarch in a powerful position in relationship to all those entering, especially all of the husbands living in the *anjuang* or *billak* inside. Houses of the highest status have front entrances that face toward the Bukit Barisan, in remembrance of the ancestral migration to West Sumatra, enhancing the division of these long houses into the front, where the *ruang* and central post, or *pangkalan*, are located, and the back with its row of *billak* for older married couples. So, the plan of the house is a diagram of the reproductive cycle of each of the women who occupy it, since the most recently married daughter and her husband occupy the end apartment until they are displaced by the next daughter to wed, ending with the matriarch, in her position of authority near the center post and the front door.

This column, or *pangkalan*, is important, but each of the others, which number about 30 in an average house, are also considered to have spiritual power, revealing the role that animism still plays in what is now a mostly Muslim society. This is especially true of columns made from an entire tree trunk, and family well-being and strength are believed to be dependant upon the sensitivity of the carpenter and his skill at interpreting natural signs when selecting the trees in the forest that are used to make them.[39] The space between the columns running the long direction of the rectangular house is called *ruang*, and across it is referred to as *lebar*. The size of the house is designated by the number of *ruang* it has, with a larger number indicating higher social stature, since this means that the number of *billak* it can accommodate, and therefore its longevity, is greater, implying a closer connection to the original Minangkabau ancestors.[40]

The *Rumah Gonjong* or "House with Horns"

While the plan of the Minangkabau house is spatially descriptive of its matrilineal organization and the reproductive life cycle of its inhabitants, its roof, which is the most distinctive feature of its external appearance, is symbolic of group identity, popularly believed to be based on a cultural legend. The roofs of the houses arch upward toward a peak at each end, which is capped with metal fittings. The legend, from which the people also take their name, is based on a battle with the Javanese, which each side eventually agreed would be settled by a contest between two water buffalos. The Javanese chose a huge buffalo to represent them, while the Minang used a young calf, which they starved before the tournament, so that it would go under its opponent looking for milk. The Minang tied a curved knife blade to its jaw to cause maximum damage and won the contest, taking their name, which means "victorious buffalo" (*menang kerbau*), from it. For this reason, the roof form of their houses represents a buffalo's horns, although there are other opinions, such as the belief that it symbolizes the ship that originally brought them

Traditional Batak style house at Lake Toba, Sumatra, Indonesia.   Courtesy of Shutterstock

to Sumatra from India.[41] Trusses with struts are used to achieve the curved slope and pointed ends of the roof. Sugar palm leaves (*ijuk*), which are extremely durable and turn black with age, are used for thatch, although corrugated metal has replaced this often.

This widely accepted apocryphal story of the connection between the roof form and the victorious buffalo is complicated a bit by other variations, described by one expert as economic symbols in which:

> Class status and identity are often associated with the composition of these forms with their projecting "*tanduk*" (horn) gable ends. A "proper" house will have four "*tanduk*," symbolic of the four main clan divisions of the Minangkabau. Houses with two to four "*tanduk*" are referred to as "*gajah mangaram*" (sleeping elephant), while those with six "*tanduk*" are the "*rumah bakajangan.*" If the steeples sit in the center, not the end, like a crown, it is known as a "*rumah bas sanggul,*" or a house with a headdress.[42]

Regardless of the mixed metaphors, the victorious buffalo story, like the legendary battle between Hector and Achilles to decide the fate of Troy, or the decision to let single combat between David and Goliath substitute for warfare between the armies of the Philistines and the Israelites, is much more compelling and memorable as a collective myth, institutionalizing the attribute of cleverness in the face of adversity, in spite of the fact that the Javanese themselves were eventually victorious.

Marantau

While Minangkabau culture has remained concentrated in and around their highland homeland until very recently, there has also been a tradition, strengthened by *adat* or custom, for young men to migrate, in search of money or identity. This is called *marantau*, which has a meaning similar to the Australian Aborigines' use of the term "walkabout," referring to a journey of self-discovery. Changes to the boundaries of the provinces by the central government of Indonesia since independence have also reduced the size of Minangkabau territory so that today there is a Minangkabau diaspora, which like the Nubians is a sociocultural rather than a geographical group.

Disseminating a Powerful Building Tradition

The tendency to migrate has also been attributed to frustration with the restrictions of matrilineal *adat*, as well as economic necessity and sheer curiosity, but for whatever reason many Minangkabau males feel the urge to explore the "outer lands" portion of their territorial consciousness, the "*rantau*," beyond the mountains. To leave "the land" for the outside is called "*marantau*," and the person who does so is called a "*perantauan*." The Minangkabau is not the only ethnological group in which the men leave the homeland while the women, preadolescent children, and elderly stay behind. The Nubians in southern Egypt and Sudan are another notable example of several ethnic groups that do the same. But for the Nubians a temporary exile is economically necessary because their homeland, which has been redistributed since the dislocation caused by the construction of the Aswan High Dam, cannot be easily farmed and there is no other way to make a living there. Their traditional self-exile is also for a finite period, from adolescence until retirement age, with frequent visits back home for weddings, anniversaries, birthdays, and funerals. In the case of the Minangkabau, there has been a historical pattern of immigration to Malaysia, as well as of men taking their entire family with them.[43]

Negri Sembilan

Malacca, which is directly across the Strait from Sumatra, has been a preferred destination for the *perantauan* from Sumatra. This pattern started in the fifteenth century when the Sultanate was at its most powerful and the city was a lucrative center for trade because of its strategic location as a meeting point for Europe, the Middle East, and Asia. There were two waves of Minangkabau immigration prior to the occupation of Malacca by the Portuguese in 1511, resulting in settlement along the Muar and Linggi river valleys and the replication there of the matrilineal society in Sumatra, but in this instance the economy was based on the planting, harvesting, and sale of rice.

After the fall of Malacca to a foreign power, the center of Malay power shifted to Johor. Eventually a group of nine "states" evolved in two rings around the royal capital. The first is Ulu Muar, the capital, with Jempol, Gunong Pasir, and Terachi surrounding it in the inner ring, and Sungei Ujong, Jelebu, and Johal in the outer circle. These states occupy an area of the Malaysian Peninsula between Selangor to the north, Johor to the south, and Pahang to the east, with Remban and Sungei Ujong having direct access to the Straits of Malacca on the west.

Similarities and Differences

The houses of the *perantauan* Minangkabau in Negri Sembilan share many attributes of the original type in Sumatra, but also differ from it in significant ways, leading to much speculation about why changes have occurred. The early settlements in the Muar and Linggi river valleys generally took the form of *kampungs*, or villages, consisting of groupings of *rumah gadang*, just as in Sumatra, which are family or clan houses under matriarchal control. There are indications, however, of an attempt by some to establish independent family groups. These *kampungs* expand as populations grow, covering the slopes of the river valleys.[44]

In general the Minangkabau houses in Negri Sembilan are not as elaborate as those in Sumatra and also incorporate local elements from the Malay house, which corrupts the original model. There does seem to have been an attempt to approximate the grandeur of the long *rumah gadang* as time passes and the immigrants became more established and economically stable, but the "victorious buffalo" roof form along with vestiges of matrilineal *adat* in Negri Sembilan remains the most obvious indication of a cultural link across the Malacca Straits.

SHANG HOUSES IN CHINA

The Shang Dynasty is the first recorded cohesive political structure in China, lasting more than 600 years, from 1766 until 1122 B.C. It was concentrated along the middle and lower portions of the Yellow River in what are now the regions of Hunan, Hopei, Shansi, Shensi, and Shantung, in a capital city called Changzhou (formerly known as Chang-chou).

During the Shang Dynasty, remarkable works of pottery, sculpture, and painting were produced, but most notable of all are the wide variety of bronze objects that have been discovered from this period. These include bronze vessels for both religious and domestic use and weapons, many of which have inscriptions that identify their purpose. Bronze was commonly used to decorate tombs and to provide a covering for the stone substructures of public and private buildings.

The Record

The Shang Dynasty is the second of the three critically formative periods in Chinese history including the Hsia that preceded it and the Chou that followed. The Shang Dynasty lasted 644 years, from 1766 to 1122 B.C. But, in spite of its duration, documentation of the Shang Period has been scarce. It has primarily been limited to bronze ritual vessels that run the gamut in scale from huge to small personal items and bones that were inscribed with texts of various lengths that predicted the future and so are called "oracle" bones. These bones mostly include the shoulder blades of cattle and turtle shells, and have helped provide insights into Shang social customs, with 14 rulers listed prior to its official royal line and 30 kings who followed once it was established. The capital was moved several times before it was firmly established in Changzhou.

Ritual Bronzes

Inscriptions, ranging from a single word to 497 characters, have been found on only a portion of the bronze vessels and objects that have been uncovered so far. These have been categorized as those with signs and those with cohesive texts or statements. The signs often identify either a family or clan or simply the social rank of the person for whom the vessel was made. The bronzes with longer texts often describe the circumstances surrounding the making of the vessel, the king to whom it was given as a gift, the cost of producing or acquiring it, or a battle or a royal journey. These inscriptions are valuable as literary texts because of the limited amount of other historical data available for this period.

Bronze casting at the scale of these vessels was difficult, showing a high level of skill and organization. Bronze making was a major occupation and an identifying feature of the Shang culture. The huge quantity of ore that was smelted to meet the demand for bronze objects is phenomenal. More than 400 bronze objects were found in one Shang tomb that was excavated in 1976, that of a high ranking member of the royal family. About half of these were vessels used in religious rituals, the largest of which were a pair of square cauldrons weighing about 250 pounds each. The copper and tin for these bronzes was mined in northern China, about 400 kilometers away from the capital, which would have involved a month-long round trip journey to procure it.

Oracle Bones

The oracle bones that were used for divination were prepared by first cleaning and polishing them to create a smooth surface. They were then heated on the hollow or concave side to cause cracking on the reverse, upper surface. The pattern of the cracks was then interpreted in response to a question put to the oracle, and the prediction was written on the bone or shell. Turtle shells were obviously a popular item in this ritual, and mostly belong to a species found only in the Yangtze Valley, south of Anyang. The inscriptions on them often state who donated them. Almost all inquiries were requested by royal clients, since the inscriptions also usually mention the person in whose name the inquiry was made, the name of the oracle, and the prophecy. Divination seems to have played a major role in the decisions taken by the court. Inscriptions have been found that refer to sacrificial rituals, military campaigns, hunting expeditions, general predictions about the future, weather, harvests, illness, the interpretation of dreams, the extent of life, the time of death, and the best time to build a temple or a palace.

The Great City of Shang and Its Houses

In the oracle bone texts, the capital was always referred to as the "Great City of Shang." There is evidence of a moderate settlement at Changzhou in the Predynastic Period, but it was not until this city was transformed into a royal capital that a consistent house typology began to emerge with two distinct types. The first of these is a large house, which was perhaps a palace; it was based on a wooden frame structure, with mud bricks used to fill in the spaces between the columns. The discovery of the foundations of these large houses has been one of the most exciting archaeological events in the study of the dynastic phase of the Shang Period.

Changzhou

The Shang capital of Changzhou must have been very impressive, with a wide variety of large ancestral temples and palaces, as well as houses for those of various socioeconomic levels divided into different districts, with the most important of these clad in shiny bronze, glinting in the sun. Changzhou was basically rectangular, surrounded by a high wall. The city occupied an area of 3.2 square kilometers. The only part of the wall that still survives today is 9.1 meters tall and 3.6 meters wide, and its inner structure makes it obvious that it was built in two stages, perhaps having been mended after an attack. Chinese historians estimate that the construction of the wall, which is made of *terre pisé*, or compressed mud brick, took about 18 years, involving approximately 10,000 laborers to dig, transport, and compress the earth that was required to make it.

It is difficult to fully understand the exact layout of Changzhou, due to its great age and the fact that many of its houses, which were also made of mud brick, have not survived. But, archaeologists believe that the residential districts surrounded a central administrative and ceremonial center. Excavations that have gone on since the mid-1970s, which have been underway in the northeastern corner of the city near the wall, have uncovered a long ditch filled with more than 100 human skulls, which were sawn in half. Human and animal bones have also been found under similar circumstances in other parts of the city, leaving archaeologists to speculate about their use. They now believe these are the remains of slain enemies, ceremonial burials, or bone used for bone workshops, where fragments are known to have been inlaid into pottery and weapons.

A Uniform City Plan

Enough of Changzhou remains to determine that the layout of the city conforms to others built in the Hsia and Chou Dynasties, indicating that even at such an early stage, a series of urban planning principles had been adopted.[45] These are known to have been codified by the time of the construction of Chang'an, for which an actual plan, which was carved in stone, exists. These principles, which conform to the concept of *feng shui* (literally "wind and water"), begin with choosing a site on higher ground, preferably with mountains on its northern side to block cold winter winds and water to the south, with land at the confluence of two rivers being highly preferable. The presence of a river was important not just as a source of water but also as an additional line of defense against attack and a means of transporting goods.

These conditions existed at Changzhou, which had the Chin-Shui River running along its northern edge and the Hsiung-Erh River on the south. The excavation site today makes it appear as if the city and the land outside the walls around it were on the same level, but thick layers of silt have been deposited over the entire area that have created this uniformly high plateau. When it was occupied, during the Shang Dynasty, the city was much higher than the river valleys around it, and the walls were built to take maximum advantage of the change in topography for defensive reasons.

There is sufficient evidence available to conclude that Changzhou contained a highly stratified class hierarchy, beginning with the royal family, moving downward through nobles, officials, warriors, merchants, commoners, and slaves. These were each allocated a separate district in the city, based on the location of palaces and temples, commercial areas and shops, and the size, type, and material of the various dwellings, all linked by a well-designed drainage system that was used to deliver water and remove sewage.

House Types in Changzhou

The foundations of houses, other than palaces, are either square or rectangular. Those with square foundations have mostly been found in a working class neighborhood, now referred to as Ming-kong-lu, near an ancient kiln site, where bricks were made and pottery was fired. In these homes, a roughly square, shallow depression was dug first, measuring 2.5 meters on a side, and a wooden floor was suspended above it to keep it dry. Mud brick walls, about 1.2 meters high, were then erected along the perimeter, creating a foundation known as *hang-tú*, or rammed earth, which is a distinctive feature of Shang houses. Windows and a door were usually concentrated on the south-facing wall for maximum solar heat during the winter, and although the roofs, which were made with wooden beams and joists, have disintegrated, boulders or bronze discs have been formed that were placed at the bottom of columns to protect them from rotting. These columns supported an intermediate thatched roof that served as a portico around the entire house to prevent the high summer sun from overheating the interior during that season. A fireplace, consisting of a hole in the floor and a chimney built into the wall was typically built on the solid northern side of the house. This kind of foundation seems to have predated the second rectangular type. This long and narrow configuration, which appeared toward the middle of the Shang Dynasty, supported several levels above it, based on the holes for columns that have been found. These houses may have been up to four or five stories high, judging from the diameter of these holes and the weight that columns of this size could have supported. A similar kind of floor was used at ground level, but it appears that it was typically paved with glazed tile. The columns were set upon stones or pottery fragments to keep them from rotting. Partitions were built in the middle of the rectangular plan to divide it into two square spaces.

Mysterious Underground Chambers

In addition to the palaces, temples, workshops, and houses that have been excavated, several underground pits have been discovered that have yet to be satisfactorily explained. One theory is that these rectangular or round pits were used for storage, or as granaries, and that the wealth of the royal houses was kept in them. Several hundred bronze casting molds, as well as jade and stone implements, hundreds of knives, pieces of bone, and many arrowheads, have complicated the problem of identification. These have led some archaeologists to believe that they were also bronze casting workshops, while bone fragments with copper green stains on them or fireplaces and stoves found in others have confounded this theory. Other archaeologists think that a number of these pits were for ceremonial or ritual burials due to the discovery of human and animal remains in them. The sequence of layers also suggest that a number of sacrificial animals were slaughtered and put on top of the human burials, which could have been those of victims, because a wooden floor was built on top, indicating the possibility of the consecration of a foundation.[46]

In one series of underground pits found near the entrance to one house, a human skeleton was found in a kneeling position, with a bronze dagger, or *ko*, nearby. In another, a skeleton was found with a sword and shield. Pits inside the door also contained human skeletons, with two in one pit and three in another, all lying face down with their heads pointing toward the center of the room. These discoveries strengthen the possibility of a tradition of ritual sacrifice, as an act of consecration during the construction of a house, or palace for an important person, concentrating on the entrance, perhaps as a gesture of protection or of the provision of spiritual guardianship.

In one case, at a house large enough to have been a palace, the skeletons of more than a hundred people were found, along with five chariots, all buried immediately in front of the entrance, contributing to the aura of mystery surrounding these houses.

House Construction as a Spiritual Act

These discoveries suggest a society that practiced both human and animal sacrifice and also believed in the survival of the soul after death, as well as attribute a religious significance to domestic architecture. There are also cemeteries that have been uncovered near Changzhou, outside the walls, where hundreds of similar pits have been found, with the type of burial demonstrating the social status of the deceased. This indicates a value system in which wealth was highly regarded. Extensive grave goods found in these tombs include bronze vessels, weapons, and jewelry. These tombs were built in the same way as the pit houses inside the city, with the addition of a wooden chamber that protected a lacquer coffin placed inside it. This confirms a similar practice seen elsewhere in other early civilizations, in which a tomb is made to resemble the house that the deceased occupied in life, to ensure continued comfort in the afterlife. The coffins in this district held the remains of prominent citizens, with members of their household buried nearby.

Many of these tombs have been plundered, but the few articles that have been recovered are astonishing in both their workmanship and scale, including huge bronze caldrons, drinking vessels, bronze figurines of cows and deer, helmets, swords, spears, and daggers. Many of these carry identical family or lineage emblems in individual areas, indicating designated burial grounds for certain families.

The alluvial plain, on which the capital city of the Shang Dynasty was located, between the T'ai-hang Mountains to the west and the Yellow River to the east, was warmer, wetter, and more fertile then it is today. Evidence of about 30 different species of mammals have been found in the area, including water buffalo, boar, deer, sheep, cattle, and pigs, giving us a clear picture of what the Shang diet during the Dynastic Period must have been like. In addition, there were six kinds of fish in the river, and chicken, pheasant, and peacock bones have also been discovered. The oracle bones also refer to rice, wheat, and millet, and they describe wildlife that resembles rhinoceros, elephants, and tigers, which all indicate a much warmer and more heavily forested environment. The Shang also domesticated horses, dogs, cattle, sheep, pigs, and chickens, which were used in ritual sacrifices as well as for food. One oracle had recorded that 1,000 cattle were used in one sacrifice and 500 in another.[47] Horses imported from the north seem to have been highly valued and were exclusively used for riding or pulling chariots. Cowrie shells have also been found and have been identified as having been used as a means of exchange since they are often referred to on oracle bones as being "precious." Strings of cowrie shells were given as gifts, and a strand of five or ten was a basic monetary unit.

Gaps in the Record

Changzhou was burned to the ground in a massive, concluding conflagration.[48] The basin has been farmed for the thousand of years since, and the Shang tombs have been repeatedly vandalized. The record that remains in archaeological excavations of house foundations, bronze vessels, and oracle bones paints a tantalizing but far from complete picture of this highly sophisticated and complex civilization that played such a formative role in Chinese history.[49]

4

Europe and the Western Mediterranean

ANGLO-SAXON AND NORMAN HOUSES
IN BRITAIN

It is dangerous to generalize about the domestic situation of people during the Middle Ages because the time between the fall of the Roman Empire and the beginning of the Renaissance, covering a period of nearly 700 years, was one of great change, and conditions varied greatly from region to region. It is usually divided into the Dark Ages, Early Middle Ages, and High Middle Ages to reflect the change in security, personal freedom, and mercantile activity that occurred. There are some indisputable common denominators that can be identified and will be discussed at the end of this overview, which will focus on Britain.

The End of Roman Power

Because of the growing threat to Rome from Germanic tribes by the middle of the fourth century, combined with the decision of the Emperor Constantine to move the capital of the Empire to the east for more security, it became increasingly difficult to support a presence in Britain, and there is evidence of a shortage of financial resources to continue to maintain an army there by this time.[1] Roman legions began to leave; there is a record of the departure of a large group under the leadership of Magnus Maximus in A.D. 383.[2] A group of local leaders took control in A.D. 410, but were immediately faced with incursions by Picts and Scots from the north. They asked for Roman help in repelling them. Troops returned several times to do so, but by the middle of the fifth century further requests went unanswered since the Romans had problems of their own in defending their homeland. The Britons then began to use Anglo-Saxon mercenaries to repel the invaders. Although the exact date is contested, but usually given as 450, Saxon leaders Hengest and Horsa, who were famously invited by a Briton named Vortigern, arrived on the east coast with three ships full of warriors. They were followed by many reinforcements, and as they became bolder, they mutinied and demanded more pay and power. Following their defeat by a local force led by Ambrosius Aurelianus at Mount Baden in A.D. 500, they left for home.

Anglo-Saxon Britain

The respite was only temporary, however, and the Anglo-Saxons, joined by the Jutes, sensed opportunity in the power vacuum that existed following the Roman departure. They began to invade again, slowly beginning to occupy Britain, moving from east to west. This occupation was not as immediate as it is usually thought to have been, however, and for some time there were two Britains: the Anglo-Saxon east and the non-Anglo-Saxon west.

As is so often the case in many of the other societies discussed here, the houses of the average Anglo-Saxon villages were made of perishable materials, so that little evidence of them still remains and any attempt to reconstruct what they were like would be highly speculative. Evidence that has been found outside of Britain, however, allows some insights into what village life might have been like. Also, as is usually seen elsewhere, there was a clear division between classes, with those involved in fighting having the upper hand.

In 1936, archaeologist Brian Hope-Taylor excavated the so-called "Palace of the Kings of North Umbria" at Yeavering, associated with Anglo-Saxon leaders Aethelfrith (593–617), Edwin (617–633), and Oswald (635–644). The palace consisted of seven main structures, including four halls that were each 100 feet long, two of which had a porch at each end. These had smaller halls for retainers nearby and one temple. The royal halls typically have a double square plan, that is, the length is twice the width; and their walls were made of squared off, mortised planks of uniform thickness aligned vertically, with every second plank sunk into the foundation for rigidity, which is a structural system unparalleled in Europe at this time. External buttress posts supported the halls against wind, which can reach gale strength in Britain. The roof was a gable with a hip at one end and a plain façade on the other. There were opposing doorways on the long sides and colonnades running parallel to these, to shorten the span of the roof timbers. This created a spatial arrangement analogous to a nave and side aisles in a Gothic church, at a much smaller scale.

The Long Hall of Alfred

In 1961 a similarly ascribed "Palace of the Kings" was excavated in Somerset, including the ninth-century Long Hall of Alfred, which had a similar post and trench system of construction. The hall, which was 80 feet long and 18 feet wide, was boat shaped, however, being wider in the middle than at the ends, with an interior row of columns on each side that sloped inward to support an upper floor, which is similar to a house type found in Viking strongholds. Archaeologists speculate that the curve was intended to accommodate a hearth at the middle of the bulge, to allow more space around it, as well as to give the hall more resistance to the wind. These discoveries compare favorably to houses found in a reasonably well-preserved Saxon village in Warendorf, Germany, dated from A.D. 650 to

800, which had 11 such long houses amidst the 75 houses in the village, as well as with stone Norse houses in Iceland, and the Orkney and Shetland Islands.

The Typical Anglo-Saxon House

So, from these findings, it seems that the typical Anglo-Saxon hall during this time, at least the halls used by leaders and nobles, was a long rectangular wooden building, with wood plank walls and buttress poles, sometimes curved, and was multistoried. As time went on, the entrance moved from the center of the long walls to the end, with the "high table," for ceremonial dinners, located at the opposite end, presumably for protection.[3] Otherwise, more modest houses had walls made of wattle and daub, which is clay, chopped straw or cow hair, and cow dung imbedded into a woven wooden surface supported by vertical or diagonal cross bracing.

Norman Houses in Britain

Following the Norman conquest in A.D. 1066, house styles and construction methods changed, with the emphasis on stone rather than wood, and adapted to local building traditions and climactic variations, making them slightly different from houses of the same period in France. Because of the Hundred Years' War with the English, which really occurred in two phases from A.D. 1337 to 1360, and then from A.D. 1369 to 1453, there are few early medieval manor houses in France, and the preference, for security reasons, seemed to have focused on townhouses instead.[4] In Britain, however, the manor house evolved in a more measured way, in a more secure framework, with a recognizable set of fixed elements, which are the hall, the solar, the kitchen, the buttery, and the garderobe.

The Hall

The first halls were the chief room of the house and mark the beginning of the evolution of the manor house. They were built of wood, which was a holdover from the Anglo-Saxon period, in which wood was used for houses and stone for churches. Wood construction was so prevalent in this early period that the word for "to build" in Old English was "timbran."[5] A period of civil unrest under Henry II (A.D. 1154–1189) led to the hall being moved up to the first floor, with a vaulted stone base on the ground level for defense. Slowly appendages, such as the pantry, buttery, and kitchen were attached, although these were in separate buildings. The first Norman halls, like their Anglo-Saxon predecessors, were also aisled, with a row of columns running parallel to each of their two long sides, to reduce the depth of the roof trusses and to add stability. By the end of the twelfth century, separated apartments for family members and close retainers were also connected to the hall, under a single roof.[6] Most surviving first floor halls are in stone, and composite examples of a stone base and timber first floor have perished, since they rotted, burned, or could be replaced more easily. This has much to do with the materials available in various regions, since stone was more prevalent in the southeast, and timber was more plentiful and less expensive in the west. The earliest halls resembled barns, having a central high space running the entire length and side aisles, separated by columns. Of the few wooden halls that survive of those in which the ground floor was in wood, the most notable examples in Britain are from the eleventh and twelfth centuries. One is in Cheddar, built in A.D. 1000 in Somerset, which is the largest of these at 60 feet by 100 feet, and it is magnificent. Rubble footings were usually used, on which the timber-framed walls rested, which performed well in the freeze–thaw cycle of winter and spring. A huge hall at Westminster, built in 1097, is 67.5 feet wide by 239.5 feet long and still has hints of brilliant colors used inside, with traces of red and blue separated by black lines. Columns were usually circular, rather than square or rectangular.

The buttery, which was for drinks, and the pantry, for bread, usually flanked a passageway leading to the kitchen, which was relegated to one end of the house, because of the risk of fire. As conditions became more secure, the hall moved down to the ground floor, having a high roof to prevent the buildup of smoke from the central hearth. The hall became, as one historian described it,

> the social center of the estate. It was the assembly place for tenants, for legal and administrative purposes, as well as the main living room for the lord's family and personal staff, where most of them dined and, at first, some of them slept.[7]

After this, during the fourteenth century, the aisled hall died out because of innovations in structure, such as the hammer beam ceiling.

The Solar, or Great Chamber

In the early history of the hall, individual bedrooms were a rarity for the staff. Servants slept in the hall and the personal servants of the family slept in the lord and lady's bedroom for protection. This bedroom was called the *solar*, meaning a room above ground level, but is sometimes referred to as the "great chamber." It was originally over the kitchen, buttery, pantry service wing, and was used as a bedroom and sitting room by the owner and his family. From the eleventh century onward, it was heated by wall fireplaces. Its location allowed the owner to discretely retire from dinner, which was usually a busy affair, including retainers, and to go up a stairway at the end of the house without walking the entire length of the hall. A landing on this outside stair, called an *oriolum*, due to its similarity to an earlike appendage, slowly evolved into the oriel window, after it was enclosed. It was originally a covered porch at the middle or top of the stairway leading from the hall to the solar, but now means a "projecting window recess."[8]

These basic components then, of the ground floor hall, service wing, solar, or great chamber on the first floor, as well as garderobe, or bathroom and covered entry, usually located off-center of the rectangular hall, near the end of the long front wall, eventually became the essential elements of the typical Norman house.[9]

Peasant houses, on the other hand, had a simple rectangular plan, consisting of a "long house" with a living room at one end and a kitchen at the other, and separate outbuildings for the animals. These appear to have been rebuilt after each generation when a son took over a small holding from his father. There is one example in Yorkshire that was rebuilt nine times in the course of 325 years, from the late twelfth century until early in 1500, in which the plan stayed essentially the same.

While it describes a house in Flanders, and not in Britain, one classic passage by a contemporary writer named Lambert in 1117 paints a graphic verbal picture of a three-story wooden house by Arnold, lord of Ardes, near his castle.

Dogan Houses   The Dogan people of Mali build their houses of mud brick and use thatch for the roofs. Because each individual or family has a freestanding house and they are typically clustered close together, their settlements have a distinctly vertical, uniform appearance.   *Source:* James Steele

Chaco Canyon   The Anasazi terrace houses at Chaco Canyon represent an intelligent adaptation to a local climate which is extremely hot and dry during the day for most of the year and cold at night. There is also very little wood available for structural use. The builders of these communal houses used local stone and mud brick, long with pimon logs covered by reed mats and a compressed clay covering to great effect here. These allowed them to cluster their houses together to provide a buffer against the heat. The mud brick and stone also kept the inside cool during the day, but buy the early evening, it would have penetrated through the walls, making the inside very hot. The terraces provided a cool place to sleep at night as well as being a social space during the day.   Courtesy of Ken Breisch

Machu Picchu   The Spanish incursion into Peru and the destruction of the Inca Empire there forced a group believed to have been dedicated to the preservation of the legacy of the imperial line to flee into the mountains high above the Urubamba river valley. They built a village there that remained undiscovered until the early 1920s when Hiram Bingham who was the inspiration for the Hollywood action hero Indiana Jones, uncovered it again. He found individual houses placed on carefully contrasted terraces that allowed the inhabitants to grow food to support their small community. The houses were built of local stones that were put up in battered walls without mortar and the joints are so tight that it is difficult to even get the blade of a knife between them. The community seems to have been divided between secular and sacred zones. The dwellings in the more exclusive area have niches in them that are believed to have held large jars that contained the mummified remains of Inca Emperors, which the sect brought with them. One large vertical rock on the mountaintop has evocatively, but quite appropriately named The Hitching Post of the Sun.   Courtesy of Hugo Cavallo

The Nubian House   The Nubian people occupy an area that now straddles the border between Sudan and Upper Egypt, near Sudan. They placed a significant part in the Pharaonic portion of the history of Egypt because they posed a constant threat to the autonomy of their powerful Northern neighbors, on the one hand and offered them precious goods that they could trade for, on the other. Recent archaeological discoveries, such as the massive Pharaonic fortress of Buken which was built beside the Nile to prevent Nubian invasion, testify to the respect and fear that the ancient Egyptians had for their erstwhile trading partners. Eventually the Nubians did mange to control Egypt for a brief time, famously putting warlike Pharaohs such as Tarhakoe on the throne. Nubian houses then, like those today were made entirely of mud brick because there is very little wood in the region, in which the desert comes almost to the age of the Nile. The people today are also too poor to be able to afford other imparted materials, such as steel, to use as scaffolding, or centering, or the concrete it might support. So, they devised an ingenious system of construction that begins with a straightforward vertical wall at the far end of the house, using mud bricks and Nile clay as mortar. Masons then mark a parabolic, catenary arch on this wall with the same clay, before layering more bricks that are cut to an angle with an edge. The base line of these vaulted courses is kept wider than the crown at the top, to that each course will remain in compression leaning against the back wall, until they can be safely straightened out. This restricts the width of the house, or the parallel rooms in it, to about ten to fifteen feet. The mud walls create an effective thermal buffer against the extreme heat of the region and orienting the vaults to align with the prevailing breeze from the river ensures constant ventilation.   *Source:* James Steele

The Jomon House The prehistoric period of Japanese history is named Jomon by archaeologists because of the characteristic way that the people decorated their clay vessels. They wrapped them with twine or cord while they were still wet, and then removed the wrapping before they were fired, to leave deeply etched, serrated lines on the vessels The houses that they built, which have been reconstructed as an outdoor exhibition at a Museum near Yokohama, were a very practical response to the distinctly seasonal climate of Japan, which generally has very cold, snowy winters and hot, humid summers, with a great deal of rain as well. The Jomon people started house construction by digging a round, uniformly deep pit in the ground, about three to six feet below grade. Wood is relatively plentiful in the island nation, and so they then inserted poles into holes that were equally spaced around the perimeter of the pit, leaning inward, like a teepee. The difference between the form of the Jomon house and that of the Native American Plains tribes, however, beside the pit which fixed them to one spot, is that the pre-historic Japanese house used two parallel horizontal ridge beams, about ten feet above grade, supported by an additional two pairs of vertical columns in the center of the house, penetrating the pit floor, which the angled row of perimeter poles rest on. A final horizontal ridge beam, at the top pf the house, then made it possible for the prehistoric builders to make a second smaller pent roof, above the lower angled one that let a bit of light into the house at the gable ends and also let the heat and smoke from the cooking fire, which also provided the only source of warmth in the winter, escape. Jomon houses were roofed with straw thatch, as precursors of the later Minka farmhouse. *Source:* James Steele

Malay House   The Malays are a uniformly identifiable race that has historically occupied territory far beyond the confines of the Malay Peninsula. They are Muslim, and were believed to have been converted as Islam spread eastward from Arabia, by both military and mercantile means. Their traditional house type conforms to what anthropologists have labeled an Australnesia configuration, which includes a premeasured, precut wooden frame, joined by wooden pins that allows the house to be made of a raised floor deck, and a steeply pitched roof with wide eaves overhangs that keeps the windows and the interior, in shade. A master carpenter begins the construction process by measuring the distance from the tip of the housewife's index finger to the elbow of her right arm, which becomes the basic dimension used, in either multiples or divisions for all the structural members used. The carpenters prefer a hard wood like ironwood, or chengal, or teak, but each of these are now protected and when quantities are released for use, are extremely expensive. They are best in the hot, humid climate of this region, however, because they resist rot and infestation by insects, such as termites. After the measurement module is established, the trees are sawn into all of the predetermined pieces necessary. These are then brought to the home site and erected, starting with the tiangseri, which is the main column that supports all of the other structural members of the house. Before the tiangseri is erected, a religious ceremony is held, and a coin is placed beneath its base, for good fortune. Rather than being divided into rooms, the Malay house has flexible, but clearly designated areas, corresponding to public and private uses. Guests are typically received on a spacious front porch and the kitchen is detached, at the back.   *Source:* James Steele

The Minangkabau House The Minangkabau ancestral homeland is located in Sumatra, which is one of the largest islands of the Indonesian archipelago, directly across the Straits of Malaka from peninsular Malaysia. the homes of the people there are very distinctive for several fascinating reasons. The first is that the Minangkabau are a matrilineal rather than patriarchal society. The second reason is that the double peaked shape of the roofs of the houses in this region commemorates a famous foundation legend of the people in it, as does their name. When a Minangkabau woman marries, she and her husband move into her house and occupy a place of honor, to the left of the front door. If the family has more than one daughter the older ones marry first, and as the process continues, the next newly married daughter than replaces the last in the living space near the door of the long narrow house. the living area of the matriarch is to the right of the entrance, so that she can control who comes in and out, and watch over and guide the new arrivals. Each daughter's family is displaced in this way, as they move clockwise around the perimeter of the longhouse, so that the oldest replaces the matriarch when she dies. The foundation myth relates to a David and Goliath like story of a war between the Minangkabau who have gold mines in their region and the covetous Javanese, who wanted them. To settle the dispute the Minangkabau suggested a fight between prize water buffalo chosen by each side. The Javanese chose their biggest, fiercest specimen, but the Minangkabau chose a suckling calf which they starved and attached a curved knife to its nose. When the two were let loose the calf went for the soft underbelly of the bull, looking for milk, and stabbed it to death. The name Minangkabau means "victorious buffalo," and the peaks at each end of their long houses remind these people of that battle.   Courtesy of Ezrin Arbi

The Yemeni House Traditional houses in Yemen are built as towers, in either stone or mud brick, depending on their location and the availability of each material. This vertical form reflects the social stratification in this culture, in which the privacy of the family, and especially the women in that group, is sacrosanct. To ensure this, all of the day-to-day service functions of each household, such as food deliveries, parking and storage, take place on ground level. The next level, above that is reserved for the majlis, which used for entertaining male guests. The women of the family do not mix with these visitors, remaining unseen behind closed doors, where food preparation also takes place. Food for guests is pushed through an opening in the wall between the kitchen and the all male majlis, to prevent interaction with women. There is sometimes an equivalent, totally separate entertaining area for women as well at this level. Family activities take place on the levels above the second floor, but these spaces, too, are often segregated by gender. Bedrooms are at the top of the tower-like house, with those of the father and mother at the highest level. The vertical form of the house also induces natural ventilation as air flows up through the stairway by stack effect. The thick masonry walls kept the intense heat of the region at bay, and the white paint around the windows helps to reduce glare.   © Curt Carnemark/World Bank Archives

He describes a richly textured domestic situation, in which the ground floor was given over to granaries and storage rooms where large wooden boxes, cases of wine, and large implements such as corn grinders were kept. The first floor contained "the dwelling and common living rooms of the residents in which were the boarders, the rooms of the bakers and butlers, and the great chamber in which the lord and his wife slept." [10] The support staff of maids as well as the younger children occupied rooms around the great chamber, and there was also a "private room" nearby, "where at early dawn or in the evening, or during sickness or at a time of bloodletting or for warming the maids or weaned children, they used to have a fire." [11] The upper story was occupied by older, postpubescent children in a series of "garret rooms," in which were, according to Arnold, "on one side the sons (when they wished it), on the other side, the daughters (because they were obliged) of the lord of the house used to sleep." [12] The watchman and family bodyguards also lived on the upper level.

THE *DOMUS AUREA*, ROME

The *Domus Aurea*, or Golden House of the Roman Emperor Nero (Nero Claudius Caesar Drusus Germanicus), was built between A.D. 63 and 68. Nero took advantage of a fire that had ravaged Rome, which some historians believe he started to distract attention from his excesses, as well as to push through a grandiose rebuilding scheme for the city and his own palace. The great fire, which started on July 18 in A.D. 64, ravaged 75 percent of the city, so that only 4 of its 14 districts survived unscathed. The damage to the Palatine Hill and the Forum was especially severe. Nero saw this as an opportunity to seize three of the Seven Hills of Rome, the Palatine, Caelian, and Esquiline promontories, along with part of the Forum, altogether encompassing a total area of about 200 acres, for his own urban estate, displacing hundreds of thousands of people who had lost their homes in the fire in the process. Understandably, this caused a great deal of public resentment. It was intended by the emperor and his architects, Severus and Celer, to be far more than a royal residence, however, and their plans included nothing less than the conversion of the depression between the intersection of the Palatine, Esquiline, and Caelian hills into a forested valley and lake, with a green border separating all of them from the rest of the city, with Nero's house strategically placed in the midst of it. This rural villa in the middle of Rome was about twice the size of the Vatican City today, which is technically a separate state, like the District of Columbia. The site, which was shaped roughly like a triangle with its point facing south, was bounded by the Circus Maximus and Porta Capena on the left diagonal to the southwest, and the fourth century B.C. walls running along the right diagonal to the southeast, with the line of the current Via Cavour and Via Lanza, which closed off the triangle, along its northern edge. [13]

Bringing the Countryside to the City

The *Domus*, which was located in the upper right, or northeastern, quadrant of this huge site, was positioned on a hillside to take maximum advantage of the panoramic view across the lake and valley below and then over the treetops of the

Near the *Domus Aurea.*   Courtesy of Braham Ketcham. *Source:* Flickr

encircling forest to the new marble skyline of the city beyond. The artificial lake, which was the introductory public announcement of the presence of the *Domus,* above it, occupied the area where the Coliseum now stands. An arcade, which wended its way up the slopes of the three hills to the royal residence, with temples located along the way, was announced by a 150 feet high statue of Nero, dressed, or more accurately undressed, to resemble the sun god Helios, complete with radiating crown. As the contemporary historian Suetonius described the scene: "There was a lake like a sea, surrounded by buildings to represent cities, beside tracts of country, varied and plowed fields, vineyards, pastures and woods with a great number of wild and domestic animals." [14]

The plan of the residence is usually published out of context, which makes it look confusing and awkward, unless this stunning topographical setting is also taken into account. It is essentially a 450 yard long ranking of 250 rooms facing in one direction to take full advantage of the southern exposure and the view. The rooms, which are organized in *enfilade,* or series, are organized behind an arcaded cryptoportico that switches from a row of columns to a perforated wall in some places, depending on the amount of privacy desired. This provides shade and protects from glare those who are looking out at the fields, trees, and lake in the distance. The portico also provided a foreground, or frame, to the distant view and acted as a transition between the human environment and the natural worlds similar to the function of the *engawa* of the Japanese house.

Nero's desire to create a rural retreat in the middle of Rome may have come partly from his childhood, which was spent in the countryside. Because of vicious internal strife at court, his mother sent him away to live with distant relatives when he was very young, and he was raised on a farm, before returning to court as the adopted son of the Emperor Claudius, whom Agrippina had married. In their lust for power they assassinated both Claudius and his legitimate son Britannicus so that Nero could become emperor.

The Peristyle and Portico Tradition

However grand, the *Domus Aurea* still conforms to the peristyle and portico tradition used in rural Roman estates since the Republican Period, and so, in spite of the fact that it hardly represents the residential architecture of the status quo, it does offer many insights into the way in which these forms evolved and how they were being dramatically transformed at this stage of Imperial history. The *Domus Aurea* is a creative watershed, after which there was a reflexive return to more pragmatic planning, in keeping with the conservative policies of Nero's immediate successors. There was great dissatisfaction with the house even as it was being built because of its scale, level of ostentation, and the large number of poor that were displaced to make it possible. Half humorous, half sarcastic "warnings" by Suetonius at the time said that, "All Rome is transformed to a villa," and urged his contemporaries to flee before they were engulfed by it.[15]

Power to the People

The bulk of the construction of the *Domus Aurea* was completed over a four-year period, but there are records of parts of it continuing to be built after Nero's death. It only survived, however, for another 40 years before being either demolished or subsumed into public works projects intended to defray discontent with economic disparities of the kind that Nero's lifestyle made all too evident. Vespasian filled in the lake and built his amphitheatre, the Coliseum, over it, temporarily using the vestibule of the *Domus Aurea* to store some of the mechanisms used to raise and lower equipment to and from the wooden floor of the arena. For a time, the statue of Nero that had marked the entrance to the *Domus* stood near the exterior wall of the Coliseum. The main palace is now covered by the Thermae of Trajan, and the public baths of Titus were built on that part of the Esquiline Hill from which the majority of the evictions had taken place that had helped to turn public sentiment against the project in the first place. To these were also added the Temple of Venus and Rome and the Flavian Temple of Peace at the northern edge of the *Domus* with a library in which some of the artwork that Nero had assembled were put on public display. The private paradise of a luxury-loving emperor was eventually transformed, in the words of a historian who is especially knowledgeable about this period, into a "pleasure ground of the masses."[16]

A Lasting Contribution

Since the *Domus Aurea* only existed for such a short time, was so controversial when it was built, and was such a luxurious anomaly, why discuss it here? Several reasons among the many that come to mind should be mentioned. First, it is perhaps the best example among several contenders of a growing confidence in a

Roman, rather than a purely Greek or Hellenistic, identity in residential design, albeit at an elevated social level. As a *parvenu* on the stage of the ancient world in the Republican Period, Rome relatively suddenly was able to exercise the enormous power it both had wrested from others and, in the case of the Attalid Empire, had thrust upon it. It appropriated the symbolic authority it needed to convey its hard-won position from predecessors who had previously held a similar position, such as the Athenian Empire under Pericles and the Hellenistic syncretism initiated by Alexander the Great and perpetuated by his successors, of which Attalus, who founded his own empire at Pergamon, was one. Alexander's adventure began and ended in Persia, in an unprecedented attempt to convert that unbelievably vast part of the world he had conquered to the Hellenic values and traditions that his tutor, Aristotle, had instilled in him when he was a child. His last wife, Roxanne, was Persian, and he encouraged his men to follow his lead, which they did in mass marriages to Persian brides in Persopolis, before he died there. He and the Hellenistic Age that he introduced became so identified with that culture in the Roman consciousness that the luxurious residential tradition that may be traced back to it was disparagingly referred to by them as being "Persian." [17]

But, the adaptations made by the Romans were far more hedonistic than their Greek or Hellenistic predecessors ever dreamed of. The *Domus Aurea* is certainly an unrepressed example of that, as a declaration of independence from a reliance on past styles to convey authority and taste and a new trust in Roman identity alone. The stiff and formally predictable palace of Augustus, which preceded Nero's *Domus* and became the model of decorum for the more conservative emperors who immediately succeeded him, serves as a useful point of comparison. While the *Domus Aurea* is also based on axial symmetry, this only occurs in its individual parts, which are placed within a relatively asymmetrical whole. This gives Nero's Golden House a far more lively and less predictable plan, to say the least.

The *Domus* has been only partially excavated, and further archaeological work has been difficult because it has been fused in some places to the foundations of the buildings that were subsequently built on the site by Nero's contemptuous successors. The part of the plan that is clear, in what appears to be a peristyled courtyard configuration with an elongated rectilinear form, is the sequence of rooms along the northern edge of the court. These are organized in a rank on either side of an octagonally shaped entertainment center and dining room next to a *nymphaeum*, or water garden, which faces into the court, placed off axis to the east. The Romans loved fountains, but the *nymphaeum* was something more, creating nature in microcosm in a series of controlled waterfalls with a rushing sound that must have filled the courtyard and reached into every room that opened onto it. This northeastern edge of what might have been a long and narrow peristyled court terminates in the most important and memorable cluster of spaces that have been discovered in the house so far, called the "Octagon," because of the structural configuration of its central reception space. A constellation of rooms fan out from this central domed entrance, organized symmetrically around the north-south axis that runs through it. Visualizing what they must have looked like and how they might have been used is important because it gives us a keen insight into the worldview of the most powerful man in the Roman Empire at that time and the level of luxury he demanded. This was not just luxury at a material level, of marble, gilt, and jewels or other expensive finishes, but at the conceptual level as well, beyond the gold plating that gave the villa its name.

The Dome Replicates the Sky Vault

The dome covering Nero's dining room was supported by the octagonal configuration of piers that surround the reception hall. It was not just a hemispherical roof, but had an *oculus*, or circular opening, at its apex as a premonition in miniature of Hadrian's famous Pantheon, which followed it. Like the Pantheon, this *oculus* let the sun and moon shine in and the rain pour in as well. A contemporary description of a similar kind of domed space in Varro's villa at Casino gives us an idea of what this one might have been like. Varro's dome had a mechanism attached to the curved inner surface to imitate the astronomical movements of the sky vault it imitated, so that it could also be used to tell time. There was also a compass shown on the inside of the dome.

A wall painting of the ceiling plan of the *oculus* found in the *Domus* indicates that the inner surface of the dome was a *trompe l'oeil* of the sky with Helios and his entourage in the midst of the clouds above. This painting is not only a reminder that every surface in the house was probably painted, but more importantly that the Roman consciousness of three-dimensional space and how to structurally manipulate it was so well developed at this time that a ceiling plan, which is a scaled diagram of the ceiling as it looks when lying on the floor below it, would be considered to be a perfectly natural pattern to replicate on the wall of a residence and be recognized as being the spatial configuration of the Octagon of the *Domus Aurea* as well.

The Romans adopted the Greeks' habit of eating in a reclining position, possibly because they thought it was more civilized and better for the digestion, so that sitting at a table was considered to be plebian. This made it difficult for more than three people to eat together since the wealthy also had servants who had to have access to a table that the recumbent trio would share. The perfect solution was the *triclinium*, which was a U-shaped arrangement of couches, with a table in the middle and access for service at the open fourth side. The Octagon has four sets of *triclinia*, with two on opposite sides of the entry axis, near the peristyle and the door, and two splayed out like ears, on the upper sides of the domed Octagon, which were more private. These are separated by a fountain that cascaded down a stairway, placed directly on axis with the front door. This entire ensemble, of domed central space and surrounding sets of *triclinia* culminating in a stepped cascade that took pride of place at the most visible part of the composition, was flanked by a symmetrical pair of apsidal halls, presumably each used for the display of a sculpture.[18]

A Royal Dinner Party

With the location and function of each of these spaces in mind, then, it is possible to conjure up what a dinner party with Nero in the Octagon might have been like. The approach to the reception room would have begun near the lake with guests being led through the cryptoporticoes lined with temples, by the emperor's bodyguard, ending at the top of a hill. It would probably have then proceeded along the courtyard through the colonnade of the peristyle, past the *nymphaeum*, from the west. Guests would have passed a series of long narrow and extremely high vaulted rooms, open to the arcade in which they were walking, which were either shrines or exhibition niches, for sculpture. To give some idea of the scale of these vaulted spaces, the famous sculptures called the *Laocoon*, which was discovered during the Renaissance and had such a profound influence on Michelangelo and others at that time, was exhibited in one of them. Guests then passed to the large vaulted water garden that dominated the entire residential composition and served to announce the Octagon in the middle of the courtyard. They would then turn left, through a doorway in a massive, brick clad concrete wall into the central domed space, just after a brief glimpse of a major sculpture in the apsidal hall near the front door. As the host, Nero would have then taken his place in the middle of the Octagon, under the golden dome, as the living representative of Helios. The floor, which was wooden under the dome, was turned by a gear driven by the waterfall cascading down a passage opposite from the entrance and under the floor to move it. Panels would have opened above him to shower flower petals down on him, and perfume would have misted down on the assembled guests from pipes on the wall. Braziers would have provided light, and moonlight would have been streaming through the *oculus;* there would have been music, perhaps some of it even provided by him, since he played the lyre. Many servants would have been moving about with trays of food, served to those at each of the *triclinia*. Nero may have been a megalomaniac, but he may have been right in saying, when he was forced to commit suicide because of his misrule, that "what an artist dies with me."

GREEK HOUSES IN THE CITIES OF ASIA MINOR

If they are given any credence at all in histories of ancient Greece, the cities in Asia Minor are usually relegated to a secondary position of influence and treated as the grateful beneficiary of the unparalleled cultural strides made on the mainland in Attica. The truth is quite the opposite, as many of the intellectual and philosophical innovations that made this progress possible are known to have originated in Asia Minor, and then to have moved West. The litany of these influences, while not widely known, is extensive and has been recited in several other sources. The important point to reiterate, however, is that these innovations were not of a superficial nature, but penetrate to the very heart of the Hellenic ethos.

Ionia

Ionia, which was the central region of the Aegean coastline of Asia Minor that separated Aeolia on the north from Caria on the south, originally took its name from a quasi-mythical patriarch named Ion. While he is conventionally listed as having been the son of an early Athenian king named Xuthus and Queen Creusa, and of having led a colonization effort from Athens to Asia Minor in the wake of the Dorian invasions of 1120 B.C., there are less well-known and extremely tantalizing variations of this foundation myth. While most sources agree about the four Ionian tribes that grew out of the four sons of Ion, named Geleontes, Argadeis,

Aigikareis, and Hopletes, another less well-known genealogy places the origin of Ion much further to the east. In the biblical "Tale of Nations" in *Genesis*, it states that:

> This is the account of Shem, Ham, Japeth, Noah's sons, who themselves had sons after the flood. The sons of Japeth (were) Gomer, Magog, Madai, Javan, Tubal, Meshech and Tiras ... The sons of Javan (were) Elishah, Tarshish, Kittim, and Dodanim. From these, the maritime peoples spread out into their territories by their clans within their nations, each with their own language.

In his overview of the Asiatic elements in Greek civilization, Sir William Ramsay has raised the point that the Greek version of Javan is Ion, and it is also interesting to note that the area strongly indicated by tradition as the starting point for Noah's flock is Mount Ararat in eastern Anatolia. Whatever the true origin of Ion was, the region of Ionia in Asia Minor is most likely to have been the birthplace of the poet Homer, whose *Iliad* and *Odyssey* both had an incalculable impact upon Hellenic religion, mythology, and social values.[19]

While several Ionian cities have laid claim to this honor, the island of Chios, which is about five miles from the Turkish coastline, is widely acknowledged to have been his home, as well as the location of a group of his disciplines called the Homeridae, who perpetuated his poems through recitation until they were finally codified around 750 B.C. While the dramatic events that Homer speaks about were probably derived from a cataclysm that took place at Troy around 1195 B.C., those that feel that he alone composed *The Iliad* also believe that he did so about 1000 B.C. Once called "the Bible of Hellenism," *The Iliad* was such an essential part of early Greek education that it was memorized verbatim and recited aloud in much the same way that Koranic verses are recited in Islamic schools today. As in the current example recited, such readings were not only intended to teach the basic skills of spelling and reading but were also considered to be an effective way of inculcating the basic values that are contained in the verse. In the case of *The Iliad*, those values revolved around the importance of personal courage, valor, and honor and were presented in such a way as to stress continually the degree of human frailty in comparison to the immortality of the gods.

A Pantheon of Individuals

Homer, as well as Hesiod, personified vividly each deity in the Greek pantheon in such a way that their highly individualized characteristics could be understood by the common man and easily linked with the natural phenomenon they were meant to embody. As historian Michael Grant has so aptly described this important identification: "Homer and Hesiod were credited, more plausibly, with the remarkable achievement of standardizing and welding together the Olympic gods for Greece [and] Homer in particular makes of them ... a collection of perilously powerful divinities full of vices and foibles." [20] Many of the deities in that pantheon originally sprang from Eastern cults. Dionysus, for example, who may have been so instrumental in the rites behind the formation of Greek drama, is known to have had his origins in the worship of Diouns, who was the Phrygian god of vegetation. Other obvious examples are the Greek goddess Artemis, who was derived from the ancient Anatolian mother goddess Kybele, or Cybele, as well as Zeus, who bore a strong resemblance to Kronos, who was the Hittite god of heaven. This later comparison even extends to the wives of these "fathers of the gods," who were called Hera and Hepat, respectively. Such similarities can be noted for virtually every member of the Olympian pantheon, indicating the degree to which Homer did indeed manage to Hellenise many diverse religious conventions into a single tradition. As Sir William Ramsey has said: "One remarkable fact strikes every observer, and that is that the personal names in old Greek mythology are rarely Greek." [21]

With Alexander, and his love of Homer's *Iliad*, then, the influence of Ionia comes around full circle in that a Macedonian who was more Greek than the Greeks was able to bring Hellenism back to the region where its highest ideals had been formulated in the first place. The generating influence of Ionia in this circle does not stop there, however, but may be said to extend even further to the first Persian incursions into the Aegean area of Asia Minor. Their rule of this area, which followed the capture and sack of Sardis in 546 B.C. and their eventual conquest of each of the Ionian cities in their turn, was not particularly harsh and was administered at a distance through a system of local satraps or governors. Yet, even this intrusion was unacceptable and in 499 B.C. the Ionians and particularly Aristagoras of Miletus instigated a revolt to throw the Persians out. Efforts to find allies in this revolt on the mainland were not as successful as originally expected, but Athens did send 20 ships and Eretria sent 5. In a naval battle off the island of Lade, which has long since been fused by a field of silt to the place where Miletus once proudly stood overlooking its harbor, the Persians shattered the badly organized confederation, and the ensuing destruction of Miletus thus became a foregone conclusion. After this battle in 494 B.C., the Persians went on to try to punish those who had assisted the Ionians in their revolt, leading to the famous battle of Marathon in 490. This was followed ten years later by a major Persian expedition that led to the capitulation of Athens and the burning of the Parthenon, which incensed Greeks everywhere. The ensuing formation of the Delian League, with Athens at its head, and the eventual restoration of that city, which led to the Persian defeat at Eurymedon in 467, was not sufficient to erase that blasphemy. In a very real sense, the Hellenic crusade called for by Isocrates was a direct result of the painful memory of that invasion, even though nearly a century and a half had passed between the desecration of the Acropolis and Alexander's crossing of the Dardanelles to free Asia Minor from Persian rule.

Institutions Common to All Cities

The major buildings typically found in all of the Hellenistic cities of Asia Minor at this time, such as the *bouleuterion*, gymnasium, and theatre, are strategically placed to punctuate the path of movement from harbor to agora, acting as landmarks with the linked spaces that they individually dominate.

Priene

Priene, which is most memorable for the strict imposition of a Hippodamian grid upon a dramatic cliffside site, did not have a symbiotic relationship with its

Ephesus, Turkey, Asia.   Courtesy of Shuttercock

harbor, which was called Naulochos, as many other Greek cities did, but did rely upon it as a lifeline nonetheless. Because of its relatively inaccessible location, much of Priene's formidable circuit wall, as well as many of its public buildings and houses, have remained basically intact and still present a vivid image of the city, as it must have been in the Hellenistic period. The fine state of preservation of many buildings such as the bouleuterion to the north of the central agora and the theatre have greatly improved our understanding of the function of such buildings. Like Miletus, Priene is a masterpiece of open public spaces that are effectively separated from the private residential areas and is very instructive of the ways in which a regular grid can become a liberating rather than a restrictive device in urban planning.

In the private realm, the courtyard houses that have survived in the western part of the city are also in a good state of preservation, and rival those in Delos in their ability to recall the everyday life of the people who once lived there. Besides providing a clear example of what urban planner Jacqueline Trywhitt once called the "human-scale intermediary" in urban planning, in which there is a logical graduation of open spaces from public agora to private residential courtyard in the city, both the variety of scale and degree of finish in these homes show how far contemporary expectations of what can be achieved in average domestic surroundings have deteriorated.

House 22 on Theatre Street

Priene is a model of rational Hippodamian planning in that all of the blocks were identical in dimension and each had four houses, divided by party walls. One of these, designated as House 22 by archaeologists, is still in relatively good condition and gives a clear idea what life in Priene, at its height of prestige, must have been like. It is located to the west of the theatre, on the north side of the street that leads to that institution and now takes its name from it. It exemplifies the Greek respect for outward modesty, being plain in front, with only a single door in an otherwise unassuming wall facing the street. Upon entering there is a covered colonnaded walkway that leads to the open central courtyard, and this has all the major rooms of the house, such as the dining room, grouped around it, with the most prominent of these, of unknown use, being on the north. This space looks like a temple, with Doric forecourt, pediment, and gabled roof. It is believed to have been the living area, or *oecus*, with the dining room or *andron* to its left. Bedrooms were on the second level, also overlooking the court.[22]

Delos

It is a bit of a stretch to say that Delos is in Ionia, because this 5 kilometer long, 1.3 kilometer wide island is claimed by the Cyclades in the middle of the Aegean. But it played a key role in the history of Ionia because it was the headquarters and central bank of the Delian Confederacy. Pericles had established this institution as a means of defense against the Persian Empire, and its members decided that the tiny island of Delos was neutral enough to suit each of them.

Delos is also important in Greek mythology as the birthplace of the twin deities Apollo and Artemis, fathered by Zeus and borne by Leto, who took refuge there from the vengeful jealousy of Hera. A settlement is recorded on Delos as early as the third millennium B.C., on the Kinthos Hill, and another was established in the Sacred Precinct by the seventh century B.C. This was just before the island came under the influence of Naxos, and its subsequent sacralization by King Peisistratos in the sixth century B.C., involving the relocation of all tombs on Delos to the neighboring island of Rhoneia.

Its status as a sacred precinct continued to grow, attracting pilgrims from all over the Hellenic world. The main harbor was located on the western edge of the island and a sacred way led from it to the Sanctuary of Apollo. There was an impressive line of temples, high altars, and civic buildings lined up along the waterfront that must have made an arrival at the Delos harbor quite spectacular. There were eventually four temples dedicated to Apollo in this grouping, the latest of which is also known as the Temple of the Athenians. The treasury, where the combined contributions of each of the members of the Delian Confederacy were kept, was located at the northern end of the island near an Ionic temple dedicated to Artemis. Further north still is the Sacred Lake, the Terrace of the Lions, the Letoon, the Agora of the Italians, the Stadium, and the Gymnasium, near to a narrow channel that separates Delos from Rhoneia.

During the Hellenistic period, Delos benefited from the attention of several rulers who tried to outdo each other in their contributions to the sanctuaries there. Control of the island passed to the Romans, but they gave control back to Athens in 166 B.C., leading to its designation as a free port. Wealth followed and by the middle of the second century B.C., a number of elegant houses were built by those who benefited from commercial gain, on the northern end of the island.[23]

The Houses of Delos

The polyglot culture created by the transformation of Delos to a free port resulted in the polarized residential districts as well as the public facilities on the island into separate ethnic enclaves. The houses on the northern slopes differ widely depending on the financial status of the owner, but almost all of them have at least one, if not two or more, central courtyards.[24] This basic Greek typology, which may be found throughout the Hellenic world as early as the fifth century, was most notably augmented by Hellenistic and Roman influence by the addition of mosaics, which are still in place in many of these houses. They differ from their Roman counterparts in being made of finely cut pieces of stone and are more expressive. They usually cover the entire courtyard, which was placed a few steps lower than the peristyle that surrounded it to prevent the rainwater that fell into the court from flooding the rest of the house. The dining room and other domestic spaces such as bedrooms were typically arranged around the sides of the peristyle, opening up to the court.

The House of the Masks, which dates from the time of the Athenian conversion of the island to a free port, has a long offset entrance leading into a large walled-in forecourt, which then opens into the central court itself. There is a more direct, but less obvious, second entrance into this court, probably used by the family as a less formal and circuitous way of coming into the house. As elsewhere, a peristyle encloses this court, and the other rooms, now designated the Room of the Masks, because of the theme of the floor mosaic, the Room with Amphora Mosaics, and the Room with the Mosaic of Dionysos Riding a Panther, all face onto the northern end of this peristyle and the court beyond.[25]

The lifestyle that these houses supported was short-lived, however, because the island was invaded and destroyed by Mithradates in 88 B.C. The substantial insights into that brief time of luxury, provided mostly by the mosaics that still survive, indicate a period of sophistication and grace.

KHIROKITIA, CYPRUS

Khirokitia is a Neolithic settlement located on the slope of a hill overlooking the Maroniou River valley about 10 miles from the southern coast of Cyprus. It was surrounded by a massive 10 feet high stone wall that was just slightly less thick than it was high. There was controlled access into the settlement through a limited number of gates, underscoring its role as both a fortress and an inhabited village, as well as the degree of insecurity that those who lived there must have felt during that uncertain time.

A Mysterious Gap

It is curious that, while other areas of Greece to the north and east of Cyprus have evidence of Paleolithic and Mesolithic culture, no trace of these historical

Paphos historic site in Cyprus.   Courtesy of Shutterstock

periods has yet to be found on Cyprus. Some have attributed this to the relative isolation of the island, which may have deterred the growth of pre-Neolithic cultures there. The sea is known to have always been a challenge to the migration of people during the Prehistoric Period because they lacked the skills necessary to build sailing vessels big enough to navigate open waters. There is evidence of oceangoing vessels from this early period, to be sure, but nothing of the kind has yet to be found on Cyprus. The Neolithic Period there actually occurred in several stages, divided into Neolithic I, without pottery, and Neolithic II, after it appeared. The earliest evidence of pottery at Khirokitia occurred in 4000 B.C., but carbon 14 tests have shown that there was human activity on the site, before pottery was used there, as early as 5800 B.C. Since archaeologists estimate that the end of the first Neolithic Period occurred around 5000 B.C., there is a hiatus of about 1,500 years that has yet to be satisfactorily explained. No substantial evidence to solve the mystery has yet been found at Khirokitia, but at Troulli, on the northern coast of the island, pottery from an intermediate Neolithic Period has been found. There has been speculation that the island was abandoned at about 5000 B.C., and then reoccupied by new settlers about 3500, but this has yet to be substantiated.

Khirokitia is one of the most important archaeological discoveries in its region and one of the best preserved Neolithic settlements in the world. It was first excavated by Porphyrios Dikaios of the Cyprus Department of Antiquities in 1934, who has said that it is "by far the most representative example yet found of the architecture, art and social structure of Neolithic Greece." Although only a small portion of the settlement has yet to be excavated, a magnetometric survey of the area has shown that a majority of the hill was occupied.

Hunter-Gatherers and Farmers

Studies of the skeletons found there, and especially craniological analysis, have not conclusively determined where the settlers of Khirokitia actually came from, with theories running the gamut from a distinct group not related to any neighboring region, possibly from the Balkans, Thessaly, Macedonia, or Cilicia, to indigenous builders. It is certain, however, that these first inhabitants were both hunter-gatherers and farmers, fitting neatly into that transitional period between a purely nomadic existence and the stationary agricultural phase that followed it, when urban settlements were firmly established. These early Neolithic settlers were attracted to this site because it was elevated and so could easily be protected and was free from floods. It was also close to the Maroniou River, which has a fertile valley and perennial springs. These provided a continuous source of food and water for the settlement. Also, since the sea is only four miles away, to the south, it was easily accessible by traveling through the valley, so the villagers could fish from the shore or organize tentative expeditions in small boats.

Circular Houses

The houses that have been excavated in Khirokitia thus far indicate a high level of construction skill and lifestyle. The bed of the Maroniou River is dry for part of the year, and stones provided the material with which to build the foundations of the houses as well as to make tools, such as hammers and axes. The houses that have been found are all circular in plan with stone and rubble walls built up to a height of about 3 feet. Archaeologists believe that these foundations were capped with superstructures of mud brick or earth tamped down into a wooden form, now referred to as *terre pisé*.

These structures, known as *tholoi*, had either domed or conical roofs, which were additionally supported by a wooden or stone column in the center of the house. Subsequently, during the Bronze Age, elegant *tholoi* reappear in Mycenae and elsewhere throughout the Argolid, made completely of cut stone and referred to as dressed ashlar, without supporting columns in the center. This is because, by this time, builders had mastered the technique of corbelling, which involves stepping each flat stone incrementally and progressively inward as the circular wall is built, in a gradual curve, until the space is covered.

The house form found at Khirokitia has also been used in much earlier prototypes, such as in the Natufian culture in the Levant, and it persisted on Cyprus, even as other societies around it began to adopt rectangular plans for theirs. There was usually an opening at the apex of the roof for the smoke from the hearth in the center of the room below to escape. There were also built-in stone benches around the perimeter that served as tables or beds. The floor was of tamped down earth. Sometimes, in addition to the central column, there were two others made of stone that supported a second, attic story used for additional sleeping quarters or for storage, accessible by a wooden ladder.

A House with Many Rooms

Archaeologists originally assumed that each *tholos* represented an independent house, but renewed excavations have indicated that one residence may have combined several of them, with each one used for a different purpose. There is also one *tholos* that is bigger than the others, which may have been set aside for the leader of the community, or it may have been used for the production of goods of some kind, since nearly two-thirds of its perimeter was covered by a roof, as if shops were located inside.[26] The passageway covered the east, west, and north sides of this larger *tholos*, and there was an opening on the south for ventilation in the summer and the lower winter sun.

All of these *tholoi* show considerable skill in construction, but the overall planning of the village does not, since the houses seem to be built randomly, occupying every available space in an organic arrangement. The *tholoi* are so close together that there is only room for narrow pedestrian passageways between them, which wind through the entire village. There is evidence that there was one main road, which crossed through the settlement at an oblique angle from a bend in the river to the south, leading up to the top of the hill. It seems to have been the major access to the water supply, and so was the lifeline of the settlement. As houses were added along its edge, the surface of the road was raised, until today its embankments look like a wall, because some of these houses have disappeared. Since the village was also surrounded by a wall, archaeologists have found it difficult to determine just where the main street ends and the wall begins. But, they are sure that the wall turned to form the western limit of the village. There were no houses built beyond this point during the primary period of occupation, although some did appear to be added much later, as population increased, and a second defensive wall was added to incorporate and protect them. Based on the number of houses uncovered and the most recent assessment of room functions, it is estimated that at its peak Khirokitia only had a population of about 600. But, it should be mentioned that the Bronze Age cities of Homer's *Iliad*, such as Troy, Mycenae, Tiryns, and Gla, which had such an enormous historical impact on the Hellenic imagination and value system after the Dark Ages ended after their fall, nearly 500 years later, were also relatively small in scale and population.

Based on skeletal evidence, the inhabitants were fairly diminutive, with an average height of 1.61 meters for men and 1.51 meters for women. Infant mortality was high, although the life expectancy in the village was about ten years longer than that of its Neolithic neighbors averaging in the mid thirties. As in Çatal Hüyük, the dead were buried under the floor of the house, but rather than an inhumation burial, in which the body was left outside, exposed to the elements until the bones were stripped clean and then wrapped in cloth for burial inside, the dead in Khirokitia were placed in a fetal position, directly under the surface of the floor, buried with implements, such as stone bowls that were ceremoniously broken as part of the funeral rite. Cornelian bead necklaces have also typically been found on the skeletons of the women. Sometimes huge stone slabs were placed flat over the graves. Flint sickle blades have also been found inside the houses, confirming that this was mainly a farming community, but the presence of flint arrowheads, and the skeletal remains of deer indicate that hunting was still practiced. Other bones, of sheep, goats, and pigs, suggest that these animals may have been domesticated at this early date. They also indicate a very varied diet, since the seeds of figs, olives, and prunes have also been found, as well as pistachio shells.

Fine Implements

A more detailed idea of the daily life of the people in this village may also be conveyed by a description of the bowls they used for cooking and eating. These were made of andesite, a stone they collected from the riverbed, rubbed thin against another stone into perfect shapes with nearly translucent sides, with patterns engraved on the sides. Some had spouts but most did not. Some of these vessels are made of a black stone that does not exist on the island and so must have been imported or traded from somewhere else, perhaps Anatolia or Northern Syria where vessels made from this material have also been found. Spindle whorls and needles found in the houses also indicate that the people of this village wove their own textiles.

KNOSSOS, CRETE

The first advanced civilization in the Aegean basin developed on Crete in the early part of the Bronze Age and lasted until it was weakened by the eruption of a volcano on the island of Thera in 1450 B.C. This destroyed much evidence of it, except for the city of Knossos, which was destroyed much later, around 1375 B.C., possibly due to a Mycenaean invasion from mainland Greece. There is ample, irrefutable evidence of the cataclysmic destruction of Thera, now Santorini, by a volcano, since half the island, which now appears as a semicircular bay, is missing. Studies of the ash caused by the volcano on the sea bottom and on Crete have confirmed that it reached the island, and some geologists have speculated that it may have traveled as far as Egypt. There were 30,000 people on Thera at the time of the eruption, but the lack of any human remains as well as the presence of frescos depicting an evacuation by long boats indicate that they may have all had time to escape. An earthquake accompanied the eruption, which may have caused a tsunami that compromised the Minoan ability to defend themselves against a Mycenaean invasion.

An Elegant Culture

The culture that this volcanic eruption bought to the verge of extinction was highly refined and developed. It was fostered by the cultivation of grapes and olives, which also yielded wine and olive oil. This gave it an advantage over northern Greece, which was restricted to growing wheat and barley. This allowed the economy and the standard of living in this part of the Aegean to grow more quickly. Archaeologists have divided the Bronze Age, which began in 3000 B.C. and ended in 1100 B.C., into early, middle, and late periods in this region, with several subheadings in each period. On Crete, in a much simplified chronology, this translates into Early Minoan I, II, and III, from 3000 to 2000 B.C., Middle Minoan IA, IB, II, and IIIA and IIIB from 2000 to 1600 B.C., and Late Minoan IA, IB, II, IIIA, IIIB, and IIIC from 1600 to 100 B.C. The description of Minoan architecture that follows focuses mainly on the period from 1600 to 1500 B.C.

The ruins visible in Knossos today represent different historical periods. The first of them is a part of the city that was built in the Middle Minoan IA period, but was burned down around 1700 B.C. The palace was then rebuilt on a much larger scale and was remodeled and enlarged over a period of 300 years, until much of the building erected during this phase was once again destroyed by a large

Knossos ruins.   Courtesy of Shutterstock

earthquake. The palace was reconstructed again, when the Minoan culture was at its height, and finally destroyed.

Inspired by the Myth of the Minotaur

The discovery of Knossos is one of the greatest, and now most controversial, archaeological adventures in modern history. The story behind it reads like a detective thriller, including clandestine meetings in smoke-filled bars, the transfer of top secret information, and a high stakes gamble with a small fortune in the balance. Sir Arthur Evans began working on Knossos in 1900, when he was 49 years old. It was his first archaeological project. Before he became involved, however, a Cretan merchant named Minos Kalokairinos had made trial excavations on the site, digging 12 trenches that revealed parts of the palace only six feet below the surface. The pottery that he unearthed caused a great deal of excitement on Crete, to the extent that the Parliament passed a resolution forbidding him to dig any further in fear that the Ottoman government that then controlled the area would take over the project and remove all the finds to the Imperial Museum in Istanbul.

Evans learned of Kalokairinos's finds and, after meeting with him, went to examine the collection of pottery and shards taken from the trenches. This prompted him to decide to excavate the site himself, buying as much of it as possible. This involved obtaining permission from Istanbul and transferring about a million dollars of Evans's personal fortune to finalize the purchase. It was not long after he began excavation that Evans concluded that this city was built by a people of great originality, vigor, and aesthetic achievement. They had sustained their culture there for more than 1,000 years and had disappeared without a trace. They were extraordinarily gifted builders and fresco painters with an obvious love of luxury and life. Knossos appeared to him to be the epicenter of a *thalassocracy*, a maritime civilization like Athens and Britain after it, that reached and maintained ascendancy through a powerful navy and the domination of the sea. Subsequent evidence of their trade as far afield as Egypt and Western Asia supports this view, as well as

Early Minoan house at Knossos.   Courtesy of Shutterstock

the Minoans' high level of sophistication. They were an elegant and not particularly warlike people who were totally unlike the Mycenaeans, who competed with them for economic markets around the Aegean and Mediterranean Seas, as well as the Assyrians, Hittites, and Egyptians at that time. There were no battle frescos or overtly aggressive scenes of self-aggrandizement in their art, just images of a joyously happy fashion-conscious people who obviously loved life.

The palace that Evans continued to excavate was, in its prime, the center of an extraordinary culture. It was not only a royal residence, and home to the extensive retinue that the royal family required, but also a religious and administrative center. It did not resemble any other residences of similar function built during the same historical period elsewhere and so could not be easily defined. Stone, wood, and gypsum were the main materials used to build it, and at its furthest extent it was five stories high in some parts.

The palace was supported by wooden columns, which are unusual in that they taper outward from bottom to top, rather than the other way around, as classical Greek columns do. Their wide capitals made it possible to use wider spans, which reduced the numbers of wooden beams necessary to support the roof. Few of these columns remained when Evans excavated the site, so he and his team recreated them from wall paintings and from their own imaginations.

The Labyrinth of the Minotaur

During his excavation of the palace, including a *megaron* with a throne still in place against one of its walls, and frescos showing acrobats vaulting over the back of a charging bull and a double headed axe or *labrys*, which was the royal symbol,

113

Evans also uncovered a large compartmentalized chamber beneath it. He concluded that he had found the mythological labyrinth supposedly built by King Minos to imprison the Minotaur. Lacking any evidence at the time to help him determine what this culture had called itself, he decided to call it Minoan. The legend of King Minos and the Minotaur, which inspired his choice of a name for this culture, focuses on Minos who was a son of Zeus. Zeus saw Europa, the daughter of the Phoenician king Agenor, picking flowers with her friends near the seashore. He fell in love with her at first sight, but thought he would not be attractive to her, and so he changed himself into a bull and cavorted around her, tempting her to ride him. When she did, he swam off to Crete with her on his back. Three sons, named Minos, Rhadamanthys, and Sarpedon were born to them there. Minos later ruled Crete using laws given to him every nine years by his father, Zeus. Minos married Pasiphaë, and they had four sons and four daughters, living in the royal palace at Knossos. The legend goes on to say that Minos, in his desire to make a sacrifice to Poseidon, prayed that the god of the sea would send him a suitable offering. Poseidon sent Minos a beautiful white bull, but Minos decided to keep it and sacrificed another instead. As a punishment, Poseidon made Pasiphaë lust after the bull that he had sent to Minos, and the Minotaur, who had a man's body and a bull's head, was the result. Minos imprisoned it in a labyrinth below the palace that his architect Daidalos designed for it.[27]

Evans subsequently presented his theories about Minoan culture in a series of four books entitled *The Palace of Minos*, which were released between 1921 and 1936. He also wrote two books dealing with the artifacts and inscriptions, which at the time of his excavations could not be translated. These included tablets carved with a primitive form of Greek, which Evans called Linear B and which were deciphered 52 years after Evans's excavation by architect Michael Ventris, who had a passion for linguistics. There was no mention on any of the inscriptions of the name the Minoans had used to refer to themselves, but translations of an Egyptian stele refer to them as *Kiftiu*.

Evans's theories about Knossos went unchallenged for nearly 50 years, while he was the only excavator there. But after he left, others began to contest his theories and his methods, putting forward alternative views about the way the rooms in the palace had been used and about the fate of the Minoans themselves. An alternative view, that Mycenaeans who had conquered the Minoans, rather than the Minoans themselves, had been living there when it was finally destroyed, was supported by Ventris's translations.

A Palace Culture

In addition to Knossos, there were five other centers of power on Crete at this time, at Mallia, Phaistos, Hagia Triada, Keos, and Gournia. It appears that they did not fight among themselves and that Knossos possibly ruled the rest as a political and religious capital by mutual consent. The palace of Knossos, then, was the hub of a powerful kingdom, with a reach that extended over the entire region, the focal point of a highly centralized religiously based bureaucracy. The rectangular court can immediately be recognized as a unifying feature in the balance of each of the six main cities on Crete, and each has similar proportions. The courtyard of the Place at Mallia, for example, measures 165 feet by 72.5 feet compared to that at Knossos, which is 165 feet by 82.5 feet. The general rule is that each of these courts is roughly twice as long in the north-south direction as they are on the east-west axis to provide shade during the summer and to capture the lower winter sun in the winter for more warmth.

The palace of Knossos is divided into eastern and western wings. The west wing was higher, since it was located on a hillside and had fewer levels than the east wing, which terraced down a slope into a valley. The so-called "Royal Villa," which is located at some distance from the main palace complex, to the north-south, faces east, with a view over the valley toward the Kairatos River. It is two stories high, with access by a stairway connected to a light well in the southwest corner. It has a main hall with a throne located behind a balustrade on the ground floor, with a crypt, thought to have been used for religious sacrifices, next to it. The arrangement of the columned portico leading into the royal hall, as well as the use of a court or well to light the stair and lower levels, and the thick masonry construction are typical of the architecture found in the main palace. The walls are faced with white gypsum, and the floors are paved with stone slabs coated in the same way.

The Theatre and the Lustral Bath

The entrance to the Royal Villa is axial, which is one of the few instances of a straightforward entry in Knossos. The Minoans seem to have been fond of asymmetrical, indirect entrances and room arrangements that created right angles.

The main entrance to the palace, into the southern end of this rectangular plaza, is a perfect example of that, bending through opposing L-shaped turns before allowing access to a *propylaeum* and a stair that leads up and into this grand open space. At ground level, the palace is clearly zoned into formal and ceremonial spaces in the southeastern quadrant, with craft workshops and related storage relegated to the northeast quarter and "magazines" for the storage of wine olives and olive oil aligned in sequence along the entire western edge of the sloping hill that the palace stood on. Artists and workmen occupied the northeast section of the palace and specific jobs were carried out in each section. For example, olives were pressed in one room, and oil flowed away through a type of drain to a spout in a wall about 50 feet away. In other rooms, pots were made and painted, stone vases were carved, metal art was molded, sculptures were chiseled, and other types of artistic activities were carried out. The walls at this ground level are all massive to support the weight of the floors above and to keep these spaces, which are used as storage areas for perishables in some cases, as cool as possible.

Lustral Basins

An "Initiatory Area," or lustral basin, intended for ritual cleansing, is located near the northwest entrance to the palace complex and is the largest of several such basins found throughout it. It is reminiscent of a similar bathing tank found in Mohenjo-daro, also described in this volume, and Evans believed these were used for more than just communal bathing. He named the northwest lustral basin in the belief that it provided a place for those entering the city to perform an ablution before doing so. A theatre or public viewing area is located nearby, just outside the palace precinct, which is also thought to have served a ritual purpose, such as a dancing area, or may also have been a place to carry out legal sentences.

A long straight corridor, which runs directly from the *propylaeum* at the south, to the Initiatory Area near the entrance to the central plaza on the north, effectively separates the magazines from a series of shrine rooms and a throne suite, facing directly into the court.

The Royal Apartments

The royal apartments, which are concentrated along the eastern edge of the central courtyard on the upper levels, progressively overhang the rooms on the levels below to shade them. A grand staircase at the middle of the courtyard on this side provided the main means of access to these floors, and the bearing walls become increasingly thinner on the higher levels, according to reduced structural requirements. The columns used here, as throughout the palace and the rest of the city, are unique to Minoan civilization. Rather than being thicker at the bottom and tapering upward toward the capital, the Minoan column is counterintuitive and does just the opposite. This may have something to do with providing more space in a room at floor level, or is a result of using an actual tree trunk as the column shaft, which would have been prevented from sprouting any new branches by turning it upside down.[28] Whatever the reason, the tapering column profile, with its slim base and bulbous capital, has become a memorable architectural symbol of Minoan culture. It is certainly no coincidence that a single column of this distinctive profile appears between a pair of rampant lions as a symbol of Mycenaean power on the outside façade of the Lion Gate, which was the main entrance into Mycenae, as a clear example of the appropriation of power by one culture from another through the deliberate borrowing of a potent icon.

The Queen's Megaron or Hall

One of the most elegant of the residential apartments in the Palace of Knossos, as well as arguably being among the most representative of the Minoan style itself, is the Queen's Megaron or Hall. Located next to the throne room, the wall above the entry and the ceiling are a riot of colors that reflect an island culture that thrived because of maritime trade. It is predominantly covered by frescos rendered in aquatic blue. The lone narrow panel above the door that connects the apartment through a right angled corridor to the Hall of the Double Axes next to it is dominated by a playful dolphin motif, separated from the doors below by a horizontal band of blue rosettes that continues in vertical stripes of the same broad width, down each door jamb to the floor. The ceiling, on the other hand, is covered by a repetitive pattern of interlocking spirals that recall the waves of the ocean in the same way that the volutes of an Ionic capital on a column of that order do. The spirals are white on an azure field that is slightly darker than the shade of blue used on either the dolphins or the rosettes, giving it more intensity and drawing the line of sight upward.

By contrast, the other three sides of the 14 feet by 20 feet (4.3 meters by 6.1 meters) room are syncopated by a series of long narrow piers that terminate on top of a ledge on each side. This could have been used as a built-in seat, since it is about 4 feet wide and 3 feet high, projecting past the edge of the piers by about 9 inches. The piers and the frame around them are dark beige, and the panels that result from the depth of the jambs of the openings that they make possible were also used to place frescos in them, which depict a series of dancing women.

The height of these built-in seats and the frescos of women, as well as the proximity of the apartment to the King's Megaron, suggested to Arthur Evans that it was meant for a queen. That interpretation has since been questioned, but the guides that lead visitors through the apartment today are certainly convinced, avidly describing the Queen's Bathroom, on the west side of this hall, which still has a clay bathtub inside it reconstructed from pieces found near the doorway, as well as the Queen's Dressing Room, connected by corridor to it, and the Queen's Privy, which was separate from the room where the bathtub was found.

Natural Light

One of the most striking things about this apartment, irregardless of its occupant, is the use of layering, created by two light wells, on the east and south edges of the rectangular hall. A 5 feet wide antechamber, between the pillars or piers on top of the benches that flank the room and the light well on that side, accentuates this feeling of layering even more.

Environmental Awareness

The Queen's Megaron shows just how well the Minoans adapted to their environment. The room is exceptionally well proportioned, with a fine sense of human scale. Structural elements such as columns and bearing walls are substantial without being massive. They are appropriately sized for their engineering requirements, use, and aesthetic pleasure. Openings are deep to avoid glare and provide shade. Wooden shutters were used that were as wide as the square columns they were attached to were deep. They pocketed into these columns unobtrusively when open, and were closed to block out the hot sun or cold air. So they controlled natural ventilation and room temperature. Floors were tiled for additional coolness in the summer.

The orientation of the palace shows that the Minoans had a keen awareness of their microclimate. Summers in Crete are intensely hot and dry and winters are cold and wet, so the use of open internal courtyards makes a lot of sense. If oriented and configured correctly, a courtyard can mitigate extreme temperatures dramatically, allowing cooler night air to be trapped there and then slowly released by convection during the day in the summer, and allowing the warmth of the sun to be absorbed and reflected during the winter.

An Integral Organism

The most remarkable thing about the Palace of Knossos from an environmental point of view is that it was conceived as and operated like an interrelated organism, so that each part played a role in allowing the entire entity to function well in a place known for climatic extremes. The overall orientation of the central plaza, the planimetric layering of functions in the clusters of functions that flank it on its east and west sides, the overhanging of the floors as they rise, the thermal mass and performance of the materials, and the smaller courtyard or light wells that penetrate through the spaces at regular intervals make the Palace of Knossos a model of ecological sensibility.

MYCENAE AND TROY

The history and the destiny of Mycenae and Troy are so inextricably connected that it seems appropriate to discuss them together even though they were located at opposite ends of the ancient world when their power was at its height. Troy, which has captured the popular imagination because of the *Iliad* and the *Odyssey* by the Greek poet Homer, is called Hisarlik today, near Canakalle, in Turkey. Courageously deciding to contradict conventional opinion in the mid-nineteenth century and to treat Homer's poems as history rather than myth, amateur archaeologist Heinrich Schliemann excavated it first, from 1870 to 1890, removing more than 50 feet of earth and debris from the top of the mound that existed there in the process. He was followed by Wilhelm Dörpfeld in 1893–1894 and Carl Blegen from 1932 to 1938. Their work, as well as many subsequent excavations, has confirmed that there was not just one but several Troys distributed among many levels of occupation that begin with Troy I before the beginning of the Bronze Age and end with Troy IX near the end of the Roman Empire. The Troy of Homer, which is near the middle, is Troy VI, and it was destroyed around 1250 B.C. near the end of the Bronze Age.

A Memorable Epic or a Historical Document?

If it ever happened at all as Homer describes, the *Iliad* deals with one episode covering several weeks in the tenth year of the Trojan War, and to understand it, it is necessary to understand the main characters on each side. Agamemnon, the Achaean King, was the most powerful ruler of his time in the Aegean region. He was King of Mycenae and in control of all of Argos. His predecessors are believed to have come from Lydia, in Asia Minor, and to have married into the Perseid Dynasty of Mycenae. Agamemnon married Clytemnestra, the daughter of Tyndareus of Sparta and the sister of Helen, whose abduction, according to Homer, was the cause of the war. Helen, who was married to Menelaos of Sparta, was Agamemnon's sister-in-law. Troy at this time was ruled by Priam, who had two potential successors: his eldest son Hector and his son Paris, or Alexander, who was next in line for the throne. Hector and Paris were sent on a diplomatic mission to Sparta, during which Paris fell in love with Helen. Whether he abducted her or she left with him willingly on board ship back to Troy is open to conjecture, but the result was the same: Menelaos felt honor bound to avenge the act and called on Agamemnon for help. Agamemnon organized an army from all over the Argolid, which met in ships at the port of Aulis. According to Homer, 164 towns and cities sent representatives, with the bulk being from Mycenae, Sparta, Tiryns, and Pylos. In an act that would prove fatal to him later, Agamemnon sacrificed his daughter Iphigenia at Aulis to end a period of calm, which was delaying the sailing of the fleet to Troy.

After nearly ten years of a stalemate, the combatants agreed that the outcome of the war would be decided by a single combat between warriors from each side. Hector was selected to represent the Trojans and Achilles the Greeks. The passage in which Homer describes how Achilles, "like an implacable god of war," killed Hector and won the war for the Greeks is one of the most eloquent parts of the *Iliad*. The Greek victory was overturned, however, when Paris avenged his brother's death by shooting Achilles in his heel as he was dragging Hector behind his chariot around the wall of the city. His heel was vulnerable because it was missed in a spell of invincibility cast over him at his birth.

The Houses of Troy

Homer's epic poem, which was transmitted orally for generations before being transcribed, evokes a grand, gleaming city, towering above the plain and beach where the Greek ships were moored below. Real archaeological evidence, however, suggests much more modest circumstances, in which the Troy of Priam was little more than a citadel at best, with walls surrounding the royal palace and a few other buildings crammed in behind the broadly U-shaped wall around it. Excavations of earlier levels, down to what is called the "first settlement," have yielded important evidence about the beginning of a house type that eventually evolved into the Bronze Age Mycenaean *megaron*, or palace. This then evolved into the classical Greek temples nearly 2,500 years later.[29] One of the earliest houses excavated at Hisarlik has all of the characteristics of the Bronze Age palaces. It is rectangular, being nearly twice as long as it is wide, with a centrally placed door in the short wall at the front and a solid opposing wall in the back. The long sidewalls extend past the front entrance wall, creating a foreporch, and carried the flat roof to create a nearly square shaded alcove. There was a fire pit in the middle of the large interior space, and platforms were built into the sidewalls. A small oven was also built into the back wall, with a drain, which also served as a toilet nearby. Animal bones and refuse, mixed in with the clay flooring, suggests that rather than regularly removing these from the house, they were simply thrown on the floor and allowed to accumulate, until they were eventually covered over with a fresh layer of clay.

This prototype of a long, narrow house with projecting sidewalls that create a front porch, all built to a 3:1 proportion and covered with a flat roof, evolves, in Troy IIc, into one with walls projecting from the back to create another back porch that was not as deep. Since there was no door in the back wall to give access to it, it is assumed that it was intended to protect the walls, which were made of mud brick, from the rain.[30]

This discovery is exciting for architectural historians, because it seems to be the predecessor of the Greek temple form, with a long narrow *cella*, porches on either end, in *antis*; even though a direct connection is impossible to prove. The striking similarity between these houses and temples in the Classical Age, as well as between other elements such as the *propylae*, or entrance gate into the city, or the colonnades surrounding the palace forecourts are clear testimony, however, to the power of cultural memory. It confirms the compelling force of tradition, which prompts the continuous retention of typologies that work, over a long period of time. The residential adaptations that evolved in Troy, beginning with the earliest Neolithic shelters to what may have been Priam's palace at Troy VI, are also found in Mycenae, Tiryns, Pylos, Gla, and other Bronze Age cities in the Argolid. Since these reappear again after a 400 year hiatus as the first prototypical temple, they are proof of the durability of memory.

Dispersion

While the history of Trojan settlements continues on past Troy VI, as well as through Hellenistic and Roman occupation, Homeric tradition holds that Priam's city was burned, the walls were razed, the entire male population massacred, and the women taken as slaves to Greece, as commemorated in Aesculus's play, *The Trojan Women*. The historian Thucydides said that this marked the beginning of the end of the Age of Heroes because, according to Homer, Agamemnon was assassinated by his wife Clytemnestra in his bath soon after his return to Mycenae as retribution for his sacrifice of their daughter Iphigenia. Soon afterward all of the other cities in the Mycenaean league fell due to unconfirmed circumstances, and the migration of the Dorians from the north marked the end of Agamemnon's empire.

An Amateur Archaeologist and Treasure Hunter

Heinrich Schliemann made his fortune during the Gold Rush in California and Alaska in the mid-1800s, and was also an amateur archaeologist. During his excavations of Troy in 1873, he uncovered a golden cask containing a necklace and earrings, which he dramatically characterized to the assembled members of the press as "the Jewels of Helen," underscoring his real agenda in undertaking these disastrously destructive excavations.

Mycenae

Schliemann's spectacular, if not disastrous, activities at Troy encouraged him to press on to find the palace city of Agamemnon as well, undoubtedly also tempted by the prospect of more gold and notoriety. He went to Mycenae and started digging there in 1876. By cross referencing Homer with passages about the city written by the Roman historian Pausanias, Schliemann focused his attention on a grave circle inside the citadel, which he felt must be the resting place of Agamemnon and the other heroes of the Trojan War. He dug a trench inside the Lion Gate through the 90 feet diameter grave circle and found 19 male skeletons covered in gold. Their faces were protected by realistically rendered gold masks, and there were gold breastplates with sunbursts on their chests, with numerous gold swords and daggers scattered around them. With characteristic hyperbole, already well rehearsed with the discovery of gold jewelry at Troy, Schliemann announced the discovery by saying, "I have gazed upon the face of Agamemnon." But such an identification was impossible to confirm, and radiocarbon dates, taken since, do not match those of the Trojan War. Schliemann then went on to Tiryns, about nine miles north of Mycenae, built on

A model of the ancient city of Mycenae.   Courtesy of Thomas Anthony Schuman Jr. *Source:* Flickr

a rocky promontory miles away from the sea, from which Homer said that 80 ships joined the fleet headed to Troy. Schliemann was the first to dig at Tiryns, and once again his crudely excavated shafts and trenches did a great deal of damage. Carl Blegen, who was also involved with the dig at Troy, followed him here and is widely credited with salvaging most of the site.

Palace Culture

Tiryns, like Mycenae, is a good example of what is newly referred to as "palace culture," since the entire city, if it may be called that due to its modest size, revolves around the royal *megaron* in its midst.

Once again, as is so often the case in many other societies discussed here, there is a marked difference between the houses of the upper and lower classes in the Mycenae Royal City. The designation "palace culture," which relates to this period, marks it because of the development of the *megaron*, but royal subjects lived here as well.

Mycenae, like Tiryns and Pylos, was a citadel, ringed with massive walls with little room inside it for residential construction. In fact, the grave circle that Schliemann excavated had once been outside these walls, which were eventually enlarged to enclose it. The palace, which was the focal point of the city plan, was a rectilinear building facing a forecourt, with a tapered columned porch serving as an entrance.

This porch, which was open in front but closed on its other three sides and roofed over, was paved with gypsum. It led to a thin vestibule as wide as the porch in front of it and the *megaron* behind, from which subjects and visitors entered into the king's throne room, or the *megaron* itself. This was nearly square, with a circular hearth in the middle, flanked at each quadrant by four columns that held up a skylight or chimney above it. The king's throne was placed against one wall. The floor was tiled with large square glazed tiles that were astonishingly polychromed in bright colors. The walls were covered with equally colorful frescos, and the timber frame was accentuated. The ceiling was also painted in brightly colored patterns. At Mycenae, the *megaron* measured 13 meters by 12 meters, or about 40 feet in each direction.[31]

The *megarons* at both Tiryns and Pylos are similar to that of Mycenae, although each varies from it in interesting ways. At Tiryns, the citadel is most cramped, having been built on top of a rock outcropping that covers only four acres, divided into three different levels. The *megaron* occupies the uppermost of these terraces and is slightly larger than that of Mycenae, being 13.34 meters by 13.64 meters, or 43.75 feet by 45.75 feet.[32] At Pylos, the main room is more rectangular, being 12.90 meters or 42 feet long and 11.20 meters or 37 feet wide. The four columns equidistantly placed around the circular hearth support an elegant balcony in this case, which overlooks the fireplace, and then a raised portion of the roof above that, which acts as a chimney and source of light and ventilation. There were chambers for the royal couple and presumably also for a select group of their retainers at this upper level. According to Homer, guests slept on beds put out for them on the porch or in the central courtyard and servants stayed in rooms surrounding it. The royal sons and daughters had rooms opposite these, built especially for them, in polished wood and smooth plaster. These smooth white walls were decorated with frescos, and the timber was left natural. The floors were either of smooth tamped clay or gypsum, also decorated with a painted abstract pattern or scene. Because of the scarcity and high cost of wood, which was necessary to make a lintel or crossbeam at the top of a window in a mud brick or stone bearing wall, windows were small. Mycenaean palace compounds, like the Minoan cities they were informed by, had drainage and sewage systems, and bathrooms had fired clay bathtubs. During winters that could be very cold and wet, heat was provided by charcoal braziers.[33]

The poor, on the other hand, lived in mud brick or wattle and daub, single or double room huts with flat roofs and clay floors in a way that may be seen to be typical in many other cultures throughout the world at this time, as discussed elsewhere.

HOUSES OF THE ROMAN REPUBLIC AND EMPIRE

The Romans began as a disparate group of tribes in the *Latium Campania*, south of the Alps in Italy. These tribes, concentrated just south of the Tiber River, began to coalesce as a challenge to Etruscan domination of the area, then known as Etruria, between the eighth and sixth centuries B.C. The Etruscans remain something of a historical mystery, having unknown origins. What little we do know of them comes from several massive fortifications, such as the main gate to the city of Perugia, that still survive and their tombs, which were a mirror of their houses and which have disappeared.

Appropriation of Forms during the Early Republic

As the Romans gained strength, they began to chafe against the rule of the Etruscan Tarquin kings and overthrew them in 509 B.C., taking control of their center of power from the Po River Valley to the Campagnia region. The new Republic then set about making alliances with surrounding territories, or taking them over by force, until it controlled the entire region 225 years later. This then brought them into direct competition with Carthage, which was a city established by the Phoenicians on the coast of what is now Tunisia. In a famously daring raid, a Carthaginian general, Hannibal, did what was then thought to be impossible by leading an army, including attack elephants, across the Alps and up to the walls of Rome. This was followed by a protracted conflict known as the Punic Wars, between 264 and 146 B.C. It was finally won by the Roman general Scipio, who was given the honorary title Africanus because of his victory, and Carthage was leveled and turned into a Roman province. Rome then had unchallenged control of the Mediterranean, which they referred to as "*Mare Nostrum*," or "our sea."

Their next fields of conquest were the Hellenistic kingdoms established by generals in Alexander's army after his death, funded with the spoils of the wars they had fought with him. These were in the Greek and Macedonian heartland, where Alexander's kingdom had begun, the Attalid kingdom based in Pergamon founded by Lysimachus, the Seleucid kingdom in what was once Mesopotamia, and the Ptolemaic kingdom in Egypt. By 100 B.C. the Romans had taken Greece and Macedonia, and by a stroke of luck also received an offer from the last of the Attalid

Villa Adriana, Tivoli, near Rome.   Courtesy of Shutterstock

kings, who was exhausted by incessant struggles with neighboring Gallic tribes, to take over the Attalid Empire. By 44 B.C., Julius Caesar had subdued Gaul itself and Rome was poised to cross the channel into Britain.

As Roman power grew, its need for an architectural image to lend legitimacy to it did also, and they borrowed heavily from the Etruscans, as well as the Greeks, to do so. This assimilation was complicated by the fact that the Etruscans were also influenced by the Greeks, due to their proximity to them and the trade they carried out with them. The Greeks, because of being intrepid sailors, had called on Etruscan ports and had also started to establish colonies on nearby Sicily by the mid-700s B.C. The Etruscans were strategically positioned on the threshold of the Tyrrhenian and Mediterranean Seas, and absorbed all of the cultural crosscurrents around them, from North Africa, Egypt, Phoenicia, and Turkey as well.

One clear example of the way in which the Romans borrowed from the Etruscans was the temple on the Capitoline Hill, which the Roman architect Vitruvius has described. Rather than being three dimensional as Classical Greek temples were, in the sense that they were designed as objects in space that were intended to be seen from any point around them, this Etruscan temple was one directional. It had a large, open entrance portico or porch in the front covered by a roof supported by two rows of columns of what Vitruvius called the *tuscan* (for Etruscan) order, with plain sides and back. Three rectangular chambers or shrines, each similar to a Greek *cella*, were lined up in parallel sequence inside the temple and were dedicated to three different deities. A second temple, which the Romans later built to replace this Etruscan original on the Capitolium, was clearly based on the earlier building. Bronze plaques recording the history of the Roman Republic and later the Empire were kept in the Capitolium, and it was here that conquering generals, on their return to Rome, would end their triumphal marches though the city, to receive a hero's welcome from the emperor himself.

Appropriation Expands to Houses

Such appropriation of architectural forms from a political power structure, or structures that a usurper had replaced, was not unique to the Romans, of course, but an additional nuance here allows us, through analogy, to gain some insight into what Etruscan houses must have been like as well, although the main focus here is the Roman house.

The Romans, like the Etruscans, organized their cities on a gridiron plan, with a main north-south street or *cardo maximus* and an east-west street *decumanus* running through the middle. This rational organizational technique was also a highly effective way of occupying recently conquered territory and fortified military camps, which slowly evolved into cities. The Romans also adopted the *atrium* house from the Etruscans and Greeks, surrounding an open inner courtyard, or *atrium*, which usually had a water feature such as a fountain or pool inside. The *atrium* house was particularly well suited to both the gridiron plan and the climate in the majority of the regions around the Mediterranean basin into which Roman authority began to extend, as well as the basic desire for privacy of the typical family during the Republic. The house was turned inside, with solid walls to the street, in much the same way that those in a Chinese *hutong* are, and so could be conjoined more easily. The courtyard is also an effective architectural device that can be used to mitigate against heat by convection, since it captures cool evening and night air that drops into it and is trapped in the surface area of the grass and leaves of the trees, and then rises up as the sun heats up the space during the day, keeping the rooms that open onto it cool the entire time.

This cooling, convective cycle was enhanced by the use of two courtyards in tandem because if one was left unplanted and the other was green, the unplanted courtyard would heat up faster and as the hot air rose, it would pull cooler air in from the planted courtyard next to it. The typical Roman house during the Republican period, following Etruscan and Greek models, used this principle to perfection, with an *atrium* block at the front near the entrance and the street, if that were the case, and another with a peristyle and a garden in the back, separated by the *tablinum*, which served as a combination of reception space in which to meet guests or clients, record room, and the place to honor family ancestors with statuary. While the forward *atrium* was public and also included spaces for guests to sleep, the peristyle was private, reserved for family and special guests. It was also where the *triclinuim*, or dining room, *portico*, or colonnaded, roofed porch that served as a living area, and bedrooms were located. In some cases, the entrance, or *fauces* was preceded by another small courtyard called a *vestibulum*, similar to a similar kind of space also seen in the Bronze Age *megaron*, mentioned earlier in the discussion about Mycenae.

A Pragmatic People Seduced by Extravagance

As time progressed and the Republic evolved into an empire, Roman houses and their decoration became much more lavish. One of the words most frequently used in reference to the Romans is "pragmatic," and no matter how rich and powerful the society became, this trait remained a central characteristic of its architecture. The Greeks, for example, insisted on the use of a post and lintel, or column and beam, system for their sacred buildings because the straight horizontal lines of the architrave and the cornice directed the eye to the sky rather than to the earth, which they consider to be the base. The Romans, on the other hand, preferred the arch because the scale of buildings that were possible with the post and lintel system was limited, due to the restriction on the size of a span. The Romans were partial to grandiose scale, perhaps again as a clear declaration of legitimacy and masonry construction, and using the arch allowed them to achieve it. Refined sensibilities, about the visual connection it made to the ground and the implication this had of a symbolic connection to the profane world, were not a concern. They were also inveterate merchants, seeing no conflict in having commercial areas mixed with sacred zones. One of the most architecturally engaging mercantile complexes in ancient Rome, known today as Trajan's Market, was located directly behind the Forum, taking advantage of a captive audience coming out of the religious precinct. The market is a brilliant example of commercial planning, stepping up the hill behind the Forum in a series of gradually receding terraces that led people effortlessly up to the Via Biberatica at the summit, which is enclosed in a large roofed structure with several stories of shops on either side. It is easy to imagine this entire ensemble of fan-shaped terraces cut into the hillside and internal street above it with balconied shops on several levels under an all-encompassing roof, teeming with people moving up and down the stairs to and from the Forum below. Such structures were made possible by the arch, which allowed Roman engineers the freedom to build on any terrain. The Greeks used natural slopes to build their theatres, finding a gentle gradient to use as a foundation for the stepped seating placed in an arch around the stage. The Romans, on the other hand, excavated sloping ground at will, and built an arched substructure on foundations built on the level plane they created. They were also the first to develop a simple kind of concrete, using *pozzolana*, sand, aggregate, and water, which was then faced with brick, as it was at Nero's *Domus Aurea*, or stone, but rarely left exposed.

Insulae

With the arch and the increasing facility in the use of poured-in-place concrete, the Romans were able to develop multistory housing blocks, called "insulae," or islands, because they seemed to be like self-sufficient units within the urban fabric. They contained shops, or *tabernae*, at street level that provided food and drink to the residents and had running water and sewage systems as well. By the Imperial Period there were many of these, to the extent that they were the prevalent housing type from A.D. 200 onward.[34]

Surviving examples of *insulae* in the well-preserved city of Ostia, which served as a port for Rome, as well as in Pompeii and Herculaneum, give us a good idea of exactly what life was like in these ancient apartment buildings. For a start, the *tabernae* that served as their foundation at street level were completely open to the

Close view of Herculaneum excavations, Naples, Italy.   Courtesy of Shutterstock

street and could be closed at night with large wooden panels that could be fixed in place. These shops, as well as selling goods directly to the public, also housed cottage industries that produced things for sale elsewhere, and so were a valuable economic resource to both the burgeoning Republic and the empire that grew from it. The floor of these shops was usually raised a step or two above the street to avoid flooding, and there was sometimes a built-in counter facing the sidewalk. In contrast to the Greek *ergasteria*, which were concentrated in or near an *agora*, Roman *tabernae* also flanked roads that were ubiquitous arteries, linking the far-flung parts of their empire, as is visible in distant corners of it, such as Jerash, or Gerasa, in Jordan today.[35]

Houses of the Roman Empire

After a resounding naval victory at Actium in 33 B.C. over the allied forces of Mark Antony and Cleopatra, who was the last Ptolemaic ruler of Egypt, no further obstacles stood between Octavian and complete control of the Roman Republic. The Senate proclaimed him Augustus, the first Roman emperor, in 27 B.C., inaugurating a Julio-Claudian dynasty. It continued after he died in A.D. 14 and included Tiberius (A.D. 14 to 37), Caligula (A.D. 37 to 41), Claudius (A.D. 44 to 54), and Claudius's adopted son, Nero (A.D. 54 to 68).

Some historians argue that the legal, economic, and military structure of the Empire already existed long before this proclamation was made, but the judicious rule of Augustus helped solidify its structure to the point that a *Pax Romana* was established that lasted for nearly 200 years, until the dissolute rule of Marcus Aurelius's son Commodus (180–192). This period of Roman peace, admittedly sustained by Roman law and military might, meant that agricultural estates could be expanded and towns and cities could prosper. They did so throughout a vast empire that included what is now roughly half of Britain, most of Continental Europe, all of north Africa, and the Middle East. Houses at each level of the social spectrum continued to evolve naturally during this period, with slight regional accommodations to microclimate and local culture taking place.

Interchangeable Parts in a Grid

One of the advantages of the gridiron plan of the typical Roman city, which was first established as a *castrum* or military camp and then slowly built up as the territory it controlled became more secure, was that the full range of public institutions could be placed into it as the city grew. These included the forum, or commercial area, the basilica, or law court, the theatre, the public bath house, the temple, and others. These then became an indispensable part of the establishment of Roman identity in the far-flung corners of a burgeoning Empire and could be inserted at will into this rectilinear framework as it grew, like a game piece on a chess board. A quick retrospective overview of one of these cities in Algeria, called Timgad, which was founded by the Emperor Trajan in A.D. 100 for retired legionnaires, shows that these institutions were not always located in a carefully prescribed way within a regular orthogonal grid. This delightful capacity to achieve freedom within a systematic urban plan reveals a great deal about the Roman approach to domestic planning as well. This same principle of individual expression within a system of conventional typologies is also recognizable in the houses of each of the various social levels.

Roman Identity in Spite of Regional Differences

This combination of an orthogonal city plan and easily recognizable and replicable institutions meant that Roman citizens living on the periphery of the Empire near Hadrian's Wall in the middle north of Britain, on the edge of the desert on Algeria, or in Gerash in Jordan could feel just as much a part of it as someone living a block away from the Tiber River. They were each protected by the same laws and could each enjoy the same amenities of the social life of the Forum and public bath, see the latest play from Rome in the theatre, or enjoy wine, olive oil, and bread with roasted meat or fish grilled at a local *tabernae*. The Romans were accurately aware of space and its demarcation and direction, even having a god named Terminus that symbolized beginnings, endings, and the difference between them. The cardinal points at the middle of each side of the city were prominently marked with gates, and one of these, which was typically the one marking the direction to Rome, was a psychological as well as a physical connection to the capital to which they paid allegiance. The construction of Roman roads was excellent, to the extent that many of them, in these isolated, undeveloped areas, still exist today. They were dug deeper than the frost line to avoid upheaval in the freeze–thaw cycle, layered with increasingly smaller rocks as the level neared the surface, and then finally topped with finely chiseled flat slabs and raised curb stones on each side. The phrase "all roads lead to Rome" was more than a casual analogy to a citizen who lived thousands of miles away from Latium, since they all really did lead there, and everyone knew that once they started out on one they would eventually end up in the capital and be relatively safe, well housed, and well fed along the way.

Estates

The estates of landholders at the upper end of the economic scale continued to become more luxurious and refined, reflecting a life of greater leisure. No matter how much wealth they accumulated, however, there remained nostalgia for the simple agricultural beginning of the Republic and the closeness to nature that such a life entailed. This is obvious in the bucolic subjects chosen for the wall paintings that have been found in the villas that have survived, in which no wall, except for those in rooms for the most mundane purpose, was left undecorated. These pastoral scenes, which became more skillfully executed over time, were an obvious debt to set design and the screens used as backdrops for theatrical productions. They demonstrate the same growing awareness of spatial perception that is evident in the rooms of the villas as well, and the increasing willingness to experiment rather than to be totally dependent upon Greek and Hellenistic precedents.

Frozen in Time

Much of what we know of this art form, as well as of mosaics, which were also extensively used in the homes of the wealthy, comes from villas that were preserved in Pompeii by the pumice that fell on it during a deadly eruption of Mount Vesuvius in A.D. 79. Unlike cities like Timgad, which evolved out of a *castrum* built on a relatively flat and unrestricted site, the north-south *cardo maximus* and east-west *decumanus* of Pompeii intersect at much less than the usual 90 degree angle to conform to irregular topography, with the *decumanus* being about 30 degrees south of west. In the Pompeii city plan, the forum, theatre, gymnasium, basilica, temple precinct, and baths are all clustered together very close to the main Stabian Gate. Many of the most elegant houses that have been extracted from the 10 feet deep layer of ash that hardened around them are at the opposite end of the city, north of the *decumanus* near the Vesuvian Gate that provided entry into Pompeii through the wall at that edge.

Without knowing their original names, unless they have found inscriptions to identify them, archaeologists have designated these villas by a distinguishing feature or theme, or even an event related to their discovery. These include the House of the Vettii, House of Pansa, House of the Silver Wedding, and the Villa of the Mysteries, which is some distance outside the perimeter wall, on the road leading out of the Herculaneum Gate in the northwest corner of the city. The House of the Silver Wedding, for example, which was excavated in 1893, was named for the silver wedding anniversary of the king and queen of Italy at the time, who supported the dig. This villa, as well the House of the Vettii are each stunning examples of the use of an *impluvium* over the *atrium*, as well as the use of a *tablinum* to connect this more public forward courtyard to the peristyle garden in the back.

A residence of Pontius Pilate, the procurator of Judea.   Courtesy of Shutterstock

The *impluvium* is an angled roof over the open corridor that ran around all four sides of the *atrium*, sloping down to the inner edge to direct rainwater into a pool in the center of the court with no gutter to stop it. It is easy to imagine what the *atrium* must have been like during a storm, with rain cascading down like a waterfall all around it into the open cistern, which served a practical as well as an aesthetic purpose below.

The Villa of the Mysteries, built in 50 B.C., is what some believe to be a center for the imitation rites into the cult of Bacchus. It has elegant and highly erotic wall paintings that have a compelling, personalized, dramatic, and sequential documentary quality to them. These include a flagellation scene showing an innocent young woman with back exposed, being whipped while draped over the knees of a wild-eyed seated matriarch who is obviously in charge of the ceremony.

Such paintings are a vivid reminder that the Romans grew even more pantheistic as the empire grew, adopting the religious traditions of the various cultures they encountered as they conquered new territories. In one of the houses in Pompeii that could be positively identified by inscription as having belonged to Publius Fannius Synistor built in late A.D. 1005, and now reconstructed in the Metropolitan Museum of Art in New York, there is such a mosaic in the middle of the bedroom floor. It represents a priest offering a snake to Isis, who was revered in Egypt as the wife of the god Osiris and credited with magical powers because of her mythical ability to bring him back to life after he was murdered by his jealous brother, Seth. Her cult spread rapidly during the Hellenistic Age because of the wider worldview that prevailed at that time and the interaction between the leaders of each of the major kingdoms that

Ruins of Pompeii, Italy.   Courtesy of Shutterstock

arose out of the ranks of Alexander's army after his death. One of the largest temples dedicated to Isis, in fact, spans a river at the bottom of the mountainside city of Pergamon, built on a successive series of terraces above it.

Mosaics

The art of floor mosaics also became progressively more sophisticated during the Imperial Period. While they, like wall paintings, had consistently been a feature of the houses of the middle and upper classes, there was a consistent refinement that took place in the skill level of the artists who prepared the panels, or *emblemata*, of these carpets of stone, which were very often composed in wooden frames in their workshops and transported to the house in which they were to be installed, which may have been some distance away. The *Tesserae* or small cubes of marble or other stones that the artists used during the Classical Greek and Hellenistic periods, gave way to subtle shades of glass that gave the images more depth and iridescence. Other than Pompeii and Herculaneum, which suffered a similar volcanic fate, many of the other best examples of mosaic art exist on the island of Delos and in the Bardo Museum in Tunis.

Cathage

There is more than a hint of tragedy in the fact that Cathage, which is described in more detail elsewhere and which had been the nemesis of the Republic in its earliest phase, became a rural paradise for rich Roman landowners who settled there after it had been subjugated. Many of the mosaics uncovered there give wonderful insights into their lifestyle on their *latifundia* or huge estates, and the workshops that produced them were the best in the Empire.

The combination of wall paintings and floor mosaics, which increasingly came to imitate the painterly techniques used on the walls, gave each room in these villas a visual, textural richness that expanded the space of even the most generous of them. When combined with access to a garden, or at least a view of one, the effect must have been overwhelmingly luxurious.

Roman Gardens

The influence of Hellenistic worldliness and hedonism, which had not yet been able to soften the stern austerity of the agriculturally based early Roman Republic, began to make inroads after the second century B.C. This was especially true of garden design, which was an integral part of any Roman house with access to water and an open space at ground floor level, being considered to be essential to domestic tranquility. Alexander had, after all, ruled from Persepolis and breached the walls of Babylon, with its fabled Hanging Gardens, and his tutor Aristotle had written one of the most complete studies of biology of its time, so there was a heightened awareness of new exotic plant types that Alexander's explorations had brought to light. The Hellenistic fondness for *nymphea*, styled to look like caves or grottos with fountains imitating waterfalls gushing out of them, was transformed by the Romans to a source of water for an entire city. The *nymphaeum* was also reduced in scale for use in villas and was frequently used as a backdrop for the exhibition of sculpture. Expanding on the Hellenistic taste for *follies*, or mock ruins reduced in scale in gardens dedicated to the Muses, the Romans added *topia*, or artificial elements that would contribute to the image of a bucolic setting. They also continued to blur the line between architecture and nature, using scenography and forced perspective to make distant scenery seem to be connected to the house. This attempt to connect with the natural world increasingly became a defining feature of the Roman villa in the Imperial Age, to the extent that Renaissance architects and landscape architects fastened upon it as a way of establishing a historical relationship with their cultural roots.

In addition to providing a wealth of information about the architectural features that were typical of Roman villas, the houses in Pompeii have also been helpful in providing insights into what the gardens were like. They typically have one or the other of the most popular types of landscaped settings: the courtyard garden or the colonnaded peristyle. A large villa sometimes had both features, which can be seen in later Renaissance Roman villas as well. Key to later Roman villas was the idea of linking the house and garden with axial symmetry. This allowed a clear sight line from the entrance through the atrium and the *tablinum* to the peristyle garden at the back of the house. The perspective effect that this caused, of limitless green space inside the house, was frequently enhanced by *trompe l'oeil* effects in the wall paintings. In houses on larger properties this axiality was prolonged by the addition of a third and final garden, called a *xystus*, that was also surrounded by a *portico*. It typically had a thin pool of water down the middle that stretched from one end to the other in the same way that Islamic gardens in Spain and Mughal gardens in India did, seven centuries or more later. According to Pliny's *Natural History*, and the evidence provided by wall paintings and in mosaics, these gardens were planted with fruit-bearing species, creating small orchards of apple, cherry, peach, pear, quince, and pomegranate trees, as well as cypress, bay, poplar, and evergreens around the house. The Romans were fond of *espalier* and topiary techniques, and also flower gardens full of roses, lilies, violets, iris, narcissus, daffodils, marigolds, and lavender, with myrtle, boxwood, and laurel used for borders.

The Romans considered the ideal setting for dining to be in fresh air in the midst of a natural paradise, under a vine-covered pergola, with the sound of water in the background and a beautiful distant view. If this was not possible, nature was replicated at a smaller scale within the space available, as a garden.

SKARA BRAE, SCOTLAND

Skara Brae is a well-preserved Neolithic village on the western edge of the Orkney Islands, between Scotland and Norway. It is built of dry stone walls, and houses had turf roofs held up by whale bone, which have long since disappeared. This area is virtually treeless, and so this kind of construction was a logical option. The houses were clustered together as if sheltering from the cold harsh winds coming in off the ocean, due to their exposed position on the western shoreline.

When this village was occupied between 3100 and 2500 B.C., it was a bit further inland, since the position of the shoreline of the Bay of Skaill has changed, but it was still a chilly forbidding spot for most of the year. This was a farming community, with cattle, sheep, and pigs, as well as wheat and barley, imported to the island from the Scottish mainland by raft about 3800 B.C.[36]

The Comforts of Home

In spite of adverse environmental conditions, the relatively long duration of habitation at the site, which went through several phases of expansion, is confirmation of the cleverness and adaptability of the residents, who made the best of the resources they had. The different dates of the nearly ten houses that make up the compound suggest that it was almost entirely replaced about 300 years after the first houses were built there. The plans of the houses are very similar, with built-in stone furniture being a common characteristic. The fireplace, which was an essential feature for survival here, was located in the center of the house, in a rectangular depression in the earth surrounded by a low stone wall. There was a hole in the roof directly above it that let the smoke escape. Since there was no wood in this region, archaeologists believe that the villages burned turf, animal dung, driftwood, and even dried seaweed to keep warm.[37] The clustering together of the houses, the tactic of partially burying them in and behind the sand dunes, and the thickness of the stone walls also helped to conserve warmth.

One of the most prominent pieces of built-in furniture, which was typically placed across from the entrance, was what is commonly referred to as a "dresser" in contemporary descriptions, using a modern frame of reference. This is because this object, which extends about 3 feet out from the wall, has uprights that support two horizontal stone slabs that form shelves. This is generally believed to have

Visitors look at the 5,000-year-old remains of Skara Brae village in the Scottish Orkney islands.   *Source:* AP / Wide World Photos

been used for storage of clothing or utensils, but its location, on axis with the entrance, suggests a more important function, such as a place where special objects were kept, like the *tokonoma* of a Japanese house. It might have been an altar that honored the family deity, like that of a Roman house.[38] A large stone placed between this dresser and the fireplace may have been used as a seat.

In addition, beds were attached to the exterior walls, made from a large slab supported by low walls on three sides. These had a recess nearby cut into the exterior wall, where personal objects may have been stored. Tall stones, located at the outer corners may have been used as bedposts from which a curtain of some kind was hung, probably for warmth and privacy. The hardness of the stone slab was offset by animal skins or mattresses stuffed with straw. Finally, there were also stone boxes sunk into the house floor and sealed with clay that were used either to store fresh water or live fish, to keep them fresh until they were to be cooked, or to soften limpets, which were used as fish bait.[39] In some houses there are small enclosures, made out of stone slabs used as walls, which have rudimentary drains in the floor that archaeologists assume were used as indoor toilets. Other similar enclosures without drains may have been used for storage. The main door was a stone slab secured with a cross bar that fit into a slot in the outer wall. The passage to the outside, which led past all of the other houses, was very small and dark and was served by another stone door, which was also secured by a crossbar. One unit, now designated as House 8, seems to have been used for some other purpose, based on the fact that there is no built-in furniture of the kind found inside other houses. Remnants of burnt flaked stone suggest that tools were made here. In a scenario reminiscent of Çatal Hüyük in Anatolia, which is older but also Neolithic, a cow's skull was found in House 7 along with the remains of two people who were buried beneath the floor, which is the only place this occurs in this settlement.[40]

Placing the house below grade, along with the use of a sod roof, meant that there were no windows, and this, along with the smoke from the fireplace, must have meant that the interiors were dark and murky. Grinders in the houses indicate that grain was ground into flour there, so that life here, for much of the year, was lived indoors. Because of the fact that the houses were rather small and connected by covered stone corridors that ran between them, there seems to have been no alternative but to be friendly with your neighbors at Skara Brae, and there is no evident difference in social level.[41]

Short Lifespan

In spite of the facts that these houses provided their inhabitants with the essential elements necessary for survival and that food, such as fish, meat, and grain, seem to have been abundant, life expectancy was short. The social equality that seems to have prevailed at Skara Brae, and is consistent with tombs there, is at odds with other monuments in the area, such as Maes Howe, the Ring of Brodgar, and the Stones of Sternness, which all required extensive hours of labor to build and suggest a hierarchical level of organization to realize.[42] As in other such cases, at Stonehenge, Silbury Hill, and Avebury, concurrent with the theme of common dedication to the public good at the expense of personal comfort, people spent a great deal of their short lives contributing their time to the construction of these monuments, either willingly or by coercion, in addition to the hours needed for planting, harvesting, and animal husbandry. Life expectancy was little more than 30 years, and 50 percent died in their teens.

Skara Brae is exciting because it is one of the few surviving examples of a Neolithic settlement, in the same category as Çatal Hüyük in Anatolia, Khirokitia in Cyprus, and Jericho in Israel as rare evidence of how people lived at the fragile transition point in human history from a nomadic, hunting, and gathering existence to a more settled agriculturally based lifestyle. The impact that this crucial transition had is clear at Skara Brae, where human ingenuity prevailed over the elements, but just barely.

STONEHENGE, WOODHENGE, AND DURRINGTON WALLS

In late Neolithic times, a characteristic type of monument was built in large numbers in the British Isles and Brittany, in which stones were placed upright outside a circular ditch. These are called henges and are most frequently found in southeast or central England. Some of these are not entirely circular, but elliptical, with perimeters laid out as arcs of circles. This indicates advanced geometric and planning skills and knowledge of field measurements. In the henge monuments, a conspicuous feature on the horizon was used to help mark the points at which the sun and the moon rose and set, particularly at their furthest points in the summer and winter solstices, equinoxes, and eclipses. The line from the stone to the horizon gave the alignment. The first light of the sun was recorded each day with a peg in the ground, and this was done over a period of years before stone markers were erected. While the stars stay in relatively the same position, the sun and the moon change, and by marking this change, a calendar was established. The sun is important in a calendar for accuracy, but the moon is more complicated and is related to the prediction of eclipses. The tilt of the earth's axis causes deviation in the rising and setting positions of the sun each year, to either the east or the west, but by pinpointing the day when the sunset occurred at its furthest point at midsummer or midwinter, the length of the year could be established. At the equinoxes at the latitude where most of the henges in England occur, which are on March 21 and September 21, the sun rises exactly in the east and sets in the west, and days begin to lengthen or shorten dramatically. At the solstices, the sun is rising and setting at the extreme northerly and southerly positions on June 21 and December 21, respectively.

Stonehenge

Possibly the best known stone circle is on the Salisbury Plain near the River Avon, called Stonehenge, although it is technically not a henge because the ditch is on the outside of the circle. This henge was built in three stages. The first stage began about 1900 B.C. when a 105 meter diameter ditch was built with an entrance facing due northeast. Two massive stones were put up to flank the entrance, and a 5 meter high sighting or heel stone was put up outside the entrance. Fifty-six pits, called Aubrey holes after the amateur archaeologist who first discovered them, were dug in the chalk and then filled in after they were used for cremation burials, although new evidence indicates that they had tall poles in them first. The distance between the holes is 4.9 meters. When seen from the center of the circle, a vertical marker called the "heel" stone marks the place on the horizon where the midsummer sun rose in 1900 B.C., and would seem to have stood on its tip. In stage II, 82 grey-blue dolerite stones, or "bluestones," which were quarried in South Wales, were dragged and shipped the 300 kilometers to Wiltshire and put up in a double ring of 38 pairs each, with 6 extras stones used to build an entrance on the northeast side. An avenue was built from the river Avon to the site to move the stones.

In its final form, Stonehenge consisted of an outer circle of sarsen (sandstone) uprights that replaced the bluestones, for some unknown reason, and an inner horseshoe-shaped part. The outer circle had 30 uprights with continuous lintels. The inner horseshoe had five freestanding archways of three stones each, called trilithons. All stones had interlocking sockets and were curved to match the circle. This last stage took place just before the Mycenaean period in Greece, in the middle of the second millennium. This, however, is only one of nearly 100 henges scattered over Britain and Ireland. The change from bluestones to sarsens is a mystery, but evidence indicates that new leaders arose and called for a new design, which involved moving 80 sarsen blocks weighing five tons each from the site 25 miles away. To give some idea of the difficulty of this, one stone alone would

Stonehenge.   Courtesy of Shutterstock

have required the backbreaking labor of over 80 people for seven weeks to drag it by rope and log rollers to the site. The lintels were raised on a timber crib that was moved upwards by levers. In all, 30,000,000 hours of labor were estimated to have been spent on the sarsen monument alone, indicating a highly organized and, some believe, sharply divided society.

In timing then, this final stage III occurred between 1900 and 1600 B.C., which is 1,000 years after the Great Pyramid of Giza. The Bronze Age began in Britain in 1700 B.C., and the people who built the final stage, referred to as the Wessex people, were commercially minded, trading with Egypt, Mycenae, and Phoenicia, unlike the people who built stage I. The total time of all three stages of construction was 300 years.

The People behind the Monument and Its Purpose

Why was Stonehenge built? Who built it, and why? These questions have haunted professional archaeologists and the public alike since the monument first came to popular attention in the eighteenth century. Theories about why it was built have evolved rapidly during the past four decades, beginning with what may be termed the Stonehenge as astronomical computer model, best represented by Gerald Hawkins. Hawkins, who has written *Stonehenge Decoded*, asked five important questions after seeing Stonehenge for the first time. First, why was the heel stone alignment with the midsummer sunrise so important? Second, why were the trilithon archways so narrow, the view through them restricted to such a narrow angle, and the grouping arranged in a horseshoe? Third, was there a connection between the trilithon horseshoe and the sarsen ring, which restricted this view even more? Fourth, why did the height of the outer circle seem to be specifically chosen to allow a sight line to the horizon? And finally, why do the station stones form a rectangle that is specifically aligned? To answer these questions, he programmed a computer with 120 pairs of points around the circle and calculated the compass azimuth and direction that each line established. He approached the problem like an astronomer, with the idea that if the stars and planets are considered to be laying in a hollow sphere, like a planetarium above the earth, the circles on that sphere correspond to the latitude circles on the earth and can be tracked as declinations. In other words, he told the computer to stand at each selected point inside the Stonehenge circle, look across the other points into the sky, and record which declination it saw.

Hawkins found there were 27,060 possible alignments between 165 possible positions. After making some admittedly subjective value judgments, he selected 120 positions. This was the early period of computer use, and checking just one pair of positions by hand took Hawkins four hours. He tried the positions of the stars in 1750 B.C., and the computer found no match. He then tried the positions of the sun and moon and found many coincidences, with astonishing accuracy. He thought that what the builders did was to align the circle, horseshoe, and rectangle so that between all of them, when paired, 16 alignments could be used to sight the 12 unique points of the sun and the moon. This shows great economy of design in that one position can be used for more than one alignment. As Hawkins describes his impression of the purpose of Stonehenge:

> This provided a calendar for planting crops, maintained priestly power, and served as a kind of intellectual game. According to the laws of probability, there is less than one chance in ten million that these alignments could have happened by accident.

Hawkins then looked at eclipses, especially the most spectacular show of a solar or lunar eclipse over the heel stone. "If the sun were considered a god, or the moon a goddess, this society would have been terrified to see them swallowed up. The Aubrey holes served as a computer for this and a stone was moved around them."[43]

The Latest Theory

Current interest in the pervasive influence of fertility cults during the Neolithic period, which characterizes each of the cultures included here, has redirected theories about the purpose of Stonehenge and similar mysterious monuments of its period in Britain, such as Avebury and Silbury Hill, into less abstract and more erogenous territory. Rather than being an astronomical calculator, these new theorists submit, Stonehenge was symbolic of the union between the earth and the sky. In this more subjective scenario, the horseshoe in the middle of Stonehenge represents or symbolizes a womb, and the shadow cast on each solstice is the cosmic phallus impregnating the earth, represented in its circle of stones yet again. In this line of thinking, the alignments mentioned by Hawkins are taken for granted, but are a secondary condition of the use of the monument.

Where the People Came From

The stone construction on Salisbury Plain represents an enormous expenditure of human labor, requiring a high level of organizational skill and resources. Who were the people who achieved this? Where did they come from? Archaeologists differ on their origins, almost equally split between what may be characterized as Diffusionists and Non-Diffusionists. The Diffusionists propose that early monuments were begun by indigenous people who were agrarian, but that this local culture was then dominated, and some believe subjugated, by outsiders. One prominent theory is that these invaders came from Malta, in the Eastern Mediterranean, which has well-preserved evidence of a highly advanced Neolithic culture with some of the earliest freestanding roofed structures in the world located there. More than 30 temples have been uncovered on Malta, built of huge rectilinear stones, with trilithon doorways of the same type used at Stonehenge. The plans of these temples are usually U-shaped, and the walls are typically cobbled. Coral limestone is plentiful in Malta and was typically used, because it is easily worked, splits into flat slabs, and can then be cut and polished quickly. Temple building appeared rather suddenly on Malta, around 400 years before the unification of Egypt by Menes in 3100 B.C.

The Diffusionists also point to the appearance of similar kinds of structures in other areas, such as *menhirs*, which are a single standing stone, and *dolmens*, which are freestanding megalithic chambers covered by a roof or capstone. They also point to the presence of passage graves, which were built of dry stone walls or megaliths, or both, ending in a round burial chamber. There are many passage graves, concentrated in certain areas in Brittany, dating from between 4600 and 4000 B.C., with some of these extending up to 85 feet long. Some have side chambers, while others turn at a right angle.

A Communal Society

In England itself, the distribution of collective graves is also substantial, as it is in Scotland where there is also a heavy concentration of them. In England, inhumation burial of kin described here in the discussion about Çatal Hüyük in Anatolia was also common, in which bodies were exposed to the elements and scavengers until they decomposed, and the bones were then stacked in a mass grave. Passage graves have been found at Maes Howe in Orkney that are just as sophisticated as those in Malta, made of easily worked sandstone. Some of these are more than 100 feet in diameter. At Quanterness, there is a collective passage grave that was built in the form of a wheel, with six chambers radiating out like spokes from a round central hall. Each of these chambers is roofed over with a triangular roof of a kind similar to that used by the Maya 300 years later, as an example of an independent invention of the same construction technique used to solve a similar problem. At both Maes Howe and Quanterness the high standard of construction indicates the possibility of professional, and perhaps even an itinerant class of, builders, as well as an accumulation of construction knowledge over time that concentrated on leveling, fitting, and joining huge stones. It also implies a professional priesthood that directed and financed construction by means that are still not clear. Understanding a bit about this piece of the puzzle of what the people who lived near Stonehenge were like is essential to an appreciation of them, as is an awareness of the second piece called Woodhenge.

Woodhenge

Knowledge about the human context surrounding Stonehenge has expanded rapidly in recent years due to a startling discovery made by a pilot in 1925. Just before Christmas that year, Gilbert Insall, who was a World War I veteran, flew over Stonehenge in a single seater Sopwith Snipe, following the River Avon at an altitude of 2,000 feet. From the open cockpit he saw a large circle that he later described as having "several rings of white spots in the center."[44] He returned later to photograph the site from the air, confirming the presence of concentric rings of white dots. He looked the site up in the *Wiltshire Archaeological Magazine* and saw that it was listed as a circular burial mound. He showed his photographs to a friend, Maud Cunnington, who, along with her husband, Benjamin, and nephew Robert, did an accurate survey over the next three years. In 1928, they excavated on the site and found something as significant and impressive in its own way as Stonehenge itself.

There had apparently been a single building on this site, held up by six concentric rings of wooden columns, surrounded by a 5 meters wide, 2 meters deep ditch. The 168 columns were each nothing less than the trunk of an oak tree weighing about 5.5 tons, making them 75 percent of the weight of the sarsens at Stonehenge. After the columns were erected, they were backfilled with chalk, which was what made them visible from the air after they disintegrated.[45] Speculation about the possible use of this building has continued unabated since, fueled by similarities between this new find, which has been labeled "Woodhenge" and "Stonehenge," nearby. These similarities include the fact that the long axes of the four minor rings at Woodhenge, which are really more elliptical than circular, are similar to that of the horseshoe configuration at Stonehenge in that each are consistent with the

Woodhenge.   © Macduff Everton / CORBIS

alignment of the midsummer solstice.[46] Each used lintels, one of stone and one of wood.

A Social Space or a Commune?

In 1940, archaeologist Stuart Piggott theorized that this one enormous thatch-roofed building had an open central court. A similar structure, now called the "Sanctuary," was later uncovered near Avebury in 1930, discovered by Maud Cunnington. In this instance there are six concentric circles of wooden columns combined with two stone circles. In each case, Piggott surmised that those structures were a communal adjunct to the circles that were near to them. The discovery of what appear to be communal buildings near the sacred circles of Stonehenge and Avebury evokes the image of a tightly knit society that lived, socialized, and celebrated in one place and then worshipped in another. But, the prospect of communal living was short-lived because of yet another startling discovery following Woodhenge and the Sanctuary.

Durrington Walls

In 1966 a plan by the Wiltshire County Council Roads Committee to build a highway through a prehistoric site known as Durrington, or Long, Walls prompted an investigation of the site by archaeologist Geoff Wainwright. The Ministry of Transport delayed construction until September 1967 to allow archaeological work. The site is about 500 feet, or 150 yards, north of Woodhenge, just west of a significant bend in the River Avon at that point. What Wainwright found was two circular structures, which in their first phase were constructed with five rings of slight, but often quite deeply set, poles, or columns. These were subsequently replaced by six additional rings, the widest of which was nearly 40 meters across, in which the largest posts were more than 1 meter thick.

Wainwright, along with archaeologist Chris Musson, imagined this as being one large rotunda, which also had a open central court, similar to the theory that Piggott had proposed about Woodhenge and the Sanctuary. Similar compounds have subsequently been found at Mount Pleasant, Arminghall, and Belfarg, near Fife, Scotland, and now there are believed to be more than 40 such timber circles in Britain. While the thought that they may have been communal domestic enclosures has yet to be conclusively disproved, archaeologists are now increasingly dubious of a residential use for these megadendritic structures.[47]

Where did People Live?

As of January 2006, we finally have confirmed evidence of what the houses of those living at Durrington Walls, the builders of Stonehenge, might have looked like. New excavations have uncovered the village that archaeologists believe housed these workers.[48] This is the largest Neolithic village yet uncovered in Britain. Eight houses in this village were uncovered in September 2006, and a new survey indicates that there were many more on this site. They are all just slightly rectangular, with the average size being 15 feet on a side, or 225 square feet. The sides were wattle and daub, or sticks woven together and filled with a paste made with crushed chalk, which is prevalent just below the thin layer of topsoil on the site. Each house had a tamped hard clay floor and a central fireplace. The middens in some of the houses were neater than others, in which broken pottery and animal bones were found strewn all over the floor, leading to speculation that religious leaders as well as builders may have temporarily occupied the structures.

Postholes as well as slots in the clay floor seem to indicate that there was also built-in furniture in the house. There are examples of built-in furniture in other Neolithic settlements in the British Isles, such as Skara Brae, discussed elsewhere, in which stone slabs are stacked between stone uprights to create cabinets in the houses, presumably used for storing clothing.

The houses that are now being excavated at Durrington Walls have been dated to between 2600 B.C. and 2500 B.C., which is exactly contemporary with the radiocarbon dates that have been established for Stonehenge 10 years ago. Some of the dwellings were set apart by having their own individual ditch and wooden palisade around them, and there are preliminary indications that there are several more of these, confounding speculation of who may have used them and for what purpose. A road that was paved with flint once led directly from this village to the River Avon nearby. And it, like the avenue leading up to Stonehenge, is aligned to the summer solstice. The avenue, however, aligns with the sunrise, while the Durrington Walls road lines up with the solstice sunset, to "midsummer night's eve."

The evidence of feasts held in some of the houses, combined with the possibility of Woodhenge being used as a social hall connected to the religious precinct of Stonehenge, presents the image of a hedonistic people celebrating life while honoring and respecting death. Dr. Parker Pearson, of the University of Sheffield, who is leading this most recent excavation, speculates that Stonehenge, because it was made of more durable material, was intended to be "a memorial and final resting place for the dead," while the wooden architecture of Woodhenge and Durrington Walls, "symbolized the transience of life," so that people from all over the region went there "to celebrate life and deposit the dead in the river for transport to the afterlife." [49]

5

East and Southeast Asia

THE FAIRY CHIMNEYS OF CAPPADOCIA

Cappadocia is in the center of Anatolia, in Turkey, near the city of Kayseri, which was once called Caesarea. The natural environment is harsh in this remote area, particularly near the volcano Erciyes Daği, south of Kayseri, which has created a moonscape of tufa. This has eroded into peaks and valleys over time, depending upon its density. The softer varieties of rock vary in color from bleached white and shades of grey to light red, and they change in hue according to the light. The eroded rock has become sand and gravel as the floor for the crevasses and valleys between the pinnacles, so that this along with an arid climate does not allow the landscape to support much vegetation in most areas. In spring, after the snow melts, springs run through these valleys or gaps between the conical outcroppings, which fall into underground channels and caverns.[1] This region was vulnerable to political and military vicissitudes in the past, beginning with the relative security of Roman control, followed by Arab invasions in the seventh century, then received Byzantine protection, disrupted by Turkish invasion in the ninth century followed by the Seljuk Turks in the eleventh century, who conquered Kayseri.

Houses, Carved out of Stone

The visual confusion caused by the similarity of the pinnacles and the relative softness of the tufa that made it possible to burrow into them made this a great place to hide while opposing armies fought it out down below or, occasionally, up above. All that was required to live here was having enough energy to carve a house out of the inside of one or more of the tufa towers, which seemed to be the preferred place of residence for those who did so, while the subterranean caverns were relegated to storage. The other advantages to living in these conical rocks was that, in addition to being a lifesaving place to hide, they were also environmentally responsive, being cool during the hot summers in the high desert and warm in the winters.[2]

Cappadocia is a portion of the Hittite heartland lying to the south of Hattusas and Yazilikaya, and the cylinder seals found throughout the area prove it was heavily populated by them. Called Katpatuka by the Assyrians, which changed to Cappadocia by the time of the historian Herodotus, this province occupies a very large section of central Anatolia, from the flats of Lake Tuzgőlű in the west, past Malatya in the east, and from Yozgut and Sivas in the north to Niğde in the south. Geothermal activity from both Mount Argaeus, now Erciyes Daği, near Kayseri, and Hasan Daği near Aksaray, first covered this entire area with a deep layer of volcanic dust millions of years ago. This was then followed by a top coating of lava that cooled into harder rock. Slow erosion at weak points in the rock mantle has led to valleys of varying width having been cut into the tufa or softer solidified ash. This has created the characteristic moonscape here, which is called *peribacalari* or "fairy chimneys" locally. The high potassium level of the tufa in combination with rainwater has ironically made parts of this wasteland a fertile area for growing fruit, especially grapes, apples, pears, plums, and apricots, and making parts of Cappadocia some of the best wine-producing areas in Turkey. Oxidation of the minerals in the tufa also creates an ever-changing spectrum of colors in each area, from the reds of Ŭrgŭp to the pale blues of Ihara and the rich creams of Gőreme.

Kayseri, or ancient Caesarea, which was the nearest city to the majority of these valleys in classical times, was an important Christian outpost in Central Anatolia because of its position on the trade routes from the south and the east. The commercial activity here attracted Greeks, who were in turn supplanted by Arabs during the Islamic invasion in the seventh century. Armenians fleeing the Seljuk move from the east added another ethnic layer in the eleventh century followed by Turks, Mongols, and then Turks again who finally established control over the city in the mid-fourteenth century, never to lose it again. The final upheavals in Caesarea were devastating for the Christian community there, and an exodus, similar to that caused by the Latin occupation of Constantinople, began as people fled east into these barren valleys for protection.

Many saw isolation here as the only safe alternative in an uncertain time when solitary *akritoi*, who were the Byzantine equivalent of Turkish ghazi warrior knights, were the only law in this frontier region. A monastic movement begun by Saint Basil of Caesarea in the fourth century gradually started to increase by the seventh century and became a flood 300 years later. In contrast to the strictly separated coenobitical units seen in the southeast and elsewhere, the monastic communities set up in Cappadocia centered around the Lavra system, which originated in Palestine and did not require constant, self-sufficient separation from society, but allowed mixing with the secular world. For this reason, the monasteries of Cappadocia usually existed side by side with nearby villages, and were much smaller than those seen at Alahan, Anavarza, Sion, and Sumela because they had no sleeping facilities. The small scale of each unit was also in keeping with Saint Basil's original belief that a good monastery should have no more than 20 monks. As Spiro Kostof has said,

> despite the lack of large corporate organization, or is it really because of it, monasteries were central to the life of the secular society. In an area where isolation from the influence of the capital was acute and danger from the outside a constant threat, the

villages and small towns looked to the monk, imitator of Christ and the embodiment in theory at least of selflessness, for pre-eminent leadership in all aspects of their difficult existence.

A Monastic Haven

The four main areas of monastic activity that have been studied in Cappadocia to date are Gőreme, Soğanli Dere, Açik Saray, and Ihlahan or Peristrema. Gőreme and the network of valleys near Ortahisar, Üçhisar, and Zilve were the centers of Christian activity here, containing hundreds of small churches in between. Many of these, such as the Apply Church (Elmali Kil) and the Dark Church (Karanlik), are decorated with beautiful frescos, made from the vivid colors of the local pigments. Soğanli Dere, like Ihlahan, is in a deep gorge, but differs in that it is surrounded by a natural wall of tufa and has a wider valley floor and sides that are not as steep as Peristrema. Because it is far from the main center of tourist activity at Gőreme, Soğanli Dere is still relatively pristine and undiscovered, making it far less commercialized. Of the more than 50 churches here, one of the most intriguing is the Yilanikilise or Snake Church, named from frescos in the interior showing women, supposedly representing the progeny of Eve, wearing real boas instead of feather ones. While their faces have been chipped away, the bodies and the snakes remain. Soğanli Dere is also close to the underground troglodyte cities of Derinkuyu, which means "deep well," and it held more than 20,000 people at one time and was connected to its sister city Kaymakli with a tunnel that was over 9 kilometers long. These underground cities offered nearly complete safety and comfort to all those living there, and they were virtually undetectable. Smoke from cooking fires as well as openings for ventilation were carefully hidden, and if an invader did happen to stumble upon one of the openings to the tunnels, it was sealed by a massive stone disk that rolled in grooves cut into the rock. Both cities have been empty since 1965 when the Turkish government opened them as museums.

Açik Saray, which is the third monastic center in Cappadocia, was not as extensive as the others, with its main claim to fame being a rock-cut church that is not made out of tufa, meaning that its intricate designs were even more difficult to execute. The Ihlahan Gorge, once known as Peristrema, is the fourth and last of this group and is located about 70 kilometers west of Soğanli Dere close to Hasan Daği. Created by the Melendis River, this valley stretches from just below Selime on the north through Yaprakhisar and Belisirma to Ihlara on the south, covering nearly 6 kilometers in its course. While not long ago this was totally uncharted territory, the churches in this valley are today dutifully marked with signs that call out strange names such as the Church of the Black Collar, the Fragrant Church, or the Church of the Crooked Stone. Yet, the atmosphere here is still primitive compared to other parts of Cappadocia, and the long walk along the river still has a feeling of high adventure.

Troglodytes

But churches and monasteries aside, the majority of the inhabitants of the fairy chimneys were people who were trying to escape persecution and death at the hands of one enemy or another. There is evidence that there were many of them, to the extent that entire cities that were carved into the tufa have been uncovered.[3] These were warrens of carved spaces connected by steps, often with only one entrance linking them to the outside world, closed off with a circular millstone that could be rolled into a groove cut into the opposing wall. In 1965, three separate, intact settlements were uncovered here covering an area of 6 square kilometers inside the rock, accessed through a single entrance.[4] Leo the Deacon, who was a historian in the tenth century, quoted Nikephoros Phokas, who was later to become a Byzantine emperor, as saying that the people living in these rock-cut houses were called "troglodytes." [5] This conjures up an image of gnarled gnomes living in dark holes underground who only poked their heads out now and then when they wanted to do evil. But this image is far from the truth, given the evidence provided by the interior of the houses. Life was not as easy in these houses as it was elsewhere, but there were considerable creature comforts. Many occupants had fireplaces, with hidden channels used to hide the smoke as much as possible. Several houses also had more than one level, reached by staircases cut into the solid stone. Carpets on the floor and mattresses and blankets on the shelves that served as beds would have done much to soften and add color to the hard rock surfaces. The underground caverns served as pens for sheep and goats that were a constant source of meat, milk, cheese, and wool. The rock itself helped to mitigate temperature extremes. The only negative that could not be offset, other than the constant fear of being discovered, was the lack of natural light.

ÇATAL HÜYÜK

In the early 1960s, archaeologist James Mellaart defied the conventional belief that no significant settlement had ever occurred on the Anatolian plateau by excavating a town there that dated from 6500 to 5300 B.C. The site is called Çatal Hüyük or "forked mound" because of the shape of the tell, or earth mound, that covered the houses. The settlement, which is located on a wide expanse of fertile land southeast of Konya, Turkey, covers about 25 acres and is about three times the size of Homeric Troy, near Canakalle, to the west. The houses that Mellaart found were all made of sun-dried mud brick in a wood frame, joined together with common walls, and entered through openings on the roofs, which were flat. Several clusters of houses shared a communal courtyard, which appears to have served as a shrine, since each of these was decorated with the skulls and horns of cows, either real or cast in plaster. Wall paintings, similar to those found in Lascaux caves in France, indicate that the people who worshipped there may also have believed in sympathetic magic, or the idea that by painting the image of an animal that they wanted to kill in a hunt ensured their success in doing so.

The difference between the people who painted the murals in Lascaux caves and those at Çatal Hüyük, however, is that the occupants of the honeycomb cluster of houses on the Anatolian plateau were at a transitional point between the hunter-gatherers of the Paleolithic Period and farmers who were trying to adapt themselves to a settled, agriculturally based life in which hunting and gathering were still practiced but were not the only means of subsistence. The murals as well as the tools, pottery, and weapons that have been found in the house all exhibit crafts-manship of a very high level, which is an advantage of a more predictable lifestyle.

Excavation has continued steadily since the site was first discovered, and archae-ologists have subsequently been able to slowly piece together a more accurate pic-ture of what the daily life of prehistoric farmers and hunter-gatherers who lived there must have been like. They have now unearthed 18 different levels of habita-tion, layered on top of each other, covering a period of 1,200 years of continuous occupation on the site.[6] The initial discovery and continuously surprising revelations that have emerged have forced a reevaluation of conventional ideas about the progress and network of Neolithic development in western Asia. The unparalleled artistic achievement displayed at Çatal Hüyük is a significant tribute to human skill and ingenuity before the invention of writing. Like Jericho in the eighth century B.C., Çatal Hüyük may seem like an isolated exception, but archae-ologists are becoming increasingly aware of the fact that they have now uncovered only a fraction of the site and have upgraded the status of the settlement from a town to a city. There is still much more to find. Based on the evidence of artifacts collected, they now believe that there was active trade between this settlement and another that is a hundred miles away and that Çatal Hüyük may end up being three times larger than Jericho at its height.

Aerial view of Çatal Hüyük tumulus in Cumra, Turkey. © Images&Stories / Alamy

Vulture Shrines

In addition to the burial of the remains of deceased family members inside each house, Mellaart also found some minor discrepancies between the objects buried with the deceased in the houses and those found in the shrines. This, he thought, "suggests that the privileged dead buried in the shrines had been people who during life had enjoyed affluence, respect or authority; in fact members of a higher social order or distinction than their relatives buried in the houses." [7] The use of red ochre, which has been found in the excavation at many other Neolithic settlements elsewhere, and was sprinkled on the bodies of those of especially high regard, was found in about 5 percent of the individuals buried in the shrines. Some bodies were also decapitated, which is thought to have been done in the case of a distinguished ancestor who began a lineage.[8] A similar practice was carried out in Jericho, in which some skulls were kept apart, plastered over and colored to look lifelike, as if to preserve the memory of special individuals in a tangible way.

The Houses of Çatal Hüyük

The approximately 2,000 houses of the Çatal Hüyük settlement had solid walls on all sides, both to conserve heat during the winter, which can be extremely cold on the windswept Anatolian Plateau, and to provide defense against wild animals, since attacks by outsiders do not seem to have been a problem. The trapdoors into the houses were on the roof and were usually located on the south side of the house. They also served as a chimney for the hearth and oven placed directly beneath them and had a wooden canopy, or pergola, above them, which protected the interior of the houses from rain and snow. Access into each house was by ladder, but the side rails and rungs were squared off and the size of each step was quite substantial. The lack of windows on the sidewalls means that the interiors must have been relatively dark, mostly lit by oil lamps and the fireplace. This fireplace was formed of mud packed into a container with a circular base, sloping sides, and an open top, with a U-shaped cutout in front to place the wood inside it.

The walls of the house were made of sun-dried brick, formed in a wooden mold. Apparently the technique of *terre pisé*, or rammed earth, which involved building wooden shutters into which the earth was placed and then pounded until it was compact, after which the shuttering could be moved up to make the next course of the entire wall, was unknown. The bricks were used to fill in a wooden frame of columns that held up the wooden roof girders.[9] Bundles of reeds were then placed across the roof beams and covered with a layer of mud, which was the roof. Woven mats were placed on top of the beams before the reed bundles were placed on top to prevent the infiltration of dirt and dust into the house below. Black mortar made from ashes from the hearths and crushed animal bone from the refuse dump was extremely strong, and the brick courses were bonded, or interlocked, for stability.

Parallels with the Anasazi

Since this house type is so similar to that of the Anasazi in North America, built 6,000 years later, it begs comparison with it in some key areas. First of all, such common party wall compartmentalization, with entrance from the roof and no windows in the walls, meant that the interior of the houses was very dark and smoky. The Çatal Hüyük houses were only one story high, compared to the Anasazi pueblos that were stacked up on terraces several levels in height, which meant that the earlier Anatolian houses did get some light through the opening in the roof, but only a minimal amount. Second, the woven mats above the rafters that were intended to stop the mud dust from the roof from entering the house were not perfectly tight and did allow dirt to fall in. All those who have been involved in investigating the Çatal Hüyük houses, however, have commented on how scrupulously clean they must have been, even though there was no drainage system of the kind found in the Indus River cities of around 2800 B.C., nearly 3 millennia afterwards. Refuse was removed to a dump outside the wall on a regular basis and covered with ash, and the walls were renewed annually. Third, the fact that both Çatal Hüyük and Anasazi settlements had no streets as such, because there was no space between the houses to allow them, meant that the roof terraces became the public space for work and play as well.

The platforms, which were used for sitting and sleeping as well as to inter deceased family members, were also covered in woven mats, before being laid with carpets and pillows.[10] Wall paintings in the houses at Çatal Hüyük varied in location and subject, but sometimes were clusters of circles or circles within circles that seem to represent stars or constellations.

CONSTANTINOPLE, "THE NEW ROME"

In early July 1203, the Venetian Doge, Enrico Dandolo, led a fleet of 200 ships and 25,000 men up the Dardanelles toward Constantinople, which, as the historian Procopius had once described it, rose from the water in front of them like "an exhalation in the night." Unlike the Crusaders who accompanied him, the blind Doge was undaunted by the sight of the 14 miles of land and sea walls that had previously repelled rapacious armies of Avars, Sassanids, Arabs, Bulgars, Russians, Attila "the scourge of God," and assorted Turkish tribes before him. The land walls that had been enlarged to their final configuration by Theodosius II, the grandson of Theodosius the Great, were undoubtedly a marvel of military construction. They were arranged in a double row behind a wide moat, with a formidable no-man's land between them. In addition to this lethal combination, there were nearly 100 huge towers along the walls, which were placed at regular intervals. They protected the main gates to the city that were placed between them, so that any invaders could be attacked diagonally from above to best advantage. Each of the gates, in turn, was named according to either an identifying characteristic or the section of the city that they gave access to, such as the White Gate, or the Gate of the Life-giving Spring. While one of the Byzantine names for Constantinople itself may have been Theophylaktos, or "Protected of God," equal credit for the 1,000 years of safety before the Venetian invasion should also be given to the cliffs of brick and stone that combined with a naturally defensive topography to keep the city secure. The bronze equestrian *quadriga* that had crowned the main doorway of St. Mark's Basilica in Venice (until it was removed recently to protect it from air pollution) had originally been brought from Rome by the Emperor Constantine

The ancient city walls of Constantinople.   *Source:* Steven Daenens; Flickr

as a centerpiece for the Hippodrome of the new city that was to bear his name. It was based on a Greek work done in the second half of the fifth century B.C., and it was just a small fraction of the treasure that the Venetians carted out of the city after a desperate nine-month long struggle that had brought about its tragic destruction. It is sad to think that the richness of the Piazza San Marco, which has been so admired for centuries, was gained through the desecration of what had been the only existing repository of the classical traditions of Greece and Rome, and that this represents only a hint of the treasure that was taken.[11]

Greek Beginnings

Byzantium, the city that the Crusaders and Venetians of 1203–1204 had looted, had its beginnings in the seventh century B.C., when King Byzas from Megara in Greece first saw it to be a uniquely defensible location on which to establish his small kingdom, surrounded as it was by the Marmara Sea on the south, the Golden Horn on the north, and the swift deep waters of the Bosphorus at its tip. This wall of water on three of its sides made only subsidiary walls along the shore and a single land wall necessary in order to make any settlement totally secure. A legend surrounding Byzas's choice of this site for the new city relates that after he consulted Oracle at Delphi, he was told to build opposite "the land of the blind," in clear reference to the lack of vision of the Greeks in Chalcedon, who failed to seize it first. Byzas established the first settlement at the tip of the peninsula at a place now called Sarayburnu, or "the Nose of the Palace," because a royal residence has been there ever since.

Because of its strategic location between the Hellenic West and the Persian East, with the power to control sea and land traffic between two continents, the new city quickly took on a key role in the Persian Wars of the fifth century B.C., as well as in the Peloponnesian War between Athens and Sparta that followed. Byzas's city, which was then nearly 200 years old, suffered several invasions by each side in the later war, as each tried to gain the upper hand in the important political arena of Anatolia. It was eventually the Persians, who, by using their navy to help the Spartans, managed to turn the tide against the Athenians, leaving the city at rest. The whirlwind passage of Alexander the Great through Byzantium on his way into central Anatolia and beyond, at the beginning of the Hellenistic Age, opened up a new chapter in the history of this entire area, of which few indications except fragments in the Istanbul Archaeological Museum now remain.

The Roman Phase

The Romans were not far behind Alexander with the establishment of the province of Asia in 133 B.C., and their greatly expanded ambitions, matched with unparalleled engineering ability, had a much bigger impact on the city than anything before. After 300 years of relative quiet during the Pax Romana, ill-conceived political alignments in a Roman factional struggle brought retribution in A.D. 196 by Septimus Severus, who leveled and burned nearly everything standing in the city. Following this conflagration, a new wall was built that stretched from the entry of what is now the Galata Bridge across the peninsula to the Sea of Marmara, nearly doubling an urban area primarily restricted in the past to the Acropolis. The rapidly increasing inability of the Roman Empire to defend and hold its far-flung frontiers against outside incursions as well as the agitation of a growing Christian population within it led to a momentous change in the historical course of what had been, until then, a relatively small city within its control. Having succeeded his father Constantius Chlorus as one of the tetrarchs in the tripartite system set up by the Emperor Diocletian, Constantine was not content to share power but methodically set out to eliminate the other members of the ruling faction. His final victory over his brother-in-law Licinius, ruler of the West, at Chrysopolis, now Üsküdar, in A.D. 324 left him as sole ruler of both the eastern and western factions of the Roman Empire, clearing the way for his decision to move its capital and establish a New Rome at Byzantium.

The New Rome of Constantine

This decision was not made lightly, but was the culmination of Constantine's long experience in this part of Asia Minor during the reign of Diocletian, when he had held a government post in Nicomedia and had overseen an extensive building program carried out there. Constantine's New Rome was intended to be not just a substitute for its famous Latin counterpart but a superior mirror image. Where Rome had seven hills and 14 regions, its new replacement was to have them as well, even if a seventh hill had to be partially built to maintain the similarity. Constantinople was also not to be deficient in riches and glory, as thousands of pieces of sculpture and other works of art were imported and manufactured to adorn the new city, which used the Severan plan as its base.

This plan already included temples, a hippodrome, and the baths of Zeus-Xeuthippes, a hyphenated deity of Thracian and Anatolian origins, and all of these played an important part in Constantine's decision to move his capital here. His plan augmented the preexisting Roman structures in several important ways, which are instructive of his long range intentions for both the character of the new city and its role as the center of his new empire. Constantine first altered the combination of temple, circus, and bath that he had inherited from Septimus Severus by replacing the pagan religious building with a pair of Christian churches that he named Hagia Sophia (Holy Wisdom) and Hagia Eirene (Holy Peace) in order to subtly ease the transition from old customs to new. Figures representing the concepts of wisdom and peace had been used in Roman buildings like the Celsus Library in Ephesus, which predated the naming of these two churches and thus would have sent out a crystal-clear message that Constantine intended this city to be the heart and conscience of a new Christian empire, just as Rome had been the epicenter of a pantheistic one. To extend the revision even further, he linked his own palace directly to the twin churches, which, along with an elongated hippodrome whose form can still be traced today, set up what Constantine felt to be the Utopian triumvirate of palatium, sacerdotium, and circus, or palace, church, and stadium. Virtually nothing of the great palace remains now, but it has been suggested that it was probably very similar to Diocletian's huge residence in Split, which was a city within a city. By inserting the palace into the old reciprocal relationship between temple and circus that had effectively replaced the theatre as an institution of social gathering and entertainment at this time, Constantine symbolically put himself in the position of arbiter between the church and the people. Considering himself to be a thirteenth apostle who was destined by God to expand the mission of Christianity on earth, he saw himself as the leader of both the Church and the State, without favoring one to the exclusion of the other.

Streets Adapted to a Different Topography

From this metaphorical head, located at the peninsular tip of the city, a spine, or *regia*, ran through the old barrier of the Severan walls to an oval forum of a size and form similar to that found in Jordanian Jerash (Gerasa) today. Like the *cardo maximus* of that almost perfectly preserved Roman city, its sides were lined with columns with shops behind them, continuing a late Roman trend toward the extension of the commercial activity of the old Greek *agora* along the street. This oval forum, which was later transformed into the Forum Taurii during the reign of Theodosius I, was the first major processional event prior to the square Philadelphian Forum to the west, where the main *cardo* branched into two in order to conform to the widening of the peninsula at that point. The northerly branch of the two ran parallel to the Aqueduct of Valens, past the Constantinian Mausoleum and the Church of the Holy Apostles to the Charisian Gate in the land wall.

The second branch turned along the coast of the Sea of Marmara to the south, running through the Forum Bovis and the Forum Arcadii to the Golden Gate, which was the main entrance into the city from the landside. The Constantinian plan for New Rome was remarkable for both the speed with which it was implemented and its adaptation of what had become a standard gridiron formula onto a challenging, hilly topography. It is important to note that Constantinople did not spring up *de novo*, but rather was an extension of both the early city plan of Byzas and the Severan rebuilding of that plan. As such, it reused the main elements of the middle avenue or *mese*, the tetrastoon *agora*, which became known as the Augusteion under Constantine, the Zeus-Xeuthippes baths, and finally the major north-south orientation of the Hippodrome, which was greatly enlarged to fulfill a wider social function. In spite of its Christian basis, the city was not, however, totally organized around religious foundations as was its Ottoman counterpart, but closely followed the template of Rome.

A Long Succession

The subsequent long line of Byzantine emperors that followed Constantine in a continuous 1,200 year succession that was broken only by the Venetian interregnum considered itself to be the rightful heir to a classical tradition that had been saved from certain extinction after the fall of Rome. For the Byzantines, the physical resemblance of their city, in its final form inside the Theodosian land walls, was too close to that of its fallen parent on the Tiber to be mere coincidence and was instead considered to be Divine Will. The gradual evaluation of that classical heritage, during a remarkably long period of political stability threatened only by internal theological debates, was characterized mainly by a constant embellishment of Constantine's original concept of the unified duality of Church and State. The emperor and the patriarch both continued to refine their roles based on the original idea of a delicate balance between the two.

The Hagia Sophia remains as the best formal expression of the wish to perpetuate a classical heritage in the Byzantine East. The form commemorated separate but equal status of the emperor and patriarch meeting beneath a great dome and also symbolized the witness of heaven above. Ranking as one of man's greatest architectural achievements, the plan of the Hagia Sophia clearly expresses the blending of the classic Roman basilica with a circular Byzantine dome fitted to a square base. Anthemieus of Tralles, who became the architect of record after the death of Isidorus of Miletus, was a past director of the Academy of Athens and a noted geometer in the best Platonic tradition, making him the perfect bridge between the traditions of ancient Greece and those of Byzantium. Transcending its role as a purely religious building, the Hagia Sophia has become one of those rare monuments that now represent an entire culture, not merely a single function. The domed typology of the Hagia Sophia, due to its great imperial symbolism, was thus eagerly adopted as a model for all future mosques in Istanbul, regardless of the purely canonical origin of its centralized form.

From Constantinople to Istanbul

In 1253, Constantinople was conquered again, but this time the invaders intended to stay. The first act of the Turkish commander Mehmet the Conqueror upon entering the city was to march to the Hagia Sophia and claim it for Islam. The Ottoman Empire, which grew from here and at its zenith almost encircled the Mediterranean Sea, encompassing the Tigris and Euphrates valley as well as Syria, the Balkans, and Greece, ruled that world from the "Sublime Porte" of Istanbul for nearly 500 years. Each of the highly visible tops of its seven hills became a preferred building site for sultans or emirs who wished to build a mosque or charitable foundation, which led in turn to a radical alteration of the skyline of the Byzantine city. Research into the documents involved with the building of these monuments, however, shows that the only criteria used for site selection was the desire for clean air or a clearly visible elevation rather than any comprehensive plan for a unified, domed, and spired silhouette running the entire length of the peninsula. The final result, then, while extremely impressive, is another of history's fortunate accidents, a series of events totally unrelated to uniform aesthetic concerns or a comprehensive urban strategy.

153

Physical Changes

It is understandable that an event as cataclysmic as the Turkish conquest of the eastern capital of Christendom would bring about other major adjustments in both the form and population of the city, which took about a century to be fully realized. Since Constantinople's population had gradually but steadily diminished prior to the conquest, Mehmet II found himself the sovereign of a virtually empty city. After some tentative attempts at resettlement that were generally resisted because of the sultan's initial refusal to grant ownership of real estate, a dual policy of land grants to prominent citizens and *waqfs* (religious endowments), as well as forced deportation and resettlement, totally reorganized the existing urban fabric, giving it a new social mix. New districts, bearing the names of origin of people resettled from Karaman, Trebizond, Belgrade, or elsewhere, began to spring up throughout Istanbul as people began to pour into the vacated city. Eventually this chaotic and somewhat haphazard policy of repopulation became more systematic, once the essential need for a basic citizenry had been satisfied. Certain classes or trades from various areas throughout the Ottoman Empire also began to be relocated en masse specifically because they could be of some exact service to either the court or the city.

In addition to this influx of culturally diverse ethnic groups, Mehmet also drastically altered the Byzantine makeup of the city by introducing the Ottoman *külliye* into common use. Basically a self-contained village unto itself, the *külliye* is a complex providing social services symbiotically related to a mosque and providing housing facilities, kitchens, hospitals, schools, and libraries, which are meant solely for the welfare of the public. This new institutional type had within it the seeds of a totally distinct urban organization, and it progressively transformed Istanbul into an Ottoman city. The imperial *külliye* gradually occupied the key points of the urban fabric and the city's continuously linear structure, which had been virtually fixed since the time of Theodosius, but was progressively replaced by a discontinuous, point-by-point configuration that has left an indelible mark upon it.

THE HITTITES

The Hittites, who referred to themselves as "the people of Hatti," exercised great power in central Turkey at about the same time as the Trojan War, ruling an empire that stretched from the Euphrates to the Aegean. Recent intensive research into the daily lives of what had previously been a mysterious people has uncovered a fascinating picture of what we now know to have been a great Bronze Age civilization, which was destroyed around 1200 B.C. Awareness of Hittite culture is relatively new, since it was only in 1923 that ruins found at Boghazköy, Alacahöyuk, and Yazilikaya were agreed to be common to it and that archaeologists finally agreed that it was the Hittites that Ramses II was referring to in his stele at the Temple of Karnak, which he erected to celebrate his victory over "The Great King of the Hatti" at the Battle of Kadesh fought in 1275 B.C. in what is now Syria.

Background

Excavations at the Hittite capital of Boghazköy in central Anatolia have unearthed cuneiform tablets, and among these was the treaty between Ramses II and Hattisilis, the "Great King" that Ramses referred to, using wording that is identical to that found at the Temple of Karnak. There are also records of the Hittites' dealings with Troy, referred to as "Taruisa," in which there are also references to Priam's son, Paris, personally. This extensive clay archive also shows that the Hittites, in addition to being in constant contact with the Egyptians, also had diplomatic relations and trade agreements with the Babylonians and Assyrians as well as with city-states such as Mycenae, Tyre, Sidon, Byblos, Jerusalem, Megiddo, and Knossos, or Crete. Evidence from an inscription on a statue base from Thebes confirms this heretofore unrecognized level of interaction, since it describes a diplomatic voyage to both Mycenae and Knossos, in 1300 B.C. This explains the Mycenaean pottery found in Amarna of about the same date.

Such evidence shows that globalization is nothing new, since these kingdoms were involved in diplomatic intrigue of a kind that would be very familiar to us today. At the time of the Trojan War the Hittites were involved in a war with the Assyrians to the east of their empire, so they wanted to keep peace with the Greeks, to the west, to avoid a war on two fronts. When the Greek forces under the leadership of Agamemnon landed on the coast of Asia Minor, they raided villages and towns along the Aegean coast, upsetting the delicate alliances the Hittites had established in the region. The Hittites conceded control of Miletus, which the Hittites called "Millewanda," to the Greeks. Some historians and archaeologists now speculate that the Achaeans, under Agamemnon, fought with the Hittites for control of Troy after the Achaeans had captured it, which conjures up the image of two great Bronze Age armies, representing two completely different cultures, meeting on the battlefield after Troy had fallen. The date of the Achaean attack in 1240 B.C. dovetails almost exactly with the disappearance of the Hittite capital city of Hattusas, as well as with Pharaonic Egyptian records of an invasion by "peoples of the sea," whose origins are still unknown. The result of the collapse of both Troy and Hattusas was disastrous for Anatolia, marking the end of the Bronze Age there and causing a Dark Age that lasted for two centuries.

Before their passing, however, the Hittites left an indelible physical record of their culture on Anatolia and the kingdom that they ruled from it. It is now believed that their culture, which was very rich, was a blending of the Indo-European people, who first arrived on the plateau around 2000 B.C. and settled near Kultepe, about 200 kilometers to the southeast of present day Inkara, and the Hatti, who were indigenous to the region. Five temples have been uncovered at Hattusas and Alacahöyuk, as well as a very sophisticated religious center at Yazilikaya.

The Yazilikaya temple, which consists of a built, introductory section that acts as a protective gateway placed in front of an open ravine on which a continuous mural depicts the entire pantheon of Hittite gods and goddesses, provides a fascinating insight into their hierarchical society. The shrine takes its name from the Hittite words for "carved rock," since more than 1,000 deities are etched into the cliff face that is only accessible after first passing through the primary temple in front of it. This is a remarkable integration between human-made and natural forms. The long, linear gateway building was organized into a series of nonsymmetrical spaces that appear to have served as places of worship and administration for the shrine. It closes off the north of a rocky defile whose walls have been turned into two sequentially ordered sculpture galleries. The story that they tell weaves the lives of King Hattus or "the one from Hattusa" and King Tudhaliya IV, who commissioned the construction of the gallery, with those of their gods, who are depicted as being very humane and loving.

Hittite civilization passed through two principal phases, now referred to as the Old Kingdom and the Empire, with the historical dividing line being the middle of the fifteenth century B.C. During the Old Kingdom period, Mursilis I incursions reached as far as Syria and Babylon, which he occupied in 1595 B.C.

Hittite Houses

The mystery surrounding the Hittites is beginning to be revealed, as excavation at important sites has continued yielding a great deal more information about their daily lives. While not always on a grid, the main streets of Hittite cities were usually straight, and images of chariot-riding royalty, such as those on the walls at Yazilikaya come to mind when walking on their ground covered surfaces. Sites for the Hittite cities, such as Boghazköy, were typically chosen with defense in mind, so they are usually on steep slopes, making it necessary to use terraces.[12] Like the early cities of the Indus River civilizations, these also had a well-integrated drainage system to take rainwater and water from melting snow off the slopes efficiently, as well as the sewage from the houses, and those clay pipe systems have been found. Unlike Mohenjo-daro and Harappa, however, the individual houses seem even more haphazardly oriented, with units of many different shapes and sizes facing in different directions being the norm. Courtyards are a ubiquitous organizing device, but beyond that it is difficult to determine a consistent typological pattern. Even they are used differently than they are in the Mesopotamian, Egyptian, Chinese, and Indus Valley cultures included here, being pushed to the front of the house and used more as a buffer between the entrance and the street than an internal temperature regulator and microcosmic symbol of a natural paradise.[13] This is the case at Boghazköy, but in other cities such as Beycesultan, the courtyard is used differently, once again with an upper floor supported by columns, overhanging it like a porch or sometimes simply as a roof. The houses we have been discussing that were joined together using party walls within a roughly rectangular block system in various cities were generally for the less well-to-do, while those at the upper end of the social spectrum preferred to live in freestanding houses outside of these precincts, often on rocky, easily defended promontories. The royal palace on the cliff-side site of Buyukkale, near Boghazköy, protected by steep mountainsides on the north and east, and massive walls on the south and west, is a good example of this preference. This palace dates from 1,500 years before the reign of Hattuslis I, but reached the apogee of its magnificence in the mid-1600s B.C., during his residence there.

Hattusas was divided into two sections, with a smaller lower portion on the northern side of a mountainside, a higher portion on the south, and a citadel at the top, in between. This citadel, known as Buyukkale, was an elliptically shaped fortress, protected by a massive castellated wall placed along the top of a cliff, with three levels that corresponded to the slope of the hill it was built on. These levels, in turn, were organized around a series of courtyards that became progressively

Cave dwellings in Cappadocia, Turkey.   Courtesy of Shutterstock

smaller as the slope rose, and these acted as incremental filters between public and private areas. The lowest courtyard column was open to the general public and was used for general administrative functions, followed by a more restricted religious section in the middle and the King's palace in the smallest and most secure level at the top.

Unfortunately, because of the steep site and the need to build the palace up on a strong structural base to accommodate the heavily contoured site, the foundations that archaeologists have uncovered are fairly repetitive and mundane, telling us very little about the room arrangement of the above residence that they supported, which has long since disappeared. What they can decipher from these thick and repetitively compartmentalized foundation walls, however, is the overall configuration and enormous scale of the complex, as well as some indications of its various functions, entrances, and exits, which all give a fairly clear pictures of how it was used. Shaped roughly like an elongated fan to conform to a terrace on its hillside site, the palace is divided into four clearly identifiable zones, which are the citadel entrance court immediately inside the main citadel gate, followed by the lower, middle, and upper courts, with walled gates at each corresponding to the break in the various terrace levels as the palace steps up the hill. With the exception of this topographical relationship, the divisions are reminiscent of those used by the architect Sinan in the design of Topkapi Palace, which he realized from the first Ottoman Emperor Mehmet (the Conqueror) in 1425 at Sarayburnu, in Istanbul. The reasons for the compartmentalization in each case, however, are the same, related to the protection and privacy of the ruler and his family, although is it not clear if Hattusilis I also had a harem as Mehmet did. His residential quarter of Hattusilis I no longer exists at the highest and most imposing final quadrant of Buyukkale, but the gate that the king used at its southeast corner still does, leading to a second gate and a ramp for his chariot that would make it easier to leave the citadel without going through all of the other sections. Archaeologists believe that each of the four courts was faced with arcades, but beyond that no substantial architectural evidence remains.

Assyrian influence is evident in both the construction techniques that were used and the introspective, internalized approach taken in the design, which carries over to houses within the city as well. The only difference is that the Hittites tended to surround courtyards with spaces that had a diverse range of functions rather than to group similar activities together as the Assyrians did.

MESOPOTAMIA

Mesopotamia is the northern tip of the Fertile Crescent; its name is derived from the Greek words for "between the two rivers." Those rivers, the Tigris and the Euphrates, have their source at Lake Van in Turkey. They begin nearly 250 miles apart, but gradually move closer together as they approach what is now Baghdad. They then begin to separate again on their way to their delta at the Arabian Gulf.

The Hit-Samara Line

A limestone escarpment that cuts across Mesopotamia from the contemporary cities of Hit on the west and Samara on the east divides it into two distinctly different geological and topographical zones, and this difference had a significant impact on the kinds of houses that were built there in ancient times and on our present ability to study them. Because of the deep channels they have cut into the limestone substrate above the Hit-Samara line, the sites of ancient cities such as Carcamish, Nineveh, Nimrud, and Ashur, which are near their banks, have been left undisturbed. South of this line, many cities are covered in sediment, since the rivers were free to meander across a broad, flat, muddy plain. In each case, either with the rivers in deep channels, or flowing freely across the plain, extensive irrigation was necessary to make farming feasible and the construction, control, and protection of these essential systems had important political implications for the region in the past.

As armies spreading Islam approached the Tigris and Euphrates river valley from Arabia, moving in from the desert to the southwest, they ended up on top of the divisive escarpment, looking down on the valley and to the Zagros Mountains to the east, in Iran, in the distance. They called the escarpment "*al-Hajara*," or the cliff, and the barren limestone plateau that separated the two rivers above it "*al-Jazirah*," or the island, since it kept them apart in individual valleys. To the south, they could see an enormous, flat, fertile plain extending all the way to their common delta, which has no equivalent in the Near East.

A Land of Extremes

This region typically has temperatures between 110 and 130 degrees Fahrenheit in the shade during the summer, with no rainfall for eight months of the year. The rivers flood when the snow in the Taurus Mountains in Turkey melts in the spring, providing a reliance upon an annual cycle similar to that existing in Egypt in ancient times. In Mesopotamia, the floodwaters arrived in unmanageable quantities and at the wrong time for planting. This, along with the relative depth of the water in its various valleys, meant that irrigation canals and reservoirs were necessary, forcing the development of a governmental system capable of organizing, building, and maintaining them. Because of extensive cultivation and irrigation, salinization began to increase. As saline water began to evaporate on the soil, salt was deposited, which lowered fertility. Salinization started in Mesopotamia in the Tigris River in 2400 B.C., spreading up into the Euphrates soon afterward. By 1700 B.C. it had affected the harvesting of wheat, which has a low tolerance for salt, to the extent that it was reduced from being 20 percent of the total source of food to being about 2 percent. It was replaced by barley, which has a higher saline tolerance.

In spite of the challenges presented by irrigation systems and salinization, the development of a sophisticated civilization in Mesopotamia represents as much of a success story in the early advancement of the agricultural revolution as that of Egypt, at the other end of the Fertile Crescent, to the southwest. As indicated earlier in the discussion about Çatal Hüyük in Anatolia, the transfer from a hunting and gathering culture to agricultural communities is one of the most momentous events in human history. This transformation did not happen all at once, occurring in layered stages in different regions around the world. It was initiated by climatic changes that took place after the Ice Age. The progressive rise in temperature encouraged agriculture, which demands a stationary, rather than nomadic, lifestyle, good organizational and planning skills, a knowledge of astronomy, the use of mathematics for record keeping, as well as writing, which is the most important advancement of all, since it is one of the criteria for the establishment of civilization. Cuneiform writing was well established in Mesopotamia by 3000 B.C.

The wheat that succumbed to salinization was derived from several wild varieties and was the foundation of that civilization until it was replaced with barley, and it was supplemented by legumes and lentils. This basic diet was augmented by milk and meat from domesticated cattle, sheep, and goats as well as meat from pigs. As people began to rely on agriculture, social behavior began to change. A year's supply of grain for a family of four can only be harvested during a brief period in the spring when the crop ripens and needs tending. It also cannot be carried around very easily, meaning that people had to remain in one place.

Three Early Cultures

Archaeologists have identified three early cultures that existed in Mesopotamia between 6000 and 4000 B.C., which they have named after the contemporary place names where they were discovered: the Hassuna, Samarra, and Halaf civilizations.[14] Hassuna was an agricultural grouping characterized by clusters of mud brick courtyard buildings joined together by party walls, which, due to recent interpretations of cuneiform tablets and cylinder seals, seem to have been privately owned.[15] There is evidence of weaving and exquisite jewelry that has been related to this culture.

In the case of Samarra and Halaf, a wide range of residential structures have been discovered that range from circular, domical homes to larger detached houses that indicate a wide range of social levels.[16]

In part because of the geological differences that have just been described as defining this region, it subsequently divided into the Tepe Gaura culture in the north and the Uruk culture in the south.

The Marsh Arabs

Because of changes in elevation and the existence of promontories, the northern cities were often designed like citadels with walled enclosures on the heights and villages typically housing farmers below in the valleys where the fields were located. In the south, because of the predominantly flat river plain, the settlements were dependent upon irrigation canals. Even further south, in the delta region now called the Shatt al Arab, people lived on islands in woven reed houses and used reed boats to go back and forth from them to the banks of each of the rivers. These houses and the way of life of the Marsh Arabs who built them have remained remarkably similar over the centuries, threatened only by the retaliatory damming and draining of many of these lakes by the regime of Saddam Hussein. In spite of the hardships that both accompanied and followed in the wake of his overthrow, the Marsh Arabs have been persistently working to undo the damage done to their ancient ways of life during the 1980s and 1990s and have made remarkable strides in doing so.

Uruk

Warka, which is about 150 miles southeast of Baghdad and now 12 miles from the Euphrates River, was once the site of Uruk, which emerged in 4000 B.C., and was home to one of the first literate urban societies in Mesopotamia. It was one of a number of cities in Sumeria that had a high degree of economic independence. It thrived between 3500 and 3200 B.C., but even then it only occupied an area of 12 hectares, or 3.5 square miles, with a population of about 10,000.

It is perhaps best known for the White Temple that has been found there, one of the best examples of a high temple built on a platform with battered walls. The columned hall takes its name from parallel rows of round 2 meters wide supports. These columns, like walls, are made of mud brick, decorated by black, white, and red ceramic tiles organized in complex patterns.

While this temple obviously falls outside the topic of houses, there are aspects of the construction techniques needed to build it that are relevant to the domestic architecture of the city and to Mesopotamian houses in general.

First of all, the lack of wood in the region meant that Sumerian builders had to be extremely ingenious in their use of mud. Sir Charles Leonard Woolley recounts the way that they strengthened it, first by using bitumen, which is also plentiful in the region, to stabilize the soil used for the bricks. In addition these bricks are tapered at each end for additional durability. The ceramic tiles that cover and protect the massive columns inside the White Temple are actually cone-shaped, with the sharp end pushed into the mud brick while it was still soft, up to the edge of the ceramic surface. These techniques, when adapted for domestic use, meant that walls and decorative ceramic surfaces were very beautiful but also very tough.

Sumer

Sumer, which means "the land," crystallized into individual city-states by the third century B.C. There was the Dynastic Period during which various powerful kings ruled from their cities before Mesopotamia was unified by Sargon of Akkad in 2370 B.C. For obvious reasons this Dynastic Period is also called Pre-Sargonid. Sargon's kinship marked an important transition from Sumerian to Akkadian rule and a revolution in political ideas. In the Dynastic Period, Sumerian city-states competed for power and each had its own patron deity who was seen as possessor of all physical things, with the king as an agent. Cities continually fought to adjust boundaries, and yet there was general allegiance to "the land" of Sumer itself. In this early period, there were a dozen or so cities with a finite amount of land bounded by the mountains and plateaus on each side, with no ambitions for territory. When Sargon took over, there was dynamic authority and statesmanship as well as a concept of absolute monarchy. The Akkadians were of non-Sumerian, Semitic origin, with a different language. The story of Sargon is similar to that of Moses in many ways in that he was an orphan who eventually became an advisor to the king of the city of Kish and was then named king when his mentor died. Once he became king, he started on a spectacular military career, subduing each of the other cities in Sumeria one by one. He founded a new capital at Agade, which has been mentioned in ancient texts but has not been discovered yet, north of Sumerian territory. It was used as a base for conquests outside of Mesopotamia, going deep into Anatolia and Arabia, and as far west as Cyprus. Sargon established a Mesopotamian empire. His reign lasted 55 years, but his dynasty was brought to an end by an uprising of Sumerian cities in 2120 B.C.

Ur

After this, Ur became the urban center of Sumeria. It is located beside the Euphrates River, which surrounded it on three sides, with dry land on the fourth. A second, heavily buttressed wall surrounded a sacred precinct inside the city, which also contained a colossal three stage ziggurat. The core of this ziggurat is mud brick with a skin of baked brick set in bitumen, and it has triple stairways converging at a single tower. The presence of drainage canals indicates that it may also have been planted with trees.

Because of an extended period of documentation of Mesopotamia by British archaeologist Sir Charles Leonard Woolley, Ur has also been well studied. It covered about 90 hectares, or 200 acres, with a density of 150 people per acre and had two peaks of prosperity from 2474 to 2398 B.C. and then from 2112 to 2095 B.C.[17] Once again the courtyard typology predominated in Ur, and houses for the more well-to-do usually had more than one level, with stairs typically located near the main entrance. Service-based spaces, such as the kitchen and storage rooms, as well as guest and servants' quarters were located on the ground floor, while areas requiring more privacy, such as family living and bedrooms, were located on the upper floors.[18] If a house had more than one story, its mud brick walls were thicker. Since wood was scarce before Sargonoid times when conquest and extensive trade made it more accessible, there were few windows, because these required wooden lintels, and interiors were dark. Lighting was provided by oil lamps. Roofs were structured with palm tree trunks, which are fibrous, but strong. These were covered with a mat of woven reeds and then a layer of clay.[19] Houses had toilets and bathtubs connected by drains to a main sewer. There was also a wide selection of furniture in a typical house, with cuneiform inventories listing chairs, tables, beds, stools, and storage chests. Water and wine were stored in clay jars.

Mashkan-shapir

Somewhere around 2000 B.C., Larsa, along with a partner city called Mashkan-shapir, eclipsed Ur as the most powerful and prosperous urban area in Mesopotamia. Mashkan-shapir had an especially fortuitous location near the Tigris River, south of what is now Baghdad. It was a thriving political center and the focal point of an extensive network of trade, surrounded by a wall and a secondary moat, inside which the inner precinct of the city was located. It remained powerful for about

An 8,000-year-old fortress right in the middle of the Kurdistan regional capital, Hewlêr (Erbil).   Courtesy of James Gordon; Flickr

275 years, until the ascent of Hammurabi. The city had five districts, with one large one in the center framed by others on the north, south, east, and west all divided by canals.[20] The most monumental building in the city was a ziggurat temple dedicated to Nergal, the god of death, and the separate graveyard indicates the city may also have been a religious center. There is no indication of economically segregated residential districts, since highly prized objects, such as stone bowls and utensils, were distributed evenly across the site.[21]

There is a strong possibility that there was an artisanal population living throughout the city, since, as archaeologists have said, "the production of goods seems to have been in the hands of artisans who lived with in broader residential neighborhoods that housed both commoners and members of the elite."[22]

Centralized Rule

In 1900 B.C. Hammurabi set up a strong centralized government in Mesopotamia, destroying other cities and ruling from Babylon. His code of laws is well known. His dynasty held power until the Hittites invaded in 1595 B.C., followed by the Kassites and then the Assyrians, who also used Babylon as their capital. The Kassite period lasted for about 300 years (from 1595 to 1235 B.C.) and is differentiated by the use of molded brick. The Assyrians built the city of Ashur at a bend in the River Tigris for protection and maintained it as a capital for over 2,000 years. The Assyrian approach to religion was coldly formal, with deities represented by symbols rather than humanistic forms. Like Sargon, they created a military empire and trade routes. Sargon II, an Assyrian, built Khorsabad in 705 B.C. The city was square, with sides a mile long. It had seven gates and lowered walls, and the main palace was planned around two main courtyards, showing a total transfer from religious to secular authority at this point in time. The city walls here are 20 meters thick, and roofs were barrel vaulted. The zenith of activity for this city was between 625 B.C. and 562 B.C.

Babylon

Babylon became powerful in its own right as a city when King Nebuchadnezzar extended it across the Euphrates River. The king's palace was in the northwest corner of the city, which was organized around a processional street. His palace had five courts.

Following 539 B.C., the Persians, under Cyprus, began to dominate the area from their capital in Persepolis, bringing the brief glory of Babylon to an end. Persepolis had no temples but only secular buildings such as the hundred columned halls, which were later burned by Alexander the Great.

TOPKAPI PALACE

The Topkapi Palace stands at the highest point of the tip of the peninsula, where Istanbul juts out into the Marmara Sea and where the ancient Greek acropolis had been. After Sultan Mehmet II conquered Constantinople in 1453, he first thought to build his palace in the Bayezit area because the *Saray-i Atik*, or "Old Palace" as it was called, was already there, having replaced Constantine's Great Palace as the residence of the Byzantine emperors after the eleventh century. Not totally satisfied with this choice, however, Mehmet decided to build at the *Sarayburnu*, perhaps because of its almost mythical connections with the city's imperial past. After the Byzantines had abandoned it, a hospital and a home for the elderly had been built there in the twelfth century, as well as several monasteries that stood on the Marmara side of the hill. Construction of a new palace, or *Saray-i Cedid*, was started in A.D. 1467, on a slope overlooking the water, which ensured a constant breeze and sweeping views of Galata, Üsküdar, Marmara, and the juncture of the Golden Horn and Bosphorus below. Continuously altered during the following 400 years of its use, the palace constantly evolved into the eclectic complex seen today. In the course of that evolution an extension of one of the pavilions built over the sea walls took the name *Topkapisi*, or Gungate Pavilion, because of the cannons strung out along the shore below. With the building of the railroad in this area in 1863, this pavilion was removed, but the name remained and eventually replaced that of *Saray-i Cedid* for the whole complex. In 1478, Mehmet the Conqueror ordered the construction of the 3 meters thick *Sur-i Sultan* or Sultan's Wall around the palace, which joined with the old Byzantine walls to encircle the entire site.

A Series of Courtyards

Having more or less arrived at its general form by 1465, the palace complex is characterized by a series of compartmentalized open spaces. Those progressively decrease in size and degree of public access in successive courts that are each surrounded by its own wall and each entered by a grand gate. The first of these is the *Bab-i Humayun* or Imperial Gate, which leads to the *Alay Meydani* or procession center, the scene of countless opulent audiences and reviews of elite Janissary corps in the past. The Janissaries, whose name is a corruption of the Turkish phrase *Yeni-Ceri* or "new force," were an elite army recruited to serve the sultan. The *Alay Meydani* was relatively accessible to the public during ceremonies and was rimmed with utilitarian spaces such as bakeries, armories, servants' residences, and storage rooms, which must have filled it with a buzz of activity.

One of the most beautiful buildings in the *Alay Meydani*, or First Court, is the *Cinili Köşk*, which is sometimes referred to as the *Şişe Saray* or Glass Palace in court documents of the past. Having been built in 1472, prior to the palace wall itself, the kiosk is set above a high platform, which acts as its base, and is fronted by an impressive colonnade that precedes a center court flanked by four *iwans*. The blue tiles that decorated this interior, which are flecked with gold and alternated with white, provide an unusual catalogue of faience styles from different regions of Turkey, which are all brought together here. The *Jerid* field, which once preceded the kiosk, now holds the Istanbul Museum of Archaeology, which is frequently overlooked, but holds great treasures. The transition from the First Court to the Second is marked by the middle gate or *Bâbüsselâm*, which is flanked by towers on each side and capped with turrets. A macabre attraction of this gate is the *Cellâd Çegmeşi*, or Executioner's Fountain, where he used to wash his axe after each execution. The sultan alone was allowed to proceed past this gate on horseback to enter the divan court beyond, which was, in reality, a large garden surrounded by arcades and galleries. Written evidence in the palace library indicates that this court was heavily planted with large shady trees and laced with curving stone pathways that were then commonplace in Turkish landscape planning. Looking at the straight, flat concrete pedestrian expressways that have now been installed to handle the large crowds that visit the palace each year, it is hard to imagine just how different this enclosure must have been in the past.

The *Divan,* or Imperial Council, met in this court, as did the Janissaries, for ceremonies and financial allotments, in a monthly display calculated to impress all those present with the incredible wealth of the empire. Regiment by regiment, the troops would march past the reviewing stand of the sultan to receive their *ulufe,* or salary, in front of the seated ambassadors and foreign dignitaries invited to attend. Coronations or *culus,* would also take place here, reinforcing the ceremonial character of the space.

On the right-hand side of the court, three gates gave access to the kitchens, as well as the housing of the staff that ran them. The kitchens, whose domes and chimneys are an unmistakable part of the palace skyline, were built by architect Sinan in the sixteenth century and are an organizational masterpiece, divided into units that were meant to serve separate groups of people reported to reach 10,000 or more on certain days. Today, the kitchens are quiet, only housing one of the world's most valuable collections of Chinese porcelain. At the far end of the court are the barracks of the Tasselled Halberdiers who were charged with taking care of the fires in the Harem. The tassels on their helmets, which gave them their name, were not only decorative, but were meant to prevent them from seeing the *odalisques,* or women of the Harem, as they carried out their tasks.

The Harem

As one of the oldest sections of the palace, the ward of the Tasselled Halberdiers is exquisitely decorated with floor and hearth tiles, lacquered flowers engraved in wood, and a technique of working in gold, called *edirnekari,* which is used on the windows. On the left side of this court, beside the imperial assembly that gives it its name, is the Carriage Gate or *Araba Kapisi,* which leads to the Harem and which is also the most popular part of the palace today. A square, 40 meter high tower, meant to be a watchtower for all of the palace grounds, marks the entrance to the legendary seraglio, which is a maze of nearly 300 rooms, only a small portion of which are open to the public today. Containing not only the women's quarters, the Harem also housed the Black Eunuchs who guarded them, the sultan's private apartments, and those of his family and relatives. Not originally a part of the palace complex, the Harem was built by Sultan Selim's son, Murad III, in 1574.

A complete world unto itself, the Harem was in reality not the scene of the hedonistic orgies it is often imagined to have been, but was instead the domain of the *Valide Sultan,* the sultan's mother, who had complete control over it and introduced only the few girls she found favorable to her son, using the *Kahisa Kadin* or Head Stewardess as her instrument. As may be imagined, such an arrangement led to a great deal of intrigue among the women there, who were chosen from all over the Empire. Tales of bored women being placated by drugged sherbets, while true, are exaggerated. The Harem was instead a closely knit matriarchal society, into which the sultan could only intrude following carefully prescribed etiquette, on special silver shoes whose unmistakable clanking on hard tile floors would announce his presence. The Harem also effectively served as a jail for relatives and offspring who were deemed to be a threat to the sultan, and even those young princes not thought to be so were confined there for schooling until they were quite far into manhood. Because the Harem as an institution was felt to have effectively isolated future leaders from both the outside world as well as the day-to-day decision making of the court, it has been cited by historians as one of the prime causes for the weakening of the Ottoman Empire in later years.

The Harem consisted of three main divisions, the first of which belonged to its guardians, the Black Eunuchs. The second belonged to the *Valide Sultan* and the *Haseki Sultan*, his primary wife, as well as ladies-in-waiting, concubines, and servants. The third and last section was given over entirely to the sultan's private apartments. Directly after the Carriage Gate, which got its name because of the charmed few Harem residents who left there by carriage to go shopping in Istanbul, was the *Nobetyeri*, where the Black Eunuchs stood guard over the main entrance. A small prayer hall, called the Black Eunuchs' mosque, stands close to the *Nobetyeri*, as does their main court, which is accessible through a large metal gate and is among the most impressive spaces in the entire Topkapi Palace complex. The court is also surrounded by the chambers of the *Hazinedar*, or treasurer, and the chief of the Black Eunuchs.

The Princes' School also located here deserves particular mention in that its extremely ornate, baroque revetments were designed in 1749 by *Beşir Aga*, who was the chief of the Black Eunuchs at the time and who was later executed in 1752 for unspecified reasons. The beauty of the decoration indicates that these men were more than just mindless guards, armed with huge curved scimitars, as they are so often portrayed. Beyond the courtyard of the Black Eunuchs is the *Cariyeler*, or inner court of the concubines, which gives access to their quarters above. These are far less extravagant than those of the Black Eunuchs, almost resembling a prison. Below the court is the concubines' hospital, whose size indicates that their life was less than idyllic. As a further confirmation of this, a stairway running down from the hospital leads to a morgue in the basement whose only exit is the *Meyit*, or Gate of the Dead.

The Third Court

The *Bab-i Sa'adet*, or Gate of Felicity, is the entrance to the Third Court of the Topkapi complex and is contemporary with its founding. The entrance itself is domed and framed by extended arcades that give it a more delicate feeling than the *Ortakapi* that precedes it. The throne of the sultan was placed under the domed canopy of the gate on ceremonial occasions, and it was here that he, as commander in chief of the army, would receive the holy banner of Islam before each military expedition. Also called the *Akagalar*, or the White Eunuchs' Gate, after the troops that were used to guard it, it leads to the *Enderun* and *Arz Odasi*, which is the throne room of the sultan where foreign ambassadors and dignitaries were both presented to and took their leave of him. Moving in from the Gate of Felicity on the left-hand side of the Third Court is the *Kutsal Emanetler*, or Treasury of the Sacred Relics, which is a square building divided into four sections, each covered with a dome. Known to those inside the palace as the *Hirkai Sa'adet*, or Pavilion of the Holy Mantle, this section housed not only the garment it was named for but also other sacred relics of Islam specifically brought here from Egypt by Sultan Yavuz Selim, who was known in Europe as Selim the Grim. Carefully guarded, the *Kutsal Ema-netler* was ceremoniously visited only on certain special holy days, when the sultan and his retinue would stay in the *Arzhane*, or Presentation Room, and have the relics brought out to them. A number of the relics belonging to the Prophet Muhammad and the four caliphs that succeeded him still survive here, so that many people from all over the Islamic world come to visit this section of the palace. In keeping with the religious nature of this section of the palace, the Agalar Mosque, as well as the Harem Mosque, were also located here. The Agalar Mosque, which was intended for those in the *Enderun*, was an important school for the higher education of Janissaries who showed great promise. It has since been turned into a library for rare manuscripts and houses many exceptional and priceless miniatures. Noted historian of the early phase of Muslim life in Istanbul Hilary Sumner-Boyd, in describing the crucial role of the *Enderun*, has said:

> This elaborately organized school for the training of the Imperial Civil guard appears to be unique in the Islamic world ... the pages who attended it came from the Christian minorities of the Empire ... and received a rigorous training, intellectual and physical, which in contrast to the usual Islamic education was largely secular and designed specifically to prepare the students for the administration of the Empire. There can be no doubt that the brilliant success of the Ottoman state in the earlier centuries was to a large extent due to the training its administrators received in this school.[23]

The Fourth and Final Court

Vaulted passageways at the rear of the Third Court lead into the fourth and final compartment of the carefully differentiated succession of spaces that make the Topkapi Palace so unique. While the Second and the Third Courts are enclosed, the Fourth Court at the tip of the peninsula is planned around the spectacular panoramic views of the Golden Horn far below. A series of kiosks are strategically placed on different levels across the narrow expanse of the terrace that both complement and contrast each other in form and personality, making this stepped garden a sculpture court of broad-eaved pavilions. Perhaps the most famous of these is the Baghdad *Köşk*, which was built in 1639 in honor of the Ottoman conquest of that city in the same year. Attributed to the architect Kasim Ağa, this broad-eaved kiosk rests on a high podium and is supported by many columns. Like the *Revan Köşk*, it has four *iwans* that radiate out from a doomed central space, all of which are covered with the most beautiful tiles and lit with colored glass windows that create ever-changing patterns on the walls and floor of the interior. The kiosk has been placed at the extreme right-hand side of a paved area called the Marble Terrace, at the center of which is a delicate canopied viewing pavilion called the *Iftariye*, or Feast of Ramadan Pavilion, because it has been used by sultans in the past to receive guests during the festivities associated with that period of the Islamic year. Built by Sultan Ibrahim in A.D. 1640, the exquisitely worked and gilded roof, which is inscribed with verses related to him, is supported by extremely thin columns, allowing an open view of the Incirlik, or Fig Park, immediately beneath it and the city far beyond. Acting as a hub for the other pavilions on the terrace that wheel out from it, the *Revan Köşk*, also called the *Sarik* or turban room in the past, was built by Murad IV to celebrate the capture of Erivan in the expedition against Persia in 1635. The *Revan Köşk*, rather small in scale, is faced inside and out with exquisite tiles that line the curved interior face of its central dome and the ceilings of its four *iwans* as well. The kiosk is historically significant as the scene of a bloody massacre in 1730, when Sultan Mahmud I lured Patrona Halil and his followers there on the pretext of conferring the title of Grand Vizier upon the revolutionary leader. When they arrived, they were all killed by the sultan's huge bodyguard, Pehlivan Halil Ağa, who was also a famous wrestler of the time. This was in revenge for the overthrow of Sultan Ahmed III, and the assassination of his own Grand Vizier, Nevşehirli Ibrahim Paşa, two months earlier. The basement of the kiosk, which is always cool because of its massively thick stone walls, was also used for the preparation of the bodies of dead sultans, adding to the dark shadow that the slaughter of Patrona and his group has cast on its beauty.

A wide, shaded arcade separates the *Revan Köşk* from the Pavilion of the Holy Mantle behind it, linking it with the *Sunnet Odasi*, or Circumcision Room. This single space was used for the ceremonies marking the entry of a young prince into manhood. The Iznik tiles, which are remarkable throughout the palace, are outstanding here. On the Marmara side of the Fourth Court a sense of enclosure is achieved by a linear complex of buildings, the first of which is called the *Esvabi Odasi*, or the Room of the Robe, followed by the Sofa Mosque, which was built in 1859, along with the *Yeni Köşk*, which is next to it. The *Mecidiye Köşk*, which effectively turns this line of buildings, creates an enclosure called the *Lala*, or Sultan's Tutor garden. In a slight play on words, this name was later changed to the *Lale*, or tulip garden, in recognition of the flower that was to become an obsession in Istanbul in the beginning of the eighteenth century. In contrast to other famous Islamic gardens, such as the Alhambra in Granada, or the Royal Meydan in Isfahan, Iran, the Topkapi Palace is unusual because of the progressive unity of its spaces. In the Alhambra, for example, each open space and the accompanying buildings that surround it, are conceived as separate and distinct units that are aesthetically self-contained, having little or no visual or physical connection with those adjoining them. In the Topkapi, however, the spaces, which are also interiorized and compartmentalized, are sequentially linked in scale, proportion, and overall character, based on the desired degree of public or private access to them. An oriental philosophy, similar to that found in the Forbidden City of Peking, and which seems to indicate the common ethnic root of both designs, judges the royal procession from exterior to interior to be the unifying link in the spatial chain of spaces, rather than the highly individualized character of each.

YEMENI HOUSES

Traditional houses in Yemen, in both the cities and the villages, are highly individual. A thorough study of each by architect Rasem Badran led to the key insight that Sanaá, which is the capital, is an aggregation of elements found in villages throughout the rugged terrain of this frontier nation and that these elements both mirrored and were adaptations of those found throughout the region. The advantage that Badran's study has over others that have been done on Yemeni houses is that he has gone beyond the similarities, toward the particular elements that make them unique. The elements discovered in the early part of the study revolved around the verticality of the individual house, generated by familial climatic defensive considerations. Stacking of floors within the house allows for a hierarchical separation related to increasing degrees of privacy. Badran recorded this segregation, noting that houses in Yemen are usually five to six floors in height with vertical separation of the floors according to the function and the users of the space. Usually the ground floor, which is called the *masam*, is used for small commercial purposes or for keeping the livestock while the first floor is used for storage. The second and the third floors are the male areas with guest rooms while the fourth and the fifth floors, called the *marawh*, are for the women, with the kitchen and the family living areas located there. The *mafrag*, or the lookout point, is on the top of the house, which is a combination of a covered and an open space.

The tower form also allows the top floors of the house to receive the cool breezes that flow through the high mountain passes and elevated desert regions that are a typical feature of the Yemeni landscape. Such tower houses are also found elsewhere in the Arabian Peninsula, most notably in the port city of Jeddah and in the Hijaz. While the social determinants for vertical stacking are the same in Jeddah and Makkah as they are in Yemen, and the houses look similar in many ways, climactic variation, as well as the availability of local materials, has resulted in different external expressions in each case. In Yemen, the prevalence of stone makes it a logical building material while wood has been used in the northwestern part of the Arabian Peninsula. Wood is scarce in Saudi Arabia, but as a port city, Jeddah has access to it through trade, primarily with India, and nearby Makkah shares in this supply. The defensive component of the house is also unique to Yemen, since it has historically been a tribal society with settlements primarily identified with one family or group. This means that conflicts between settlements are a frequent fact of life. Agricultural land

The traditional Yemen house is built of local materials and is organized in a vertical tower-like structure based on consideration for family privacy. © Curt Carnemark/World Bank Archives is scarce in Yemen because of the large amount of rocky soil, and so the tower form allows the use of the land to be maximized and protected. Jeddah was originally a walled city until the mid-1940s, when the walls were removed and replaced with a ring road; the tower house form helped conserve land, but the defensive aspect was no longer a consideration.

Further investigation into the environmental implications of the tower house in Yemen reveals interesting and surprising implications related to certain details. One of these is size, location, and ornamentation of the window openings, which are far from random. The placement of internal spaces and the openings to the outside in each are directly related to the daily sun path, "to the extent," Badran has recorded, "that people themselves classify houses according to the amount of light they receive." [24]

Comparisons

Badran began his study of the Yemeni house by looking at similar urban situations in Cairo, Tunisia, and Morocco. This comparative analysis led him to conclude that the city center, with its large mosque, the Masjid al Jami'i, and its commercial activities, was a constant, but that Sanaá had developed very differently from cities in the two other countries. The reason for this, he believes, is that, "in other cities, the residential neighborhoods have spread out horizontally and are based on the internal courtyard, which creates a private space for each house." But in Sanaá, the verticality of the houses, which developed because of the need of an agricultural society to protect its land, crops, and herds, creates a more direct interface with nature, since sunlight and natural ventilation are more prevalent at the higher levels of the house. Traditional Arab houses in other countries are typically found to be modest and plain on the outside, while having a rich series of spatial arrangements within. In Yemen, however, the exterior elevations of all of the traditional houses are richly decorated, and this ornamentation, which looks like icing on gingerbread, serves several important functions. First of all, it provides a means of social differentiation, sending key clues to everyone in each neighborhood about the status of each family. Second, this ornamentation contributes to environmental mitigation, since it reflects the sunlight away from the windows and thus reduces both the heat and the glare.

The tower, as opposed to the party wall typology, perpetuates an individual or family mentality rather than a group or communal one, and this ornamentation underscores that individuality.

The Space of the Yemeni House

The *mafrag*, similar to a *majlis*, or reception room, is the highest and most prestigious space in a traditional Yemeni house, and its scale and magnificence is also broadcast by external decoration. Because of the isolation of individual families in tower houses, this *mafrag* also serves the function of a courtyard in the sky, as open as possible to light and air. Light is augmented and controlled by *kamriya* (the use of colored glass) similar in appearance to large panels of stained glass, which visually enhances the house interior.

Part of the prestige value of any house in Yemeni culture depends on its orientation. Since the best direction, environmentally, is toward the south, the Yemenis call a "complete house" one facing in that direction. A house facing east or west is "semi-complete" and one facing north is "deficient." The allocation of functions inside the house changes in each case.

The house's vertical growth is a gradual process, and it happens according to the family's means. In order for a house to look finished at each phase, it is capped with a wide white band that serves as a horizontal marker on the elevation. Vertical growth of the house also requires an efficient drainage system, which the Yemenis have developed as external channels incorporated into the ornamental system.

Translating the Analysis

Badran translated his investigations into the formation of rural villages and towns and residential districts in cities such as Sanaá into a list of generational aspects that are responsible for form. He found that each residential neighborhood is a result of the following constants.

The first, the most important of these, is the *abiyar*, or well, since a

Mud house at Dar al Hajar, Yemen.   Courtesy of Shutterstock

source of water is obviously necessary to sustain life. The amount of water available also governed the size of the community it could support, as well as being a socializing element, where people of the village or residential district in the city would meet outside the house. Egyptian architect Hassan Fathy, whose translation of a traditional village at New Gourna near Luxor will be discussed in Volume III of this series, has been criticized for only providing wells in each neighborhood, rather than having running water in each house, since it was available at the time of construction. He replied that in traditional villages the well served an important function in allowing young men and women to meet and interact outside of family restrictions, and this was one of the few times they could do so. Step wells in villages throughout rural India, which are no longer used now that mains deliver water to individual houses, were known to serve this purpose of presenting women of marriageable age to prospective husbands, who watched them collect water in loti jars and carry it home on their heads.

The mosque is equal in importance to water in each Muslim neighborhood. Before the advent of broadcasting systems, the call to prayer, which is given five times a day in such settlements, was originally given by a *muezzin*, who climbed up to the top of the minaret to sing it out. In addition, there are three other consistencies:

1. The *bustan* is supervised by the same family that takes care of the mosque.
2. The mosque, *Al-Jami*, is located on or close to the *bustan*.
3. There are specific commercial districts, called *samsara*, in which the *suqs* or markets are located. The number of *samsara* in a city reflects its culture status because trade requires interaction with other towns, cities, and districts; this exchange brings a transfer of knowledge along with it. The *samsara* include places for traders to stay, similar to the *cravanserai* or *khans* in other cities.

One major environmental advantage of the Yemeni way of building that Badran recorded, in addition to the extensive use of local materials, is that the vertical house has a very small footprint and thus occupies a minimum of the already scarce agricultural land. He also noted that this organizational system and the ornamental additions that result from it create neighborhoods in a human scale.

Notes

INTRODUCTION

1. Henri Lefebvre, *The Production of Space* (Oxford: Blackwell, 1991).
2. Pierre Bourdieu, "The Berber House," in *Rules and Meanings*, ed. Mary Douglas (Suffolk: Penguin, 1973), 133.
3. Donald Sanders, "Behavioral Conventions and Archaeology: Methods for the Analysis of Ancient Architecture," in *Domestic Architecture and the Use of Space*, ed. Susan Kent (Cambridge, U.K.: Cambridge University Press, 1990), 43.
4. Ibid., 44.
5. Ibid., 44.

CHAPTER 1: THE AMERICAS

Houses of the Adena Tribe in the Ohio Valley

1. Ephraim George Squier and Edwin H. Davis, *Ancient Monuments of the Mississippi Valley* (New York: AMS Press, 1973).
2. John W. Reps, "Urban Redevelopment in the Nineteenth Century. The Squaring of Circleville," *The Journal of the Society of Architecture Historian* 14, no. 4 (1955), 23–26.
3. Roger Kennedy, *Hidden Cities* (New York: Macmillan, Inc., 1994).
4. Eric Hinderaker, "Archaeologists Question Existence of Hopewell, Adena Cultures," *The Ojibwe News*, May 16, 1997.
5. S. Allen Chambers, *The Buildings of West Virginia* (Oxford, U.K.: Oxford University Press, 2004), 14.
6. William S. Welch and Raymond S. Baly, "The Adena People," No. 2 (Columbus, OH: Ohio State University Press, 1957), 15.
7. Raymond S. Baly, "Cowan Creek Mound Explorations," *Ohio Historical Society*, *Museum Echoes* XXII (1949), 54–55.

The Anasazi

8. Stephen Lekson, *Great Pueblo Architecture of Chaco Canyon, New Mexico* (Albuquerque, NM: University of New Mexico Press, 1984), 30.

9. Ibid., 32.

10. David E. Stuart, "Power and Efficiency in Eastern Anasazi Architecture," in *Anazasi Architecture and American Design*, ed. B. H. Morrow and V. B. Price (Albuquerque: University of New Mexico Press, 2000).

11. Steven D. Schreiber, "Seven Engineering Feats of the Anasazi," ed. J. M. Coheri, in *Architecture and American Design*, ed. B. H. Morrow and V. B. Price (Albuquerque: University of New Mexico Press, 1997), 83.

12. Ibid., 77.

13. Robert H. and Florence C. Lister, *Aztec Ruins on the Animas: Excavated, Preserved and Interpreted* (Albuquerque, NM: University of New Mexico Press, 1987), 35.

14. Schreiber, *Engineering Feats of the Anasazi*, 81.

15. Ibid., 81 and 78.

16. R. Lister and F. Lister, *Aztec Ruins on the Animas*, 35.

17. Ibid., 45.

18. See Anna Sofaer, Rolf M. Sinclair, and Joey B. Donahue, "An Astronomical Regional Pattern Among the Major Buildings of the Chaco Culture of New Mexico," paper published in the *Proceedings of the Third International Conference on Archaeoastronomy* (St. Andrews, Scotland: University of St. Andrews, 1990); as well as Ralph Knowles, *Energy and Form* (Cambridge, MA: MIT Press, 1974), 20–46.

19. Ibid.

20. Ibid., 59

21. R. and F. Lister, *Aztec Ruins on the Animas*, 37.

22. Stuart, *Power and Efficiency in Eastern Anasazi Architecture*, 45.

The Inuit Snow Houses

23. "The Igloo of the Innuit," *Science* 2 (November 31, September 7, 1883). JSTOR, 804.

24. JSTOR, 804.

25. JSTOR, 806.

26. Molly Lee and Gregory A. Reinhardt, *Eskimo Architecture* (Fairbanks, AK: University of Alaska Press, 2003), 21.

27. Ibid., 18.

28. Ibid., 55.

The Aztecs

29. Bernal Diazand and J. M. Cohen, eds., *The Conquest of New Spain* (New York and London: Penguin, 1988), 36.

30. Warwick Bray, ed., *Aztecs* (London: Royal Academy of Arts, 2002), 20.

31. Ibid., 19.

32. Michael E. Smith, "Life in the Provinces of the Aztec Empire," *Scientific American* 15, no. 1 (March 2005): 92.

33. Ibid., 93.

34. Ibid., 91.

La Galgada and Casma and Moche Vallies of Peru

35. Terence Grieder, Alberto Bueno Mendoza, C. Earle Smith Jr., and Robert M. Malina, *La Galgada, Peru: A Pre-Ceramic Culture in Transition* (Austin, TX: University of Texas Press, 1988), 18.

36. Ibid., 18.

37. Ibid., 31.

38. Shelia Pozorski and Thomas Pozorski, *Early Settlement and Subsistence in the Casma Valley* (Iowa City, IA: University of Iowa, 1987).

39. Ibid., 53.

40. Garth Bawden, "Domestic Space and Social Structure in Pre-Colombian Northern Peru," in *New Direction in Archaeology, Domestic Architecture and the Use of Space*, ed. Susan Kent (Cambridge, U.K.: Cambridge University Press), 154.

41. Ibid., 155.

42. Curtis T. Brannan, *Investigation of Carro Areana, Peru; Incipient Urbanism on the Peruvian North Coast* (PhD diss., University of Arizona, Tucson, Proquest, Ann Arbor, MI, 1977).

43. Bawden, "Domestic Space and Social Structure," 154.

44. Ibid., 159.

45. Ibid., 163.

The Inca and the Chimu

46. William Allman and Joannie M. Schrof, "Lost Empires of the Americas," *U.S. News and World Report*, 1998, 41.

47. Ibid., 53.

48. Ibid., 53.

49. Ibid., 54.

50. Henri Stierlin, *Art of the Incas and Its Origins* (New York: Rizzoli, 1983), 166.

51. David P. Werlich, *Peru: A Short Story* (Carbondale, IL: Southern Illinois University Press, 1978), 32.

52. Stierlin, *Art of the Incas and Its Origins*, 157.

53. Ibid., 157.

54. Ibid., 166.

55. Hiram Bingham, *Lost City of the Incas* (New York: Duell, Sloan and Pearce, 1948), 5.

56. Bingham, *Lost City of the Incas*, 184.

57. Kenneth R. Wright and Alfredo Valencia Jegarra, *Machi Picchu: A Civil Engineering Marvel* (Reston, VA: ASCE Press, 2000), 72.

58. Bingham, *Lost City of the Incas*, 9.

The Iroquis Longhouse

59. Bruce Johansen, *Encyclopedia of the Haudenosaunee (Iroquois)* (Westport, CT: Greenwood Publishing Group, 2000), 1.

60. Ibid., 14.

61. Ibid., 15.

62. William Engelbrecht, *Iroquoia: The Development of a Native World* (Syracuse, NY: Syracuse University Press, 2003), 68.

63. Ibid., 68.

64. Ibid., 88.

65. Ibid., 90.

66. Ibid., 94.

67. Dean R. Snow, *The Iroquois* (Cambridge, MA: Blackwell, 1994), 122.

68. Engelbrecht, *Iroquoia*, 71.

69. Snow, *The Iroquois*, 43.

70. Engelbrecht, *Iroquoia*, 72.

71. Ibid., 76.

72. Ibid., 79.

73. Lewis Henry Morgan, *League of the Iroquois* (Secaucus, NJ: Corith Books, 1962), 318.

74. Johansen, *Encyclopedia of the Haudenosaunee (Iroquois)*, 145.

The Maya

75. Mary Ellen Miller, *Maya Art and Architecture* (London: Thames and Hudson, 1999), 8.

76. Ibid., 17.

77. Michael Coe, *The Maya* (London: Thames and Hudson, 1999), 36.

78. In Miller, *Maya Art and Architecture*, 22.

79. William Gates, *Yucatan Before and After the Conquest*(New York: Dover, 1980), 144.

80. Victor W. Vonhagen, *The World of the Maya* (Colchester, UK: Signet, 1969).

81. Miller, *Maya Art and Architecture*, 81.

82. Tatiana Proskouriakoff, *Album of Mayan Architecture* (Washington, DC: Carnegie Institution of Washington, 1946), 12.

83. Ibid., 13.

CHAPTER 2: AFRICA

Al-Qahira, Egypt

1. Andre Raymond, *Cairo* (Cambridge, MA: Harvard University Press, 2000), 65.

2. Richard Ettinghausen and Oleg Grabar, *The Art and Architecture of Islam 650–1250* (New Haven, CT: Yale University Press, 1987), 172.

3. Yinong Xu, *Boundaries, Centers and Peripheries in Chinese Gardens: The Case of Suzhou in the Eleventh Century* (London: Taylor and Francis, Ltd., 2003), 21.

4. Norbert Schoenauer, *History of Housing* (New York: W.W. Norton & Company, Inc., 2000), 98.

Carthage, Tunisia

5. Serge Lancel, *Carthage: A History* (Oxford, UK: Blackwell Publishers, 1995).

6. Ibid., 164.

7. Ibid., 164.

8. Ibid., 167.

Deir El Medina and Tel El Amarna, Luxor, Egypt

9. Ian Shaw, *The Oxford History of Ancient Egypt*, new ed. (New York: Oxford University Press, 2004).

10. Ellah Nuandi, *African Architecture* (New York: McGraw-Hill, 1997), 22.

11. Ibid., 24.

12. Author's interview with Hassan Fathy, August 14, 1986.

13. Ibid.

14. Shaw, *The Oxford History of Ancient Egypt*, 277.

15. Paul G. Bahn, ed., *Lost Cities: 50 Discoveries in World Archaeology* (New York: Welcome Rain, 1999), 12.

16. Jacobus van Dijk, "The Amarna Period and the Later New Kingdom," in Shaw, *The Oxford History of Ancient Egypt*, 282.

17. Bahn, *Lost Cities*, 17.

18. Ibid., 17.

Great Zimbabwe

19. Webber Ndoro, "Great Zimbabwe," *Scientific American* (November 1997).

20. Ibid., 76.

21. Ibid., 76.

The Nubian House

22. Author's interview with George Scanlon, October 15, 1985.

23. See Yasmin Moll, "Paradise Lost," *Egypt Today Magazine*, May 2004.

CHAPTER 3: ASIA AND AUSTRALASIA

Zhouzhuang, A Canal Village in China

1. Chi-chu Tsang, "Venice of the Orient—Zhouzhuang," *People's Daily*, April 26, 2000. Available at http://english.people.com.cn/english/200004/26/eng20000426_39741.html.

2. Joseph C. Wang, "Zhouzhuang, A Historic Market Town," *Chinese Landscapes: The Village as Place*, ed. Ronald G Knapp (Honolulu: University of Hawaii Press, 1992), 139–150.

The Dai and Thai House

3. Michael Freeman, *A Guide to Northern Thailand and the Ancient Kingdom of Lanna* (Trumbull: Weatherhill, Inc. Ct., 2001).

4. Ibid.

5. Zhu Liangwen, *The Dai* (Bangkok: DD Books, 1992), 36.

6. Ibid., 36.

7. Ibid., 84.

8. S. J. Tambiah, *Animals are Good to Think and Good to Prohibit*, ethnography 1628, no. 4 (October 1969), 424–459.

9. S. J. Tambiah, *Buddhism and the Spirit Cult of Northeast Thailand* (Cambridge, U.K.: Cambridge University Press, 1975), 197.

Hutong

10. Shen Yantai and Wang Changqing, *Life in Hutongs* (Beijing: Foreign Language Press, 1989).

Jomon and Yayoi Heritage in Japan

11. Robert Treat Paine and Alexander Soper, "Architecture of the Pre-Buddhist Age," in *The Art and Architecture of Japan* (Baltimore, MD: Penguin Books, 1955), 275.

12. Ibid., 275.

13. Ibid., 276.

14. Gunten Nitachke, *Japanese Gardens* (New York: Longitude Books, 2007), 16.

15. Kenzo Tange, Yashiro Ishimoto, and Walter Gropius, *Katsura, Tradition and Creation in Japanese Architecture* (Tokyo: Zokeisha Publishers, 1960), 168.

16. Paine and Soper, "Architecture of the Pre-Buddhist Age," 277.

17. Kazuo Nishi and Kazuo Hozumi, *What Is Japanese Architecture?* (Tokyo: Kodansha International, 1983), 82–85.

The Khmers in Cambodia

18. Ian Mabbett and David Chandler, *The Khmers* (Oxford: Blackwell, 1995).
19. Ibid., 79.
20. Ibid., 78.
21. Ibid., 261.
22. Ibid., 96.
23. G. Coedes, *The Indianized States of Southeast Asia*, trans. S. Cowing (Canberra: Australian National University Press, 1968).
24. Ibid., 135.
25. Ibid., 108.

The Malay House

26. Syed Iskander, "Order in Traditional Malay House Form" (PhD diss., Oxford Brookes University, Oxford, UK, 2001).

Mohenjo-daro and Harappa, Pakistan

27. Bodo Cichy, *Architecture of Ancient Civilizations, Mohenjo-Daro and Harappa* (New York: Viking, 1966), 144.
28. Jonathan Mark Kenoyer, "Uncovering the Keys to the Lost Indus Cities," *Scientific American* (July 2003): 26.
29. Ibid., 28.
30. Cichy, *Architecture of Ancient Civilizations, Mohenjo-Daro and Harappa*, 150.
31. Ibid., 151.
32. Kenoyer, "Uncovering the Keys," 50.
33. Ibid., 49.
34. Sir Mortimer Wheeler, *The Indus Civilization* (Cambridge, UK: Cambridge University Press, 1968), 41.
35. Ibid., 21.
36. Ibid., 114.
37. Ibid., 116.

The Minangkabau House

38. Michael Emrick, *The Traditional Houses of Negri Sembillan and Malacca: Their Derivation from Minang Kabau Prototypes* (December 14, 1977, unpublished).
39. Ibid., no pagination.
40. Ibid., no pagination.
41. Ibid., no pagination.
42. Ibid., no pagination.
43. Ibid., no pagination.
44. Ibid., no pagination.

Shang Houses in China

45. Chang Kwang-chih, *The Archaeology of Ancient China*, 3rd ed. (New Haven, CT: Yale University Press, 1977).

46. Chang Kwang-chih, *The Archaeology of Ancient China*, 4th ed. (New Haven, CT: Yale University Press, 1986), 20–55.

47. K. C. Chang, ed., *Studies of Shang Archaeology, Selected Papers from the International Conference on Shang Civilization* (New Haven, CT: Yale University Press, 1986), 325.

48. Te-k'un Cheng, *Archaeology in China, Volume II: Shang China* (Cambridge, U.K.: W. Heffer & Sons, Ltd., 1960).

49. Su Gin-Djih, *Chinese Architecture: Past and Contemporary* (Hong Kong: The Sin Poh Amalgamated, 1964).

CHAPTER 4: EUROPE AND THE WESTERN MEDITERRANEAN

Anglo Saxon and Norman Houses in Britain

1. M. W. Beresford. *Medieval England: Aerial Survey* (London: Cambridge University Press, 1958), 22.

2. Ibid., 22.

3. Ibid., 208.

4. Ibid., 17.

5. Ibid., 17.

6. Margaret Wood, *The English Medieval House* (London: Phoenix House, 1965).

7. Ibid., 49.

8. Ibid., 99.

9. Ibid., 17.

10. Ibid., 216.

11. Wood, *The English Medieval House*, 214; R. A. Brown. *English Medieval Castles* (London: Batsford, 1954), 31–32.

12. Ibid., 22.

The *Domus Aurea*, Rome

13. Axel Boethius, *The Golden House of Nero* (Ann Arbor, MI: The University of Michigan Press, 1960).

14. Frederick Vreeland, "Roman Treasures Revealed," *Conde Nast Traveler* (June 1999): 35.

15. Boethius, *The Golden House of Nero*, 102.

16. Ibid., 43.

17. Ibid., 108.

18. Ibid., 110.

Greek Houses in the Cities of Asia Minor

19. Axel Boethus, *Roman and Greek Town Architecture* (Goteburg, Sweden: Wettergren and Kerbers, 1948).

20. Ibid., 78.

21. Christine Mitchell Havelock, *Hellenistic Art* (New York: W. W. Norton and Co., 1981), 76.

22. Paul G. Bahn, ed., *Lost Cities: 50 Discoveries in World Archaeology* (New York: Welcome Rain, 1999), 55.

23. Ibid., 58.

24. Havelock, *Hellenistic Art*, 77.

25. Ibid., 78.

Khirokitia, Cyprus

26. K. Karageorgis, *Khirokitia Cyprus*, Monograph Series #1 (Cyprus: Department of Antiquities, 1983), 11.

Knossos, Crete

27. Anna Michailidou, *Knossos* (Athens: Ekdotkie Athenon, 1986), 11.

28. Ibid., 81.

Mycenae and Troy

29. A. W. Lawrence, *Greek Architecture* (Baltimore, MD: Penguin Books, 1983), 102.

30. Ibid., 93.

31. Ibid., 80.

32. Ibid., 81.

33. Ibid., 82.

Houses of the Roman Republic and Empire

34. Axel Boethius, *The Golden House of Nero* (Ann Arbor, MI: The University of Michigan Press, 1960), 137.

35. Ibid., 146.

Skara Brae, Scotland

36. Chris Scane, *Exploring Prehistoric Europe* (New York: Oxford University Press, 1998), 101.

37. Ibid., 103.

38. Ibid., 104.

39. Ibid., 106.

40. Ibid., 108.

41. Ibid., 111.

42. Ibid., 111.

Stonehenge, Woodhenge, and Durrington Walls

43. John Noble Wilford, "Neolithic Village May Have Housed Builders of Stonehenge," *New York Times*, Wednesday, January 31, 2007.

44. Ibid., A11.

45. Anthony Jackson, *Solving Stonehenge, The Key to an Ancient Enigma* (London: Thames and Hudson, 2008), 38.

46. Ibid., 40.

47. Ibid., 43.

48. Rodney Castleden, *The Stonehenge People, An Explanation of Life in the Neolithic Britain, 4700–2000 BC* (London: Routledge Kegan, Paul Ltd., 1987), 151.

49. Ibid., 152.

CHAPTER 5: EAST AND SOUTHEAST ASIA

The Fairy Chimneys of Cappadocia

1. Lyn Rodley, *Cave Monasteries of Byzantine Cappadocia* (Cambridge, U.K.: Cambridge University Press, 1985), 21.

2. Ibid., 16.

3. Spiro Kostoff.

4. Ibid., 24.

5. Ibid., 18.

Çatal Hüyük

6. Ian Hodder, "Women and Men at Catal Hüyük," *Scientific American* (January 2004): 351.

7. Ibid., 207.

8. Ibid., 208.

9. Ibid., 209.

10. Ibid., 209.

Constantinople, "The New Rome"

11. See John Freely, *Byzantine Monuments of Istanbul* (Cambridge, UK: Cambridge University Press, 2004); Ross R. Holloway, *Constantine and Rome* (New Haven, CT: Yale University Press, 2004).

The Hittites

12. J. G. Macqueen, *The Hittites and their Contemporaries in Asia Minor* (London: Thames and Hudson, 1986), 79.

13. Ibid., 80.

Mesopotamia

14. Karen Rhea Normet-Nejat, *Daily Life in Ancient Mesopotamia* (Westport, CT: Greenwood Press, 1998), 101.

15. Ibid., 103.

16. Ibid., 101.

17. Sir Charles Leonard Woolley, *The Indus Civilization* (Cambridge, UK: Cambridge University Press, 1968), 43.

18. Ibid., 102.

19. Normet-Nejat, *Daily Life in Ancient Mesopotamia*, 122.

20. Elizabeth C. Stone and Paul Zimansky, "The Tapestry of Power in a Mesopotamian City," *Scientific American* 15, no. 1 (2005), 66.

21. Ibid., 67.

22. Ibid., 67.

Topkapi Palace

23. Hilary Summer-Boyd, *Strolling Through Istanbul* (London: Kegan Paul, 2005).

Yemeni Houses

24. Samar Damluji, *The Architecture of Yemen, From Yafi to Hadramut* (London: Laurence King Publishing, 2007).

Bibliography

Introduction

Bourdieu, Pierre. "The Berber House." In *Rules and Meanings*, edited by Mary Douglas. Suffolk: Penguin, 1973.

Hillier, B., and J. Hanson. *The Social Logic of Space*. Cambridge, United Kingdom: Cambridge University Press, 1984.

Kaufman, S. A. *The Origins of Order: Self Organization and Selection in Evolution*. New York: Oxford University Press, 1993.

Lefebvre, H. *The Production of Space*. Oxford: Blackwell, 1991.

Mumford, L. *Techniques and Civilization*. New York: Macmillan, 1971.

Sanders, Donald. "Behavioral Conventions and Archaeology: Methods for the Analysis of Ancient Architecture." In *Domestic Architecture and the Use of Space*, edited by Susan Kent. Cambridge, United Kingdom: Cambridge University Press, 1990, 43–72.

Schama, Simon. *Landscape and Memory*. New York: Vintage Books, 1996.

Chapter 1: The Americas

Houses of the Adena Tribe in the Ohio Valley

Baly, Raymond S. "Cowan Creek Mound Explorations," *Ohio Historical Society, Museum Echoes* XXII (1949).

Chambers, S. Allen. *The Buildings of West Virginia*. Oxford, United Kingdom: Oxford University Press, 2004.

Hinderaker, Eric. *Elusive Empires*. Cambridge: Cambridge University Press, 1997.

Kennedy, Roger G. *Hidden Cities*. New York: Macmillan, Inc., 1994.

Reps, John W. "Urban Redevelopment in the Nineteenth Century. The Squaring of Circleville," *The Journal of the Society of Architecture Historian* 14, no. 4 (1955).

Squire, E. G., and E. H. Davis. *Ancient Monuments of the Mississippi Valley*. New York: AMS Press, 1973.

Welch, William S., and Raymond S. Baly. "The Adena People," No. 2. Columbus, OH: Ohio State University Press, 1957.

Bibliography

The Anasazi

Bassett, Carol. "Roots of Regionalism: Great Stone Cities." *Architecture* (March 1984): 100.

Brewer, Steve. "Understanding the Anasazi." *Albuquerque Journal* (April 21, 1991): C-1.

Brody, J. J. *Anasazi: Ancient People of the Southwest.* New York: Rizzoli, 1990.

Cordell, Linda. *Prehistory of the Southwest.* New York: Academy Press, 1984.

Ferguson, William, and Arthur Rohn. *Anasazi Ruins of the Southwest in Colorado.* Albuquerque, NM: University of New Mexico Press, 1987.

Frazier, Kendrick. *People of Chaco.* New York: Norton, 1986.

Hayes, Alden, David Brugge, and W. James Judge. *Archaeological Surveys of Chaco Canyon.* Albuquerque, NM: University of New Mexico Press, 1987.

Judd, Neil. "The Architecture of Pueblo Bonito." *Smithsonian Miscellaneous Collections* 147, no. 1 (1964).

Knowles, Ralph. *Energy and Form.* Cambridge, MA: MIT Press, 1974.

Lekson, Stephen H. *Great Pueblo Architecture of Chaco Canyon, New Mexico.* Albuquerque, NM: University of New Mexico Press, 1984.

Lekson, Stephen H., Thomas C. Windes, John R. Stein, and W. James Judge. "The Chaco Canyon Community." *Scientific American* (July 1988): 100.

Lipe, W. H., and Michelle Hegmon. *The Architecture of Social Integration in Prehistoric Pueblos.* Cortez, CO: Crow Canyon Archaeological Center, 1989.

Lister, Robert H., and Florence C. Lister. *Aztec Ruins on the Animas: Excavated, Preserved, and Interpreted.* Albuquerque, NM: University of New Mexico Press, 1987.

Nabokov, Peter, and Robert Easton. *Native American Architecture.* New York: Oxford University Press, 1989.

Riley, Carroll L. *The Frontier People: The Greater Southwest in the Protohistoric Period.* Albuquerque, NM: University of New Mexico Press, 1987.

Wills, W. H. *Early Prehistoric Agriculture in the American Southwest.* Santa Fe, NM: School of American Research, 1988.

The Inuit Snow Houses

Lee, Molly, and Gregory A. Reinhardt. *Eskimo Architecture*, Fairbanks, AK: University of Alaska Press, 2003.

The Aztecs

Bray, Warwick, ed. *Aztecs.* London, United Kingdom: Royal Academy of Arts, 2002.

Smith, Michael E. "Life in the Provinces of the Aztec Empire." *Scientific American* 15, no. 1 (March 2005).

La Galgada and Casma and Moche Valleys of Peru

Bawden, Garth. "Domestic Space and Social Structure in Pre-Colombian Northern Peru." In *New Direction in Archaeology, Domestic Architecture and the Use of Space*, edited by Susan Kent. Cambridge, United Kingdom: Cambridge University Press, 1990.

Brannan, Curtis T. *Investigation of Carro Areana, Peru; Incipient Urbanism on the Peruvian North Coast.* PhD diss., University of Arizona, Tucson, Proquest, Ann Arbor, Michigan, 1977.

Grieder, Terence, Alberto Bueno Mendoza, C. Earle Smith Jr., and Robert M. Malina. *La Galgada, Peru: A Pre-Ceramic Culture in Transition.* Austin, TX: University of Texas Press, 1988.

Pozorski, Shelia, and Thomas Pozorski. *Early Settlement and Subsistence in the Casma Valley.* Iowa City, IA: University of Iowa, 1987.

The Incas and the Chimu

Benson, Elizabeth P. *The Mochica: A Culture of Peru.* New York: Praeger Publisher, 1972.

Bingham, Hiram. *Lost City of the Incas.* New York: Duell, Sloan and Pearce, 1948.

Burland, Cottie Arthur. *Peru Under the Incas*, edited by Edward Bacon. New York: G. P. Putnam's Sons, 1967.

Child, Jack. "Peru Chapter 1A, Historical Setting, Countries of the World, 01.01.1991." Bureau Development, Inc., 1991. Available at http://www.elibrary.com.

Donnan, Christopher B. *Ceramics of Ancient Peru*. Los Angeles, CA: Regents of the University of California, 1992.

Donnan, Christopher B. *Moche Art of Peru*. Los Angeles, CA: Regents of the University of California, 1972.

Kendall, Ann. *Everyday Life of the Incas*. New York: G. P. Putnam's Sons; London: B. T. Batsford Ltd., 1973.

Prescott, William H. *The World of the Incas*. Minerva, Geneva: Edi Editions, 1970.

Stierlin, Henri. *Art of the Incas and Its Origins*. New York: Rizzoli, 1983.

Stone-Miller, Rebecca. *Art of the Andes*. London: Thames and Hudson, Ltd., 1995.

Ubbelohde-Doering, Heinrich. *On the Royal Highways of the Inca*. New York: Frederick A. Praeger Publishers, 1967.

Werlich, David P. *Peru: A Short Story*. Carbondale, IL: Southern Illinois University Press, 1978.

Wright, Kenneth R., and Alfredo Valencia Zagarra. *Machu Picchu: A Civil Engineering Marvel*. Reston, VA: ACSE Press, 2000.

The Iroquis Longhouse

Axtell, James. "The Ethno History of Native America." In *Rethinking American Indian History*, edited by Donald L. Fixico. Albuquerque, NM: University of New Mexico Press, 1997, 11–28

Engelbrecht, William. *Iroquoia: the Development of a Native World*. Syracuse, NY: Syracuse University Press, 2003.

Johansen, Bruce. *Encyclopedia of the Haudenosaunee (Iroquois)*. Westport, CT: Greenwood Publishing Group, 2000.

Mann, Barbara, and Jerry L. Fields. "A Sign in the Sky: Dating the League of the Haudenosaunee." *American Culture and Research Journal* 21, no. 2 (1997): 105–163

Morgan, Lewis Henry. *League of the Iroquois*. Secaucus, NJ: Corith Books, 1962.

Reaman, G. Elmore. *The Trail of the Iqoquois Indians: How the Iroquois Nation Saved Canade for the British Empire*. London: Frederick Muller, 1967.

Snow, Dean R. *The Iroquois*. Cambridge, MA: Blackwell, 1994.

Sturges, William Gould. "An Exploration of the Reltaionships between Houses and Forests in American History." *JAE* (November 1992): 66–69.

The Maya

Harrison, Peter. *The Lords of Tikal; Rulers of an Ancient Maya City*. London: Thames and Hudson, 1999.

Miller, Mary Ellen. *The Maya; Art and Architecture*. London: Thames and Hudson, 1999.

Proskouriakoff, Tatiana. *Album of Maya Architecture*. Washington, DC: Carnegie Institution of Washington, 1946.

Chapter 2: Africa

Al-Qahira, Egypt

Ettinghausen, Richard, and Oleg Grabar. *The Art and Architecture of Islam 650–1250*. New Haven, CT: Yale University Press, 1987, 172.

Raymond, Andre. *Cairo*. Cambridge, MA: Harvard University Press, 2000, 65.

Schoenauer, Norbert. *History of Housing*. New York: W. W. Norton & Company, Inc., 2000, 98.

Xu, Yinong. *Boundaries, Centers and Peripheries in Chinese gardens: The case of Suzhou in the Eleventh Century*. London: Taylor and Francis, Ltd., 2003, 21.

Carthage, Tunisia

Lancel, Serge. *Carthage: A History*. Oxford, United Kingdom: Blackwell Publishers, 1995.

Soren, David, Aicha Khader, and Hedi Slim, *Carthage: Uncovering the Mysteries and Splendors of Ancient Tunisia*. New York: Simon & Schuster, 1990.

Deir El Medina and Tel El Amarna, Luxor, Egypt

Kemp, Barry J. *Ancient Egypt Anatomy of a Civilization*. London: Routledge, 2006.

Great Zimbabwe

Beach, D. N. "The Shoma and Zimbabwe, 900–1850." *The International Journal of African Historical Studies* 16, no. 2 (1983): 310–312.

Garlake, Peter S. *Great Zimbabwe*. New York: Stein and Day, 1973.

Mufuka, Ken. *Dzinbahwe: Life and Politics in the Golden Age 1100–1500 AD*. Harare: Harare Publishing House, 1983.

Ndoro, Webber. "Great Zimbabwe." *Scientific American, Mysteries of the Ancient Ones* 15, no. 1 (2005): 74–79.

Summers, Roger. *Zimbabwe: A Rhodesian Mystery*. Cape Town: Thomas Nelson and Sons, 1963.

The Nubian House

Steele, James. *Hassan Fathy*. London: Academy Editions, 1983, 33–49.

Steele, James. "Nubia." In *An Encyclopedia of Vernacular Architecture*, edited by Paul Oliver. Cambridge, United Kingdom: Cambridge University Press, 1998.

Chapter 3: Asia and Australasia

The Dai and the Thai

Chu, Valentin. *Thailand Today: A Visit to Modern Siam*. New York: Thomas Y. Cromwell Company, 1968.

Freeman, Michael. *Temples of Thailand: Their Form and Function*. Hong Kong: Pacific Rim Press (H.K.) Ltd., 1991.

Henderson, John W. *Area Handbook for Thailand*. United States of America: Foreign Areas Studies of The American University, 1971.

Liangwen, Zhu. *The Dai*. Bangkok: DD Books, 1992.

Reid, Daniel. *Bangkok*. Hong Kong: The Guidebook Company, 1990.

Hutong

Yantai, Shen, and Changquing, Wang. *Life in Hutongs*. Beijing: Foreign Language Press, 1989.

Jomon and Yayoi Heritage in Japan

Engel, Heino. *Measure and Construction of the Japanese House*. Boston, Rutland, VT, Tokyo: Tuttle Publisher, 1985.

Kopf, Jennifer Jean Schwartz. "Modern Sukiya and Its Implications." Senior thesis, University of Southern California, May 1, 2003. Unpublished manuscript.

Nishi, Kazuo, and Kazuo Hozumi. *What Is Japanese Architecture?* Tokyo: Kodansha International, 1983.

Paine, Robert Treat, and Alexander Soper. "Architecture of the Pre-Buddhist Age." In *The Art and Architecture of Japan*. Baltimore, MD: Penguin Books, 1955.

The Khmers in Cambodia

Chandler, D. P. *A History of Cambodia*. Boulder, CO, and Oxford: Westview Press, 1992.

Cowig, S., trans., *The Indianized States of Southeast Asia*. Australian National University Press, 1968, of G. Coedes original, Boccard, Paris, 1964.

Huttern, K., ed. *Economic Exchange and Social Interaction in Southeast Asia: Perspectives from Prehistory, History and Ethnography*. Ann Arbor, MI: University of Michigan Press, 1977.

Lebar, F., G. Hickey, and J. Musgrave. *Ethnic Groups of Mainland Southeast Asia*. New Haven, CT: Human Relations Area Files, 1964.

Mabbett, Ian, and David Chandler. *The Khmers*. Oxford: Blackwell, 1995.

Tarling, N., ed. *The Cambridge History of Southeast Asia*. Cambridge, United Kingdom: Cambridge University Press, 1992.

Van Liere, W. "Traditional Water Management in the Lower Mekong Basin." *World Archaeology* II, no. 3 (1980).

The Malay House

Iskandar, Dr. Syed. "Order in Traditional Malay House Form." PhD diss., Oxford Brookes University, Oxford, UK, 2001.

Mohenjo-daro and Harappa, Pakistan

Allchin, F. Raymond, and Bridget Allchin. *Origins of a Civilization: The Prehistory and Early Archaeology of South Asia*. Delhi: Viking, Penguin, 1997.

Cichy, Bodo. *Architecture of Ancient Civilizations*. New York: Viking, 1966.

Frifelt, K. "Some Problems Regarding the Forma Urbis Mohenjo-Daro." *South Asian Archaeology 1985* (1989): 247–254.

Jansen, Michael. "Architectural Remain in Mohenjo-Daro." *Frontiers of the Indus Civilization*, edited by B. B. Lal and S. P. Gupta. Delhi: Books and Books, 1984, 75–88.

Jansen, Michael. "City Planning in the Harappa Culture." *Art and Archaeological Research Papers* 14 (1978): 69–74.

Jansen, Michael. "Public Spaces in the Urban Settlements of the Harappa Culture." *Art and Archaeological Research Papers* 17 (1980): 11–19.

Kenoyer, Jonathan Mark. *Ancient Cities of the Indus Valley Civilization*. Karachi: Oxford University Press, 1998.

Kenoyer, Jonathan Mark. "Uncovering the Keys to the Lost Indus Cities." *Scientific American* (March 2005): 24–33.

Kenoyer, Jonathan Mark. "Urban Process in the Indus Tradition: A Preliminary Model from Harappa." *Harappa Excavations 1986–1990: A Multidisciplinary Approach to Third Millennium Urbanism*, edited by Richard H. Meadow. Madison, WI: Prehistory Press, 1991, 29–58.

Mittre, Vishnu. "The Harappa Civilization and the Need for a New Approach." *Harappa Civilization*, edited by Gregory L. Possehl. New Delhi: Raj Bandhu Industrial Co., 1982.

Possehl, Gregory L. "The Harappa Civilization: A Contemporary Perspective." *Harappa Civilization*, edited by Gregory L. Possehl. New Delhi: Raj Bandhu Industrial Co., 1981, 15–27.

Possehl, Gregory L. "Revolution in the Urban Revolution: The Emergence of the Indus Urbanization." *Annual Review of Anthropology*, no. 19 (1990): 261–282.

Rajan, Soundara. "Motivations for Early Indian Urbanization and Examination." *Harappa Civilization*, edited by Gregory L. Possehl. New Delhi: Raj Bandhu Industrial Co., 1982, 69–75.

Shaffer, Jim. "Harappa Culture: A Reconsideration." *Harappa Civilization*, edited by Gregory L. Possehl. New Delhi: Raj Bandhu Industrial Co., 1982, 41–50.

Vats, M. S. "Excavations at Harappa." *Annual Report of the Archaeological Survey of India* (1929): 121–131.

Wheeler, Mortimer. "The Indus Civilization." *Civilization of the Indus Valley and Beyond*, edited by Stuart Piggott. New York: McGraw-Hill Book Co., 1966, 9–52.

The Minangkabau House

Emerick, Michael. "The Traditional Houses of Negri Sembilan and Malacca, Their Derivation from Minankabau Prototypes," December 14, 1977. Unpublished manuscript.

Shang Houses in China

Allen, Sarah. *The Shape of the Turtle: Myth, Art, and Cosmos in Early China*. Albany: State University of New York Press, 1991.

Chang, Kwang-chih. *The Archaeology of Ancient China.*. 3rd ed. New Haven, CT: Yale University Press, 1980.

Chang, Kwang-chih. *Shang Civilization*. New Haven, CT: Yale University Press, 1980.

Hsu, Cho-Yun, and Katheryn Linduff. *Western Chou Civilization*. New Haven, CT: Yale University Press, 1988.

International Conference on Shang Civilization (1982: East-West Center). *Studies of Shang Archaeology: Selected Papers from the International Conference on Shnag Civilization*. New Haven: Yale University Press, 1986.

Keightley, David. *Sources of Shang History: The Oracle Bone Inscriptions of Bronze Age China*. Berkeley: University of California Press, 1978.

Watson, William. *China Before the Han Dynasty*. New York: Frederick A. Praeger, 1961.

Wu, K. C. *The Chinese Heritage*. New York: Crown Publishers, Inc., 1982.

Chapter 4: Europe and the Western Mediterranean

Anglo Saxon and Norman Houses in Britain

Addy, S. O. *The Evolution of the English House*. London: Allen and Unarin, 1933.

Barley, M. V. *The English Farmhouse and Cottage*. London: Routledge, 1961.

Beresford, M. W. *Medieval England: Aerial Survey*. London: Cambridge University Press, 1958.

Braun, H. *The Story of the English House*. London: Batsford, 1940.

Clapham, A. W. *English Romanesque Architecture before the Conquest*. New York: Oxford University Press, 1930.

Crossley, F. H. *Timber Building in England*. London: Batsford, 1951.

Faulkman, P. A. "Domestic Planning from the Twelfth to the Fourteenth Centuries." *Archaeological Journal* CXV (1958): 150–184.

Garner, T., and A. Stratton. *Domestic Architecture of England During the Tudor Period*. London: Batsford, 1929.

Holmes, U. T. *Daily Living in the Twelfth Century*. Madison, WI: University of Wisconsin Press, 1953.

Hope-Taylor, B. K. *The Saxon Palace at Yeavering*. London: Ministry of Warke, 1951.

Lloyd, N. *A History of the English House*. London: Architectural Press, 1931.

Pantin, W. A. "Medieval English Town House Plans." *Medieval Archaeology* VI-VII (1962): 202–239.

Sulzman, L. F. *English Life in the Middle Ages.* New York: Oxford University Press, 1929.
Turner, T. Hudson. *Some Account of Domestic Architecture in England.* London: J. H. Parker, 1851.
Wood, Margaret. *The English Medieval House.* London: Phoenix House, 1965.
Wood, M. E. "Norman Domestic Architecture." *Archaeological Journal* XCII (1935): 167–242.

The *Domus Aurea*, Rome
Boethius, Axel. *The Golden House of Nero.* Ann Arbor, MI: University of Michigan Press, 1960.
Vreeland, Frederick. "Roman Treasures Revealed." *Conde Nast Traveler* (June 1999): 35–37.

Greek Houses in the Cities of Asia Minor
Havelock, Christine Mitchell. *Hellenistic Art.* New York: W. W. Norton and Co., 1981.
Laidlaw, William Allison. *A History of Delos.* Oxford, UK: Oxford University Press, 1933.
Steele, James. *Hellenistic Architecture in Asia Minor.* South Bend, IN: Academy Editions, 1990.
Wycherley, R. E. *How the Greeks Built Cities.* London: MacMillan & Co., 1962.

Khirokitia, Cyprus
Karageorgis, K. *Khinokitia, Cyprus.* Monograph Series #1. Cyprus: Department of Antiquities, 1983.

Knossos, Crete
Coldstream, J. N. *The Sanctuary of Demeter.* Great Britain: The British School of Archaeology at Athens, Thames and Hudson, 1973.
Evans, Arthur J. *Scripta Minoa: The Written Documents of Minoan Crete with Special Reference to the Archives of Knossos.* Oxford: The Clarendon Press, 1952. (i) Vol. 1, *The Hieroglyphic and Primitive Linear Classes;* (ii) Vol. 2, *The Archives of Knossos.*
Lawrence, A. E. *Greek Architecture.* New Haven, CT: Yale University Press, 1996.
Mellersh, H. E. L. *The Destruction of Knossos; The Rise and Fall of Minoan Crete.* New York: Weybright and Talley, 1970.
Palmer, Leonard R. *A New Guide to the Palace of Knossos.* New York: Frederick A. Praeger Publishers, 1969.
Palmer, Leonard R. *The Penultimate Palace of Knossos.* New York: Frederick A. Praeger Publishers, 1969.
Wunderlich, Hans Georg. *The Secret of Crete.* New York: Macmillan Publishing Co., Inc., 1970.

Mycenae and Troy
Lawrence, A. W. *Greek Architecture.* Baltimore, MD: Penguin Books, 1983.

Houses of the Roman Republic and Empire
Boethius, Axel. *The Golden House of Nero.* Ann Arbor, MI: The University of Michigan Press, 1960.
Cantarella, Marguerite. *Pandora's Daughters, Roles and Status of Women in Greek and Roman Antiquity.* Baltimore, MD: John Hopkins University Press, 1987.
Detrind, Richard E. L. B. *Houses in Herculaneum: A New View of the Town Planning and the Building of Insulae III and IV.* Amsterdam: J. C. Gieben Publisher, 1998.
Pallottino, Massimo, *A History of Earliest Italy.* London: Routledge, 1991.
Youncenar, Marguerite. *Memoire of Hadrian.* New York: Farrar, Straus & Giroux, 1987.

Skara Brae, Scotland
Childe, Gordon. *Skara Brae; A Pictish Village in Orkney.* London: Kegan Paul, 1931.

Clarke, David. *The Neolithic Village at Skara Brae, Orkney 1972–73 Excavation, an Interim Report*. Edinburgh: HMSO, 1976.

Clarke, David, and P. Maguire. *Skara Brae; Northern Europe's Best Preserved Prehistoric Village*. Edinburgh: Historic Scotland Press, 1989.

Renfrew, Colin, ed. *The Prehistory of Orkney*. 2nd ed. Edinburgh: Edinburgh University Press, 1990.

Richards, Colin. "Skara Brae: Revisiting a Neolithic Village in Orkney." In *Scottish Archaeology, New Perception*, edited by William Hanson and Elizabeth Slater. Aberdeen: Aberdeen University Press, 1991.

Ritchie, Anna. *Prehistoric Orkney*. London: Batsford, 1995.

Scane, Chris. *Exploring Prehistoric Europe*. New York: Oxford University Press, 1998.

Stonehenge, Woodhenge, and Durrington Walls

Jackson, Anthony. *Solving Stonehenge, The Key to an Ancient Enigma*. London: Thames and Hudson, 2008.

Castleden, Rodney. *The Stonehenge People, An Exploration of Life in Neolithic Britain, 4700–2000 BC*. London: Routledge Kegan, Paul, 1987.

Chapter 5: East and Southeast Asia

Çatal Hüyük

Balter, Michael. "Why Settle Down? The Mystery of Communities." *Science* 282 (November 20, 1998): 1442–1445.

Hodder, Ian, ed. *On the Surface: Catal Hüyük 1939–95*. Cambridge: McDonald Institute for Archaeological Research and British Institute of Archaeology at Ankara, 1996.

Hodder, Ian. "Women and Men at Catal Hüyük." *Scientific American* (January 2004): 351–354.

Kunzig, Robert. "A Tale of Two Archaeologists." *Discover* 20, no. 5 (May 1999): 84–92.

Mellaart, James. *Catal Hüyük: A Neolithic Town in Anatolia*. New York: McGraw-Hill, 1967.

Mellaart, James. *A Neolithic City in Turkey Scientific American* 210, no. 4 (April 1964): 94–104.

Constantinople, "The New Rome"

Summer-Boyd, Hilary. *Strolling Through Istanbul*. London: Kegan Paul, 2005.

The Hittites

Lehmann, Johannes. *The Hittites, People of a Thousand Gods*. New York: The Viking Press, 1975.

MacQueen, J. G. *The Hittites and Their Contemporaries in Asia Minor*. London: Thames and Hudson, 1986.

Mesopotamia

Matthews, Roger. *The Archaeology of Mesopotamia: Theories and Approaches*. London: Routledge, 2003.

Normet-Nejat, Karen Rhea. *Daily Life in Ancient Mesopotamia*. Westport, CT: Greenwood Press, 1998.

Postgate, J. Nicholas. *Early Mesopotamia: Society and Economy at the Dawn of History*. London: Routledge, 1992.

Stone, Elizabeth C., and Paul Zimansky. *The Anatomy of a Mesopotamian City: Survey and Soundings at Mashkan-shapir*. Winona Lake, IN: Eisenbrauns, 2004.

Stone, Elizabeth C., and Paul Zimansky. "The Tapestry of Power in a Mesopotamian City." *Scientific American* 15, no. 1 (2005): 60–67.

Topkapi Palace
Summer-Boyd, Hilary. *Strolling Through Istanbul.* London: Kegan Paul, 2005.

Yemeni Houses
Damlugi, Samar. *The Architecture of Yemen, From Yafi to Hadramut.* London: Laurence King Publishing, 2007.

Index

Index

Index

Index

Shariah al-Muizz Li Din, 33
Shatt al Arab, 160
Shen Wansan, 48
Shetland Islands, 95
Shiite Fatimids, 31
Shimenawa, 62
Shinmei zukuri, 63
Shinto, 62, 65, 70, 76
Shiva, 76
Shoden, 63
Shuksheika, 35
Siam, 50–51. *See also* Thailand
Sibeyuan, 59–60
Sicily, 123
Sidon, 155
Siem Reap, 66
Si Inthrathit, 52
Silbury Hill, 134, 137
The Silk Route, 58
Sinan, 158, 165
Sindh Province, 75
Singgalang, 81
Sipapu, 8
Şişe Saray, 164
Siva, 69
The Six Nations, 23–24
Skara Brae, 132–34, 141
Snake Church (Yilanikilise), 145
Social stratification, xiv
Sociological-ecological model, xi
Sofa Mosque, 168
Soğanli Dere, 145
Solar (Great Chamber), 96–97
Somerset, 94–95, 96
Song Dynasty, 47
Sork, 54
Spain, 131–32
Sparta, 150–51
Split, 152
Squier, Ephraim George, 1
Squier (Chinese), 20
Sri Lanka, 52
Stabian Gate, 128
The Stadium, 106
St. Mark's Basilica in Venice, 149–50
Stonehenge, 134–39; communal buildings near, 140; construction of, 134, 135–36, 138; described, 135–36; Diffusionists vs. Non-Diffusionists theories, 138; purpose of, 136–37, 141; radiocarbon dates, 141

Stonehenge Decoded (Hawkins), 136–37
Stones of Sternness, 134
Strait from Sumatra, 86
Stupa, 53
Sudan, 43–44, 82, 86
Suetonius, 98, 99
Suinin, Emperor of Japan, 62
Sujin, Emperor of Japan, 62
Sukhothai, 51–52
Sultan's Wall (*Sur-i Sultan*), 164
Sumatra, 80, 86, 87. *See also* the Minangkabau house
Sumeria and Sumerians, xiv, 76, 160–61. *See also* Mesopotamia
Sumner-Boyd, Hilary, 167
Sungei Ujong, Malaysia, 87
Sunnet Odasi, 168
Sunrise and sunset, 72
Suqs, 172
Sur-i Sultan (Sultan's Wall), 164
Surou, 80
Suryavarman II, King, 67
Suzhou, 33
Syria, 111, 154, 156

Tabasco. *See* the Maya
Tabernae, 125–26, 127
Tablinum, 124, 128, 131
Takbir, 74
Taktaboosh, 35
Talatat, 42
"Tale of Nations" (*Genesis*), 103
Tandikat, 81
Tarascan Empire, 13
Tasselled Halberdiers, 165
Tatami, 73
Taurus Mountains, 159
Technology, overview, xi–xv
Tel El Amarna, 37–38, 40, 41–42, 77
Tello, 20
Temple of Karnak, 154, 155
Temple of the Athenians, 106
Temple of Venus, 99
Tenochtitlan, 13, 14, 15, 16
Teopan tribe, 14
Tepe Gaura culture, 160
Terachi, Malaysia, 86–87
Terminus, 127
The Terrace of the Lions, 106
Terre pisé, 109, 148
Tesserae, 130

Thailand, 50–58; belief in spirits, 68–69; climate, 67–68; Dai house, 51; farming, 56; geographic location, 50; houses, 51, 52–58; Lanna Kingdom, 51; origin, 50–51, 52; Sukhothai, 51–52; Thai houses, 52–53; Theravada Buddhism, 50, 51, 52–53
Thalassocracy, 112–13
Thebes, Egypt, 37–38, 39, 42
Theodosius I ("Theodosius the Great"), 149, 152
Theodosius II, 149
Theophylaktos, 149
Thera, 111
Theravada Buddhism, 50, 51, 52–53
The Thermae of Trajan, 99
Tholoi, 109–10
Thucydides, 120
Tiang seri, 70, 84
Tiberius, 126
Tigris River, 158, 159, 162, 163. *See also* Mesopotamia
Tikar, 72–73
Tilokorai, King, 51
Timgad, 127, 128
Tira de la Peregrinacion (Codex Boturini), 14
Tiryns, 110, 119, 120–22
Titus, public baths of, 99
Tokonoma, 133
Tongji University, 49–50
Topia, 131
Topkapi Palace, 163–68; courtyards, 158, 164–65; Fourth Court, 167–68; the Harem, 165–66, 167; Janissary corps, 164, 165, 167; Princes' School, 166; Second Court, 165–66; Third Court, 166–67
Topography, overview, xi–xv
Tortillas, 14
Toyuke, 62, 63
Trajan, Emperor, 127
Trajan's Market, 125
Treasury of the Sacred Relics (*Kutsal Emanetler*), 166
Tribal rituals, documentation of, 1
Triclinium, 101–2, 124
Trojan War, 118–19, 120–21, 154, 155. *See also The Iliad* (Homer)
The Trojan Women (Aesculus), 120
Troulli, Cyprus, 108
Troy, 118–22; Age of Heroes, 120; as city of Homer's *Iliad*, 103, 110 (*see also The Iliad*); excavation of, 118, 119, 120; Hittites and, 155; houses, 119–20; levels of occupation, 118; Trojan War, 118–19, 120–21, 154, 155
Trujillo, Peru, 20
Trywhitt, Jacqueline, 105
Tshudi, 20
Tudhaliya IV, King, 156
Tunisia, 170
Tupig, 13
Turkey: Canakalle, 118; conquest of Constantinople, 153–54, 163–64; Isnick tiles, 35; Lake Van, 158; Taurus Mountains, 159. *See also* Anatolia; Hittites
Tuscan order, 123–24
Tuscaroras, 23. *See also* the Iroquois Longhouse
Tutankamen, 39, 42
Tyndareus of Sparta, 118
Tyre, 155

Uadling, 10
Ubosot (*bot*), 53
Udon Thani Province, 52
Ukhaider Palace, Iraq, 34
Ulufe, 165
Ulu Muar, Malaysia, 86
Ur, xiv, 32, 161–62
Urubamba River, 21
Uruk period, xiv, 160–61
Uxmal, 30

Valide Sultan, 165, 166
Valley of Mexico. *See* the Aztecs
Valley of the Kings and Queens, 39
The Valley Ruins, 43
Varro, 101
Vatican City, 97
Venice, 149–50
Ventris, Michael, 114
Vespasian, 99
Vestibulum, 124
Vesuvian Gate, 128
Vesuvius, Mount, 128
Via Biberatica, 125
Via Cavour, 97
Via Lanza, 97
Vietnam, 56, 68
Viharn, 53

Index

Vihle, 20
Vikings, 94
Villa of the Mysteries, 128, 129
Vishnu, 67
Vitruvius, 123–24
Von Hagen, Victor W., 29
Vortigern, 93–94

Wadi Halfa, 44, 45–46
Wainwright, Geoff, 140
Warendorf, Germany, 94–95
Warka, xiv, 160
Wat, 52
Wat Chai Wattanaram Temple, Ayuthaya, Thailand, 54
Water sources, 171
West Sumatra Province, 80, 81–82, 84. *See also* the Minangkabau house
White Eunuchs' Gate (*Akagalar*), 166
The White Temple, 160–61
Wiltshire Archaeological Magazine, 139
Wolfe Counties, Kentucky, 3
Wooden halls, 95–96
Woodhenge, 134–35, 139–40, 141
Woolley, Charles Leonard, 160–61

Xuthus, King, 102
Xystus, 131

Yamato, 61, 63
Yamoto-hime-no-Mikoto, Princess of Japan, 62
Yangtze River basin, 47–50, 55
Yasod Harapura, 67
Yasovarman, King, 67
Yavuz Selim, Sultan, 167
Yayoi heritage, 60–61, 62, 63, 65
Yazilikaya, 144, 154, 155–56
Yeavering, 94
Yemen, 168–72; houses, 170–71; Masjid al Jami'i, 170; mosques, 172; water sources, 171
Yeni Köşk, 168
Yilanikilise (Snake Church), 145
Yogyakarta, 66, 67
Yorkshire, Britain, 96
Yuan Dynasty, 48
Yucatan, xiv. *See also* the Maya
Yunnan Province, 52, 56, 57

Zagros Mountains, 158
Zana battle, 37
Zeus, 104, 106, 114
Zeus-Xeuthippes, 151, 152
Zhou Di, 47
Zhouzhuang, 47–50
Zimbabwe, 43

About the Author

JAMES STEELE received a Bachelor of Arts degree, as an English Major, from Lafayette College in Easton, Pennsylvania, and both a Bachelor's and Master's Degree in Architecture from the University of Pennsylvania. He practiced architecture in and around the Philadelphia area for twelve years and became registered in Pennsylvania before relocating to Saudi Arabia where he taught for eight years at King Faisal University in Dammam. He then moved to London and served as Senior Editor of *Architectural Design* magazine, while also teaching at the Prince of Wales's Institute for Architecture. Since 1991, he has taught at the University of Southern California, where he has also received a Doctorate in Urban Planning and is now a tenured Professor there. He has written extensively about both traditional and contemporary architecture and has had several books published.

REFERENCE